The Capture of Caen

The Capture of Caen

The Fall of the City, June–July 1944

Tim Saunders

Pen & Sword
MILITARY

First published in Great Britain in 2025 by
PEN & SWORD MILITARY
an imprint of Pen & Sword Books Ltd
Yorkshire – Philadelphia

ISBN 978-1-03615-040-2

A CIP catalogue record for this book is available from the British Library.

Typeset by Concept, Huddersfield, West Yorkshire, HD4 5JL.
Printed and bound in England by CPI Group (UK) Ltd, Croydon, CR0 4YY.

MIX
Paper | Supporting responsible forestry
FSC® C013604
FSC www.fsc.org

The Publisher's authorised representative in the EU for product safety is Authorised Rep Compliance Ltd, Ground Floor, 71 Lower Baggot Street, Dublin D02 P593, Ireland – www.arccompliance.com

For a complete list of Pen & Sword titles please contact
PEN & SWORD BOOKS LTD
47 Church Street, Barnsley, South Yorkshire, S70 2AS, England
E-mail: enquiries@pen-and-sword.co.uk
Website: www.pen-and-sword.co.uk
or
PEN & SWORD BOOKS
1950 Lawrence Rd, Havertown, PA 19083, USA
E-mail: uspen-and-sword@casematepublishers.com
Website: www.penandswordbooks.com

Contents

Acknowledgements

As usual, there is a long list of those who have helped me with this project, starting with Richard Hone and his encyclopaedic knowledge of the Second World War, the German Army and his library of regimental histories. As ever, he generously came to my aid with information and clarification when needed. I am also most grateful for the assistance provided by the Lessons Exploitation Cell at the Land Warfare Centre and the staff of the Government Reading Room at The National Archives for their help in making documents available beyond the usual war diaries. Originally used for battlefield studies, insights from their documents have now found their way into this book.

I must also extend my thanks to the museums of the regiments that fought with the 3rd Division. They are, of course, valued custodians of their battalions' wartime history. The time and help provided by their staff in offering opinions, information, and photographs are hereby gratefully acknowledged. Finally, I would like to thank the members of various forums and the members of the Guild of Battlefield Guides with whom discussion has done much to shape my ideas.

In quoting those who fought in the battles for Caen, I have followed my usual practice of using the rank that officers and soldiers held at the time of the fighting. Many, of course, were promoted later in the campaign or during post-war service. Although there are plenty of references and notes, to keep them to a reasonable number, I have avoided repetition where the source is obvious within a chapter.

Introduction

This book continues the story of the 3rd British Division's capture of the city of Caen begun in *The Advance on Caen: From Sword Beach towards the City*, which covers the battle from D Day to 9 June, regarded as 'the end of the first phase of the invasion'. Caen had not been taken as hoped on D Day or in the days thereafter, with I Corps being brought to a halt by the arrival of two of the three panzer German divisions that fought Second British Army in the early days of the campaign. Of the 3rd Division's first attempts to capture the city a War Office report had this to say:

> The Division had failed to achieve the primary task which it was set, the capture of Caen. However, the wording of I Corps' order for the assault implies that this objective, though eminently desirable, could only be achieved under most favourable circumstances by 'bouncing' an enemy thoroughly unprepared, surprised and disorganised. Failure to capture it on D Day was not only anticipated but it was foreseen that thereafter probably a considerable period of build-up would be essential before a highly organised major operation could be launched on this key communication centre which the enemy would do everything possible to hold.[1]

This may be regarded as an excuse by some, but it should be borne in mind that the 3rd Division had to first break through the coastal crust on SWORD Beach, which neither 1st US, 50th or 3rd Canadian divisions managed with the planned speed. Then the 3rd Division faced the panzer grenadiers and artillery of a panzer division deployed to protect Caen, and by the early evening the beginnings of a significant armoured counter-attack. Finally, there were pre-prepared belts of barbed wire, anti-tank ditches and trench systems blocking routes into the city that far exceeded those found elsewhere.

There was a second battle being conducted, and that was to build up the force ashore and the logistics to support it. Commander Edwards noted that the assault divisions

> had had a long and far from smooth and comfortable sea passage, followed by an assault on prepared enemy positions and a day and a night of fighting. Unless the build-up of their strength by the landing of reinforcements and supplies was perfectly carried out there would be danger that these tired men would have to go on fighting without immediate or adequate reinforcement, and possibly under the handicap of shortage of ammunition, fuel for the vehicles, water and rations.[2]

Partly for these reasons, following D Day and its immediate aftermath, with I Corps halted, Second Army's main effort was transferred to the west, where XXX Corps attempted to envelope Caen via Villers Bocage. Consequently, activity on the front north of Caen was reduced, but pressure was, as we will see, maintained and attacks were launched in support of operations elsewhere on the front. This led to some bitter and costly fighting around places like Château de la Londe, which has been referred to as 'the bloodiest square mile in Europe'. As a measure of activity, even though during this period they were not committed to an operation on the scale of MARTLET/EPSOM or the fighting around Tilly-sur-Seulles, the 3rd Division's casualties were comparable to those of other divisions. As predicted by General Montgomery, the Germans had proved determined to fight for Caen and suffered irreplaceable losses as a result.

Only once the enveloping operations of PERCH and EPSOM had failed to deliver the city into Allied hands would capturing Caen by direct attack, in Operations WINDSOR and CHARNWOOD, be ordered during the first week of July. By then the German panzer divisions facing the British divisions and 3rd Canadian Division had been greatly reduced and were slowly being replaced by infantry divisions. For the British, the Second Army's build up was all but complete, with 59th Staffordshire Division joining I Corps. The final battle for Caen was fought with the aid of the RAF's heavy bombers and overwhelming strength; nonetheless, German resistance remained fierce, and the three Allied divisions experienced a stern fight. Finally, the city that was to have been captured on D Day, or immediately afterwards, was in Allied hands.

Tim Saunders MBE
Warminster, 2025

Tim Saunders is an accredited member of the Guild of Battlefield Guides

Glossary of Terms

All wars produce their own lexicon. Therefore, it is no surprise that abbreviations abound in war diaries and accounts of the NWE (North-West Europe) campaign. The main ones are listed here, but in an army where combat training took priority over staff work, many non-standard and local variations were used. The following list will help:

2iC	Second in Command
A1 Echelon	Immediate replenishment of combat supplies
A2 Echelon	Further back planned replenishment of combat supplies
AA	Anti-aircraft
ACV	Armoured Command Vehicle
ADC	Aide de Camp
Adjt	Adjutant, unit commanding officer's staff officer
Admin	Administration
Adv	Advance
AGRA	Army Group Royal Artillery, a corps' artillery 'division', consisting of heavy, medium and field regiments plus anti-aircraft guns
AFV	Armoured Fighting Vehicle
Amn	Ammunition
AOP	Air/Armoured Observation Post
AP	Armour-piercing or anti-personnel
APCBC	Armour piercing ballistic-capped
APC	Armoured Personnel Carrier
APDS	Armour Piercing Discarding Sabot, 6- and 17-pounder anti-tank ammunition
APIS	Air Photo Interpretation Section
Arty	Artillery
Assy Area	Assembly Area, where troops regroup (e.g., tanks, infantry and gunners) for an operation prior to moving to the FUP
Aslt	Assault
A/Tk	(+ variants) Anti-tank
ARV	Armoured Recovery Vehicle
AVRE	Armoured Vehicle Royal Engineer
Axis	The central direction of advance
BC	Battery Commander

B Echelon	The entry point of combat supplies into a unit's logistic infrastructure
BCR	Battle Casualty Replacement
Bde	Brigade (British) equivalent to a US or German regiment
BK	Battery Captain
BMA	Beach maintenance Area (logistic dumps)
Bn	Battalion
Br	Bridge
Bty	Battery
Cas	Casualties
Casevac	Casualty evacuation
CCP	Casualty Clearing Post
CCS	Casualty Clearing Station
Cdn	Canadian
Centre Line	Axis of Advance
C in C	Commander-in-Chief
Civ	Civilian
CL	Centre Line or axis of advance
CO	Commanding Officer*
Co-ax	Coaxial machine gun mounted in tanks alongside the main armament
Coln	Column
Conc	Concentrate, also Conc Area, where units assigned to an operation gather before moving forward to the assy area
Comd	Command
Coord	Coordinate
Coy	Company
CP	Command Post
Cpl	Corporal
CPO	Command Post Officer (artillery)
CS	Close Support
CSM	Company Sergeant Major
D Day	The day on which an operation begins
Dem	Demolition
Dets	Detachments
DF	Defensive fire, pre-planned artillery, mortar or medium machine gun target areas on likely enemy approaches, etc.
DGNS	Dragons
Div	Division
DP	Distribution Point, logistic
DR	Dispatch rider, also 'Don R' or 'Don Romeo'

*Today the distinction between CO and OC is well-defined, with the former commanding a unit such as a battalion and the latter a sub-unit such as a company, but in many British Second World War memoirs and documents they are transposed or used inconsistently.

DZ	Drop Zone
Ech	Echelon, normally referring to fighting echelon and logistic echelons of a unit
Fmn	Formation, i.e., brigade, division, etc.
En	Enemy
Enfilade	Fire from a flank
Fd Regt	Field Regiment RA
FMC	Field Maintenance Centre
FOB	Forward Officer Bombardment (naval gunfire)
FOO	Forward Observation Officer (artillery)
FUP	Forming Up Place
Fwd	Forward
Gd	Guard, typically advanced, flank or rear guard
GOC	General Officer Commanding
GPO	Gun Position Officer
Gr	Grenadier
H Hour	The hour (time) at which an operation starts
HE	High Explosive
Hy	Heavy
Inf	Infantry
Int	Intelligence
I Sec	Intelligence Section
JNCO	Junior Non-Commissioned Officer
KIA	Killed in action
KO	Knocked out
LAA	Light Anti-Aircraft
LAD	Light Aid Detachment
LCA	Landing Craft Assault
L Cpl	Lance Corporal
LCT	Landing Craft Tank
Ldr	Leader
Line	Field telephone wire
LZ	Landing Zone
MG	Machine Gun
MIA	Missing in Action
MMG	Medium Machine Gun
MSR	Main Supply Route
O Group	Orders group, assembly of subordinate commanders for the issue of orders
OC	Officer Commanding
OP	Observation Post
P Hour	Time of a parachute drop
PIAT	Projector Infantry Anti-Tank
Pl	Platoon

Posn	Position
Pt	Point
Pte	Private (rank)
PW	Prisoner of War
Pz	Panzer
QM	Quartermaster
RAP	Regimental Aid Post
Rd	Road
Regt *or* Rgt	Regiment
REME	Royal Electrical and Mechanical Engineers
RHA	Royal Horse Artillery
RHU	Reinforcement Holding Unit
RMO	Regimental Medical Officer
RPM	Rounds per minute
RSM	Regimental Sergeant Major
RSO	Regimental Signals Officer
RV	Rendezvous Point
SA	Small Arms
SB	Stretcher Bearer
Sec *or* Sect	Section
Shelldrake	Appointment title for artillery
Shellrep	Report of enemy shelling, used to locate enemy batteries
Sgt	Sergeant
Sitrep	Situation Report
Sjt	Serjeant, the old form of Sergeant still used by some regiments
SL	Start Line
Smk	Smoke
SNCO	Senior Non-Commissioned Officer
SP	Self-Propelled or support
Sta	Station
Stand-to	'Stand to arms', fully man defensive positions. Also routine at dawn and dusk
Sub-unit	Company-, squadron- or battery-sized unit
Sunray	Commander of any sized unit or formation
Sups	Supplies
Sqn	Squadron
Svy	Survey
Tac	Tactical, usually used in context of a tactical headquarters
Tac/R	Tactical reconnaissance by aircraft
Target	All guns within range when an '*xxxxx* target' was called: Mike (regiment), Uncle (division), Victor (corps), York (army)
Tgt	Target
Tk	Tank
Tp	Troop

Tpt Transport
Unit An infantry battalion or a British artillery or armoured regiment
Wef With effect
WIA Wounded in Action
X Rds Crossroads
Yd(s) Yards
Yeo Yeomanry

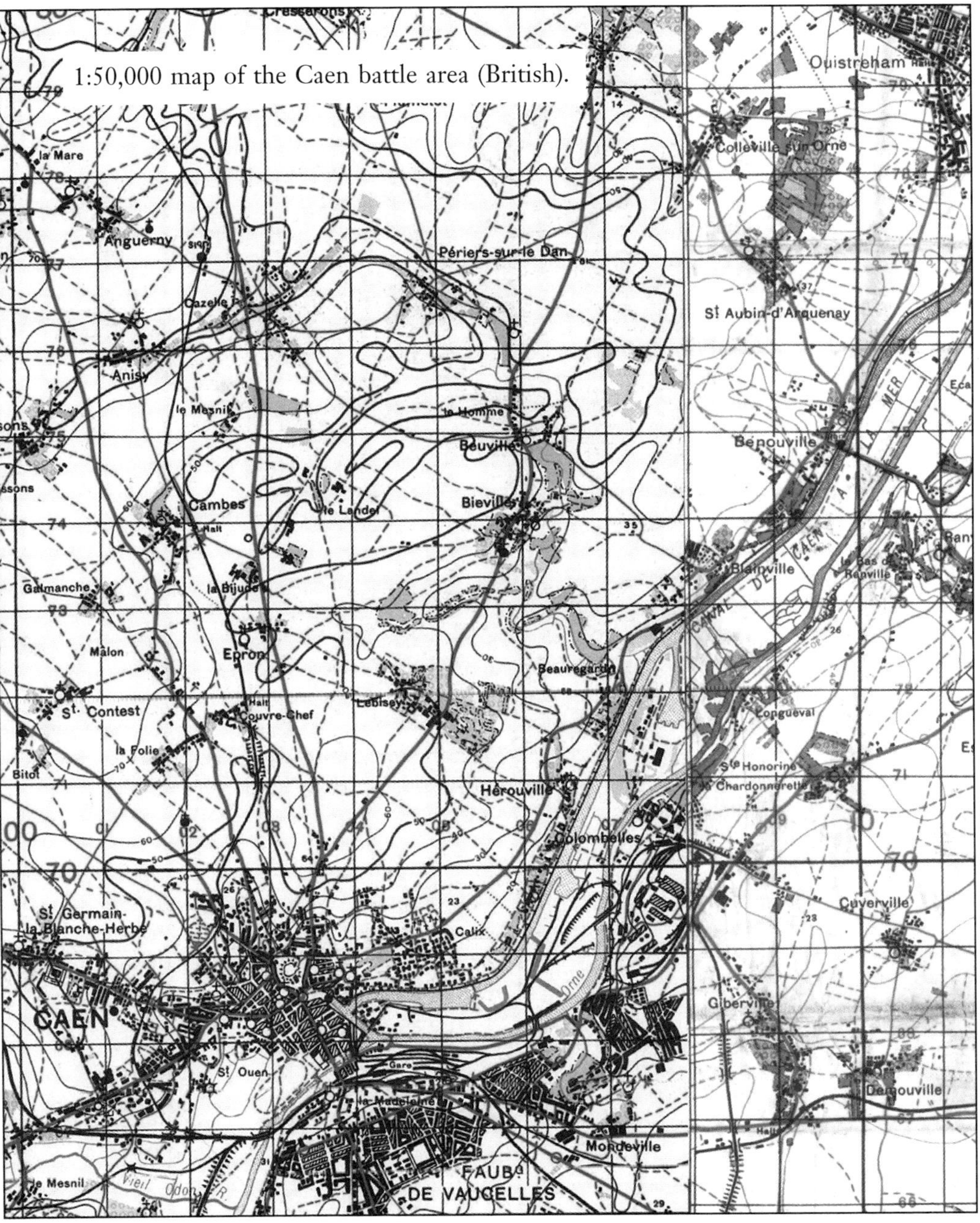

1:50,000 map of the Caen battle area (British).

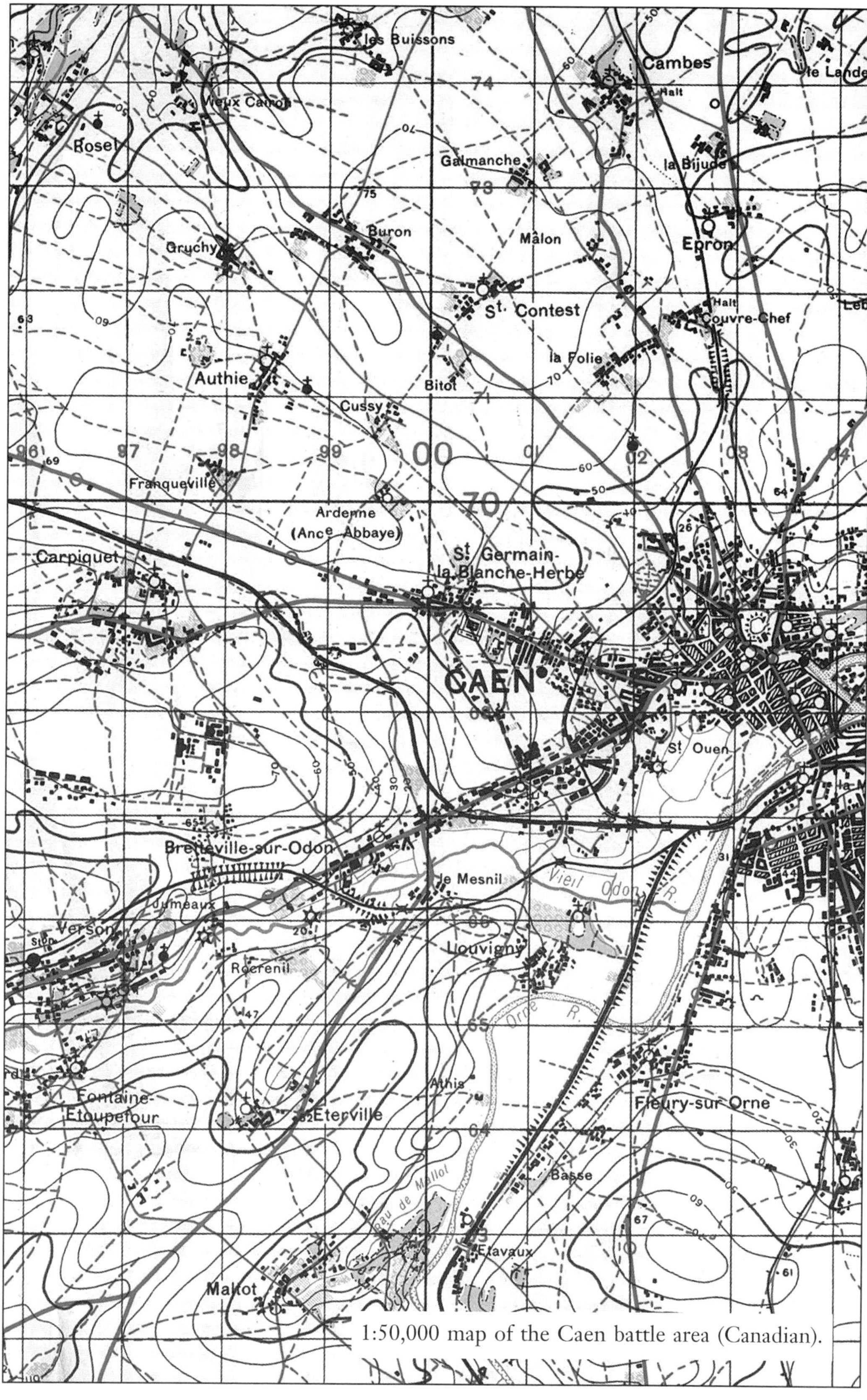

1:50,000 map of the Caen battle area (Canadian).

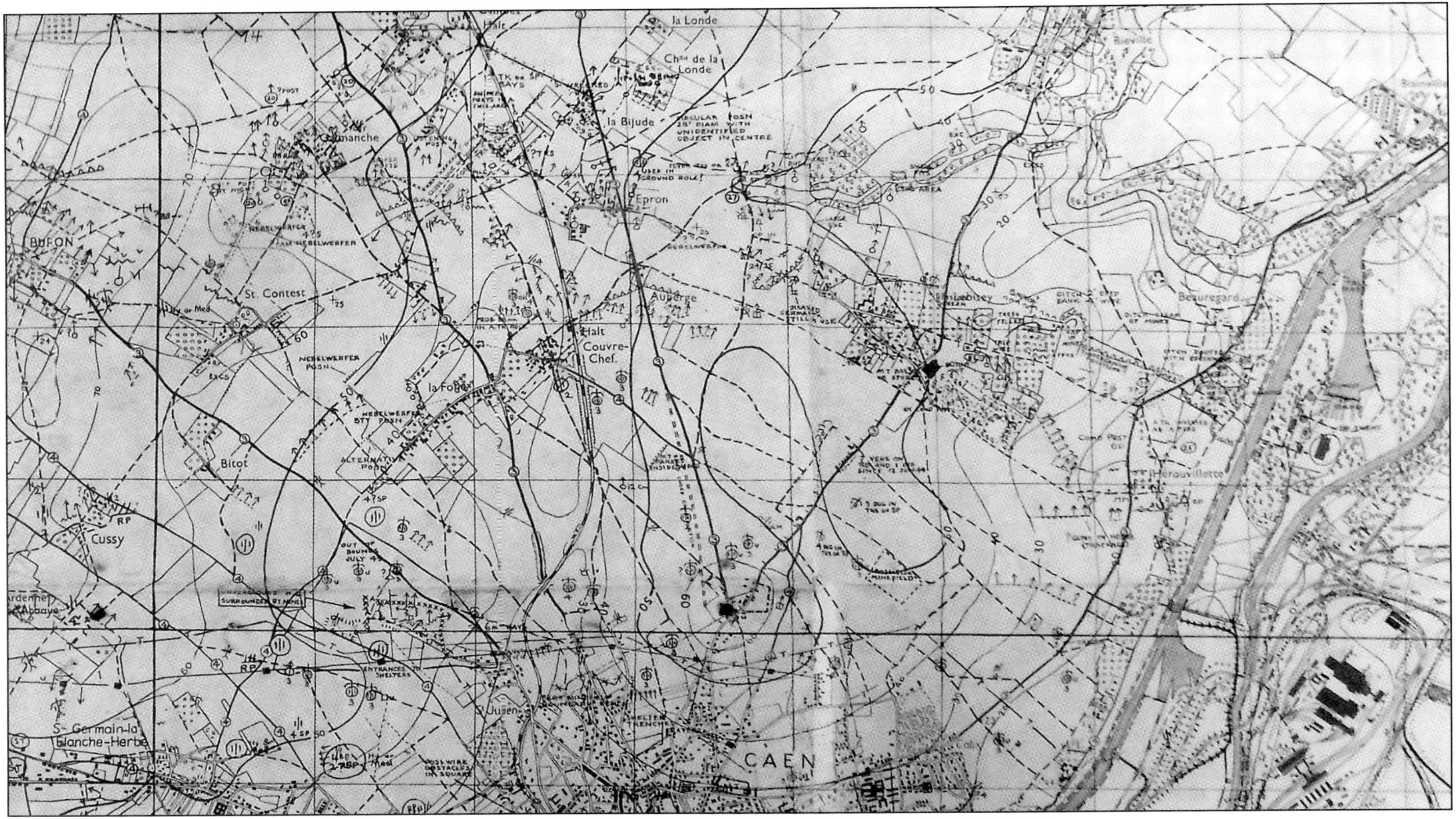

A section of the CHARNWOOD tactical overprint 1:25,000 map covering the British assault. Compilation sheet dated 2 July 1944.

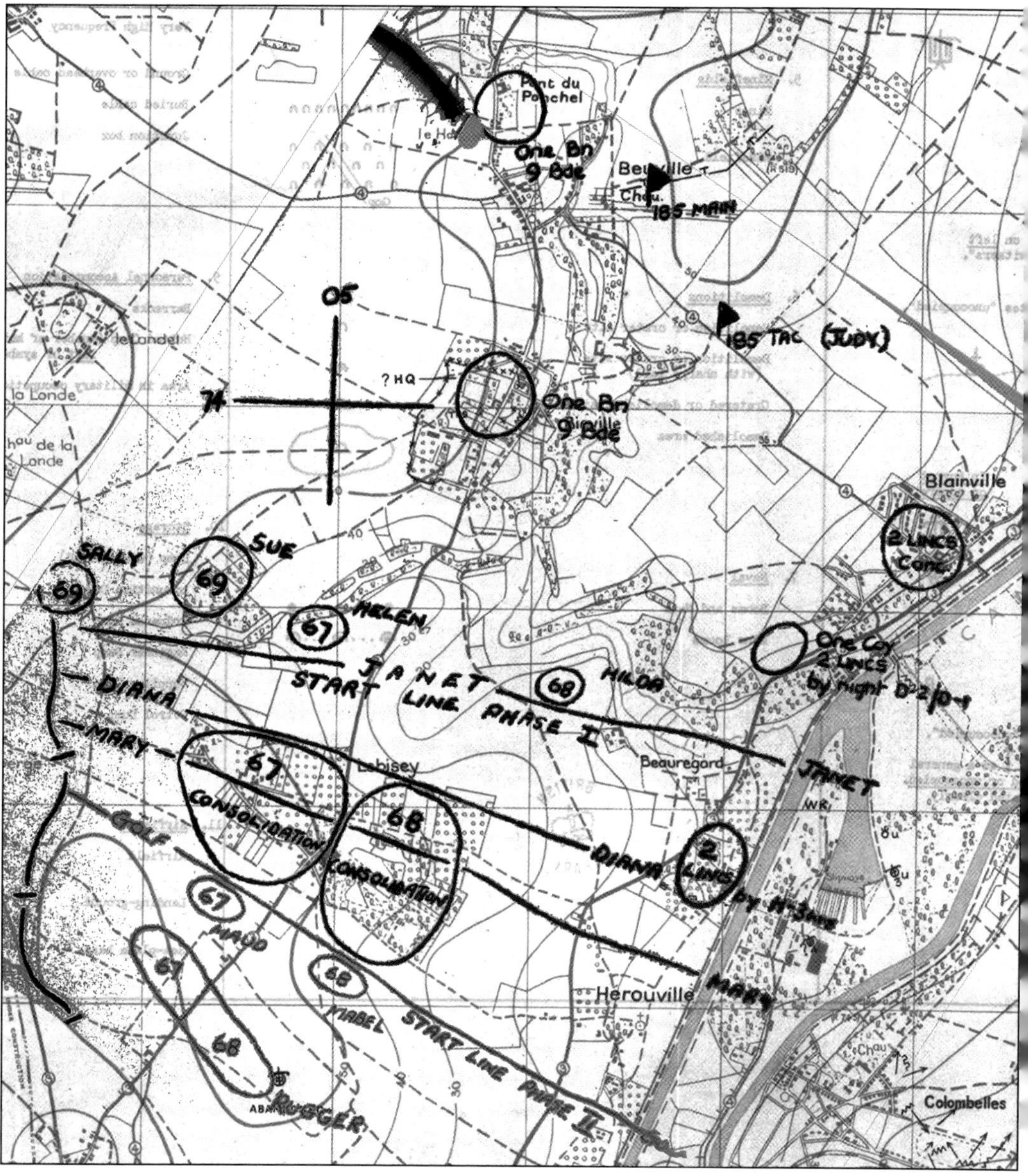

The 185 Brigade CHARNWOOD overlay applied to a 1:25,000 map showing the plan for the attack on Lebisey Wood and village. Battalion numbers: 67 = 1 Norfolk , 68 = 2 Warwick, and 69 = 2 KSL.

Chapter One

D Day and the 'First Phase'

This chapter sets the scene, summarizing, firstly, the development of the original plan that encompassed the capture of Caen on D Day, the re-planning resulting from Eisenhower's and Montgomery's concerns and the German reinforcement of Normandy; and secondly, the impact of the decision to 'go' despite less than ideal weather conditions, and the fight through German forces deployed in depth up to D+3.[1]

The COSSAC Plan

In the aftermath of the Casablanca Conference, Lieutenant General Sir Fredrick Morgan was appointed to lead the Anglo-American COSSAC team that was tasked to come up with proposals for the invasion of North-West Europe. The planners were not, however, starting from scratch but building on information gathered and work carried out on the 'return to Europe' by Combined Operations Headquarters since 1940. Working with the resources that the chiefs of staff and their service heads were willing to make available to a project that some doubted, COSSAC's initial work centred on recommending where the assault landing should take place. Their recommendation was primarily based on the suitability and capacity of the beaches, the level of enemy defence and the importance of remaining within range of fighter cover. On these grounds Lower Normandy was a straightforward choice, one that was put to the Combined Chiefs of Staff and political leaders at the First Quebec Conference (QUADRANT). Lower Normandy was significantly less well defended than the Pas de Calais, where thirty-eight enemy divisions were concentrated in mid-1943. The target date for the invasion was set as the beginning of May 1944.

Within the Normandy option, General Morgan argued that such was the importance of Caen on the Allied left flank that it needed to be taken as a part of the first act of the invasion. The city stood in the way onto more open ground running down to Falaise, and thence on to Paris and the Reich, and its capture was planned be the primary task of a British airborne division. It was originally intended that there would be just three landing beaches, eventually to be named JUNO, GOLD and OMAHA. Beach 306, which was to become SWORD, was initially discarded on the basis of its narrowness at just 800 yards, confined by flanking rocks and its proximity to the emerging defences around the small port of Ouistreham. The COSSAC plan called for a link up with the airborne troops on D Day, but it was over 15 miles from Courseulles at the centre of JUNO Beach to the River Orne bridges in the centre of Caen – a very tall order.

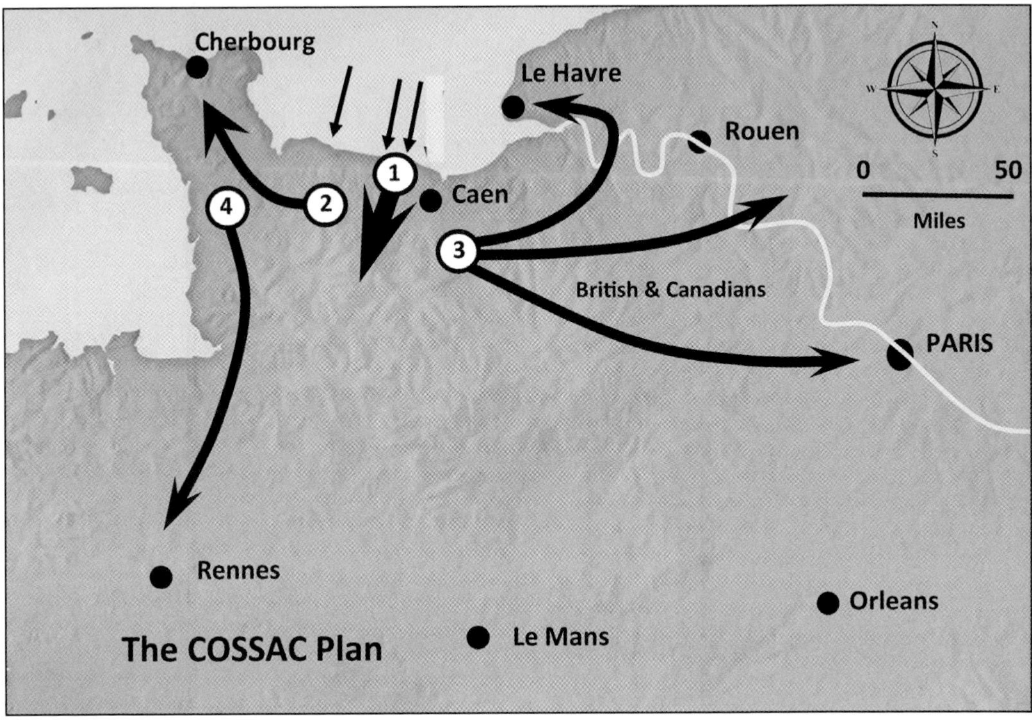

The COSSAC plan …

Montgomery Modifies the Plan

Having handed over their respective commands, but while still in the Mediterranean prior to assuming responsibility for the invasion, Generals Montgomery and Eisenhower were shown COSSAC's OVERLORD plan by Churchill. Both commanders agreed, based on intelligence available at New Year 1944, that it was under-resourced and on too small a scale to deal with the expected rate of German reinforcement. On his return to London Montgomery set the staff of 21st Army Group to reworking the plan and seeking political support for a significantly larger allocation of resources from the UK and US. In widening the frontage of the invasion Montgomery aimed to present Rommel with three challenges: not just defending Caen, but also recapturing Bayeux and defending the Cotentin Peninsula. Despite opposition from the likes of Admiral King and concerned heads of service and ministries of production, the extra resources were agreed, but the consequence was a delay of a month in mounting OVERLORD. This took D Day to the end of May or beginning of June 1944, the exact date being dictated by the coincidence of daylight for the bombardment, suitable tides for landing and moonlight for the drop of airborne troops.

In upscaling the invasion Montgomery inserted two new assault beaches to the flanks of the original three. In the west, UTAH was added at the foot of the Cotentin Peninsula to avoid having to cross the extensive inundations around Carentan in order to facilitate the early capture of the port of Cherbourg. To the east, Beach 306, previously ruled out as impractical, was adopted as SWORD, and the 3rd Division landing there would now be responsible for the capture of Caen.

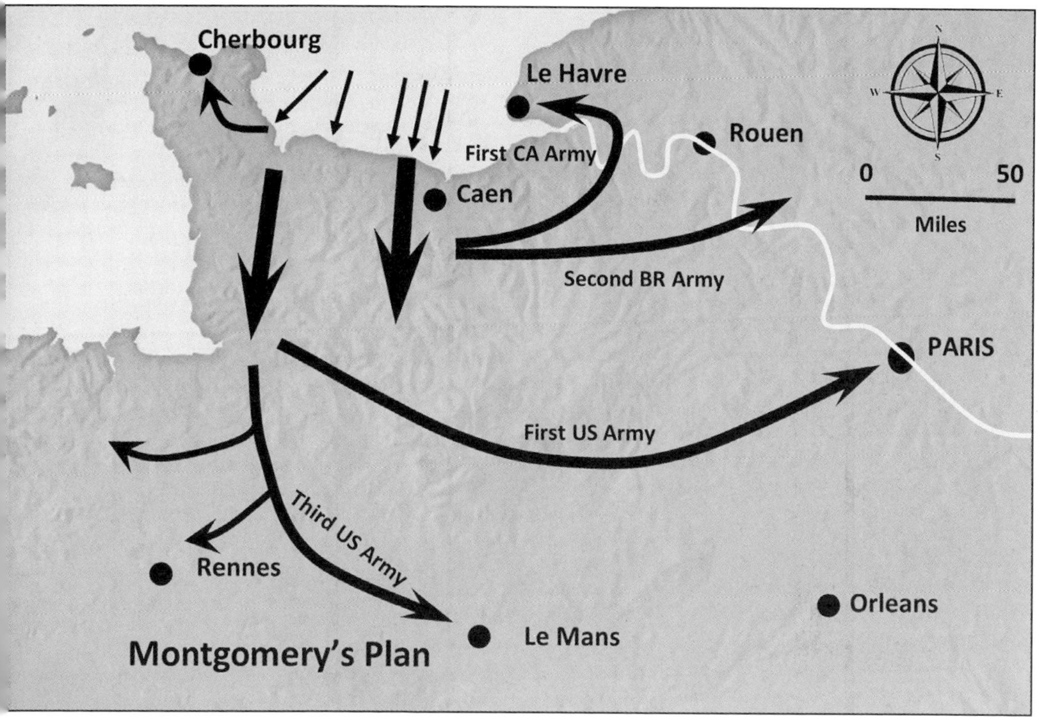

… and Montgomery's modifications of early 1945.

A convalescent Churchill meets senior Allied commanders and staff in Marrakesh, December 1943.

In the revised plan, the British airborne division would now form a buffer between the Rivers Orne and Dives. Against the opposition expected in January 1944, an assault by an infantry division followed by the advance of a mobile column based on a tank regiment and an infantry battalion to seize the Orne bridges in the city seemed entirely feasible. Outline plans were discussed, and concepts of operations were developed by army, corps and divisional headquarters, with the actual location, date and time only gradually being revealed down the chain of command.

The German Reinforcement

While the Allies were working on their plans, during the early months of 1944 Berlin was preoccupied with the Soviet winter offensive; but in March, as Allied plans were maturing, Hitler's attention turned to the west and the impending invasion. The German commanders were fully convinced by the efforts of the Allies in Operation FORTITUDE, plus their own military estimates, that the invasion would come in the Pas de Calais area. Perhaps, however, the Allied deception was a little too effective, since the number of divisions being marked on German maps of the UK continued to grow to a point at which OKW believed that there were sufficient Allied troops for a preliminary or secondary landing. The quantity of shipping that the Luftwaffe was reporting in the ports of the West Country led them to conclude that Normandy was the likely place for such an enterprise. Consequently, troops were to be moved from areas that *Generalfeldmarschall* von Rundstedt's estimate identified as being unlikely Allied targets. The redeployments have been ascribed to 'Hitler's intuition', but this is wrong; they were based on analysis of a combination of fact and FORTITUDE's fiction.

The 352nd Division came forward to the coast from the St Lo area, thus reducing the 716th Coastal Division's frontage by half, and on the Cotentin Peninsula the 91st *Luftlande* Division and 6 *Fallschirmjäger* Regiment increased defences en route to Cherbourg. On the eastern flank, a regiment was brought across from the Le Havre area, and around Caen the 21st Panzer Division was moved from Brittany to bolster the defences of the city. The division's two infantry regiments, artillery and anti-tank assets were redeployed in depth astride the Orne and Canal de Caen, behind the 716th Division. The 21st's panzer regiment was deployed around Falaise, less than two hours' drive from the coast. This highly significant reinforcement of the Lower Normandy coast was revealed to the Allies in a series of ULTRA intercepts by the code-breakers at Bletchley Park. Bletchley's Western Front Committee reported on 19 May 1944 that '21 Pz Div is moving North from RENNES to the area South of CAEN.' The source was so secret that only the three army commanders and Montgomery and Eisenhower had the details. Those in the chain of command below them were only broadly aware of the reinforcement through carefully worded intelligence summaries. The 21st Army Group's BIGOT Top Secret intsum of 4 June 1944 is a fine example of denial of knowledge followed by snippets of confirmation:

> The chief gaps in our knowledge of the enemy in the Neptune area are the strength and location of 21 Panzer Division, the location of 352 Division …

Hitler and his staff calculated that the Allies had sufficient troops for a secondary landing on the coast of France.

> Nothing more has come to light about 21 Panzer Division; but there is slowly growing evidence of tank tracks North of the Caen–Bayeux lateral [N13] . . . A single soldier from 352 Division is reported to have been making for Arromanche in March.[2]

There followed some 'supposition' about the 352nd Division, followed by obfuscation, stating that it 'is all very neat and tidy but rationalised beyond our intelligence.'[3]

Information regarding the reinforcement in April and May came too late for plans to be changed, and no further resources were available to enlarge the scale of the invasion. It followed that expectations of capturing Caen on D Day were being increasingly hedged in documents and orders, while phrases such as 'in the following days' started to appear.

Invasion

The fine settled weather of May 1944 started to break down at the end of the month, with Allied meteorologists reporting a series of frontal systems approaching across the Atlantic. D Day was eventually postponed by twenty-four hours, and rather than wait two weeks until the next combination of tide and moon in the middle of the month, with all the consequent implications for security leaks, Eisenhower decided to 'go'. In doing this he accepted that the weather conditions were not good. The air forces gave their opinion that conditions for airborne operations and bombing were marginal, and the navies said that landing was possible but would be slowed by the expected sea state. These were risks that the

Supreme Commander had to take, and it is no wonder that he had a short statement ready in his pocket, just in case, taking responsibility for the failure of the assault on Normandy.

The weather-delayed crossing of the Channel by naval Force S bound for SWORD Beach on the night of 5/6 June, along with the bombardment of the coast by the navies, went remarkably well. However, with cloud cover and the time added to bomb runs, the strike by the heavies of the Eighth US Air Force, as predicted by Leigh-Mallory, contributed little. For example, in the strike on the gun battery known as MORRIS (WN 17) only a third of the bombs were released, and most of those that were dropped fell in the open ground between MORRIS and the defended locality of HILLMAN.

As 8 Brigade, the assault brigade, approached SWORD beach aboard its various landing craft, the sea conditions were such that the Sherman DD tanks of the 13/18 Hussars that were to have swum ashore from 7,000 yards out to sea were brought in to 5,000 yards. Conditions here were little better, and the DD tanks, with less than 3 feet of freeboard, could only manage about half the speed achieved during exercises, while the waves kept the crew manning the bilge pumps. The concept was that the DDs, when their tracks engaged the sea bottom, would motor towards the beach until they were hull down in the water, from where, with the fire from seaward lifting, they would engage enemy positions that came to life in the five minutes before the breaching teams arrived. In the event, the breaching teams' Landing Craft Tank had caught up with the DDs and, as the tank's flotation screens were being dropped, the thirty-four 'funnies' of the breaching teams were disembarking not only around them but in front of them. This reduced the Sherman's arcs of fire, and consequently the overall effect of DDs on SWORD Beach was significantly reduced – a clear impact of the risky decision to 'go'.

Once on the beach, armoured vehicle casualties mounted, while creating gaps through the defences was far from straightforward and took longer than anticipated. Meanwhile, the dismounted engineers and Royal Navy clearance teams were at work. Rather than the landing taking place when the beach obstacles were fully exposed with, on SWORD, between 300 and 400 yards of beach, the Sappers arrived to find that they were working in 4½ feet of water on just 150 yards of sand. The tidal harmonics had been calculated on the nearest data the hydrographers had, which was for Le Havre and Cherbourg. This error was exacerbated by the sea state, with the result that the clearance of 250 yards of obstacles on both QUEEN WHITE and RED could not be achieved that morning. As the tide rose, the landing craft were left threading their way through not only the obstacles and drowned or knocked-out vehicles, but also damaged craft, all of which inevitably slowed the landing. Delays on the beach mounted throughout the morning, slowing the tempo of the 3rd Division's operations inland.

The level of destruction wrought by the fire of the run-in shoots fell short of expectation. For example, Lord Lovat was told that the heavy concrete fire control tower at Ouistreham to the east of SWORD Beach would be destroyed

With delays in opening exits, the beach was soon clogged with knocked-out, drowned and bogged assault vehicles, while the tide was rising around them.

by naval gunfire, but it still stands today, with barely a mark on it. In contrast, the 'drenching fire' by craft and guns of all types on the beach/coastal defences had in a number of key places ripped up barbed wire, sympathetically detonated mines and collapsed stretches of trench. This fire, which reached its crescendo minutes before the force's touchdown, may not have destroyed the enemy sheltering under concrete, but it did stun many of the defenders – temporarily.

In the centre of SWORD Beach, from where the advance on Caen was to develop, Strong Point COD (WN 20) barred the way to companies of the 1st South Lancashire and the 2nd East Yorkshire regiments and delayed the opening of most of the eight planned exits from the beach. COD was cleared around 0900 hours, but traffic was only beginning to make its way off the beach an hour later.

One significant impact of the accumulated delaying factors was to postpone the arrival of the Staffordshire Yeomanry's (Staffs Yeo) Shermans, which were, along with 2nd King's Shropshire Light Infantry (2 KSLI), to form the mobile column that would lead the dash to Caen. In the case of the Staffs Yeo, the delay was extended by German guns as far east as Le Have opening fire and causing their LCTs to turn back out to sea until the big guns of Bombarding Force D had again neutralized the enemy batteries.

Objective HILLMAN

The headquarters of the German 736 Regiment was built on the Périers Ridge south of the village of Colleville, from where its machine guns and anti-tank guns commanded the centre of the 3rd Division's axis of advance to Caen. Landing behind the two assault battalions, 2 Suffolks were to clear Colleville and MORRIS before taking on HILLMAN, which was surrounded by belts of barbed wire and mines. The Suffolks had batteries of 105mm Priests to support them, but the cruiser detailed to provide fire support could not help since the naval

Forward Officer Bombardment and his party had been lost on the beach. Crucially, the battalion with a platoon of engineers was to breach the minefield by hand, as the support of Sherman flails to the mobile column was considered more important (the main effort).

With Colleville cleared, the Polish gunners manning MORRIS surrendered quickly, but the attack on HILLMAN launched at 1310 hours with the tanks remaining outside the minefield, failed. This resulted in 185 Brigade, particularly 1st Norfolks, being shot up crossing the open country to the flanks. A misappreciation of the strength of HILLMAN, and the mistaken belief that an infantry battalion could take it quickly, added to the list of delaying factors.

HILLMAN, however, had to be taken, and Colonel Goodwin knew that close support of tanks on the enemy position would be required. To achieve this, the only option was for the Sappers to widen the breach by hand to a width of 20ft. At close proximity to the defenders, and with the Sappers working on their bellies, this was a slow process and, as a result, H Hour for the second attack was not until 1900 hours. This time, with tanks inside the mines and wire, the Germans surrendered or went to ground in the concrete bunkers. *Oberst* Krug's headquarters held out overnight beneath 2m of concrete, but the following morning, the commander of 736 Infantry Regiment and around fifty officers and soldiers surrendered to the Suffolks,

The Advance on Caen

The Intermediate Brigade, 185 Brigade, was to lead the advance on Caen, but having waited for nearly two hours, 2 KSLI set off without the tanks of the delayed Staffs Yeo. The battalion was soon under artillery fire and in action with German infantry on the Périers Ridge, one company being peeled off to the right flank to deal with a German artillery battery. Lieutenant Colonel Maurice, with the tanks finally joining the KSLI, did not allow his battalion to be pinned down but forced them on to their next objective, the straggling villages of Biéville and Beuville. These took some time to clear by two rifle companies supported by tanks and M10s on the flanking high ground. Once they were taken, Y Company and a handful of tanks resumed the advance and crossed the steep-sided valley of the Dan stream, known as the 'Anti-tank Obstacle'. By late afternoon, having fought through German positions sited in depth between SWORD and Caen, the KSLI was only able to penetrate a short distance into the wooded village of Lebisey. Having encountered far more resistance than originally estimated, the battalion lacked sufficient combat power to clear the village and woods and advance into the city. Consequently, the leading company was withdrawn. With reports of the movement of panzers around Caen, there was little option but to pull back and consolidate on the line of the Anti-tank Obstacle. Rather than allowing the division to become overextended towards Caen, the East Riding Yeomanry and the battalions of 9 Infantry Brigade were held back by General Rennie as a strong reserve to fight the expected attack of 21st Panzer Division.

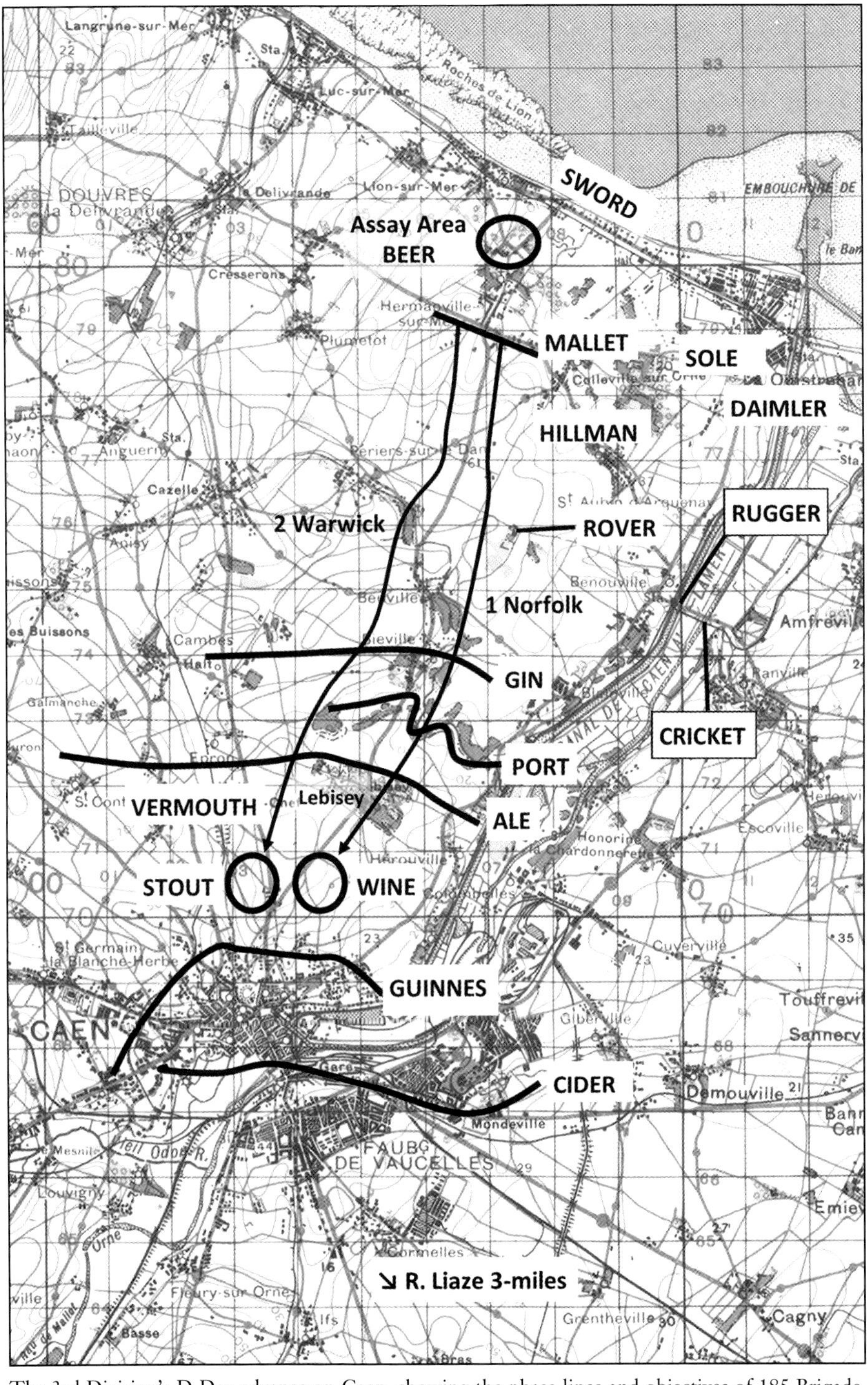

The 3rd Division's D Day advance on Caen, showing the phase lines and objectives of 185 Brigade. The KSLI's Mobile Column followed the Hermanville (Line MALLET)–Lebisey road between the Warwicks and Norfolks to the high ground of WINE and STOUT. Line PORT was the naturally steep-sided Dan valley known as the 'Anti-tank Obstacle'.

Counter-Attack of the 21st Panzer Division

> General Marcks took the leadership of the attack in his own hands and, thereupon, told *Oberst* von Oppeln-Bronikowski that the war would be lost if he did not succeed in hurling the British back into the sea.

At 1615 hours, 2 KSLI's and the Staffs Yeo's war diaries both recorded, 'German tanks seen approaching from the west.'[4] Part of the task of the Yeomanry's commanding officer, Colonel Eadie, was to cover the six-mile-long western flank of the brigade group, which was thinly held; he therefore requested the return of A Squadron from HILLMAN, where it had been deployed to support the Suffolks.

In common with a number of senior commanders from Rommel downwards, *Generalmajor* Feuchtinger was away from his division in Paris. On his return, the focus was on preparing an attack on the airborne landing east of the River Orne, but at 1130 hours (Allied time), as his attack about to be delivered, General Marcks ordered the division less 125 *Panzergrenadiers* to launch an immediate counter-attack against the British inland from SWORD Beach. This change of mission required a complete rearrangement of orders and the planning of routes to the east of the Orne, which caused additional delays.

The shortest route to the new assembly area to the east of the Orne was through Caen, but the only bridges still intact were in the city and these were being attacked by artillery and fighter-bombers. The commander of 22 Panzer Regiment, *Oberst* von Oppeln-Bronikowski, was forced to direct his tanks on a longer route west of the city.

As a result of the deployment of 21st Panzer Division in depth immediately behind the 716th it was impossible to disengage much of the division's *panzergrenadiers* from fighting with 6th Airborne Division east of the Orne. Werner Kortenhaus, a veteran of the 21st, concluded that 'The 21. Panzer Division was no longer a cohesive formation. The elements that could be assembled for the decisive counter-attack in the afternoon of 6 June 1944 amounted to less than half a panzer division.'[5] It can be argued that this was the result of Rommel's 'string of pearls' tactic; the 21st Panzer Division was not an effective operational reserve.

General Feuchtinger planned to attack with two *Kampfgruppen*, one based on 22 Panzer Regiment and the other on the available infantry of *Oberst* Rauch's 192 *Panzergrenadier* Regiment, with some regrouping between the infantry and the panzer companies. *Oberst* von Oppeln-Bronikowski's armour heavy *Kampfgruppe* on the right was to swing around the wood at the end of the Anti-tank Obstacle and head north-east via the crest of the Périers Ridge towards SWORD Beach. The infantry-heavy *Kampfgruppe* Rauch on the left was to strike north via Mathieu and Cressons to the sea between Lion and Luc-sur-Mer.

Generalleutnant Marcks, the commander of LXXXIV Corps, now arrived and berated Feuchtinger for the delays, objecting 'strongly to the division's approach march and the manner in which the division had been commanded in battle up to this point.'

First in action were Oppeln-Bronikowski's twenty-four Panzer IVs. The Staffs Yeo and a troop of anti-tank guns on the Périers Ridge opened fire as they came into range at 1,000 yards. Despite moving fast, the Germans lost six tanks, so this first attack was halted and the panzers resorted to a 'horizon crawl' to the north. Meanwhile, further west, *Kampfgruppe* Rauch were advancing into the void between the British and the Canadians, who were advancing from JUNO Beach. By 2000 hours the leading troops had reached the coast and were turning east and west. In the area to the west of Lion-sur-Mer, an East Riding Yeomanry squadron assisted the Lincolns and knocked out a half-track and another light armoured vehicle for the loss of one of their tanks. At this point the deep throbbing sound of massed aircraft could be heard approaching from the north. Landing astride the River Orne, these were the glider-and-tug combinations of 6 Airlanding Brigade (Operation MALARD) and a re-supply drop for 6th Airborne Division (Operation ROB ROY). Kortenhaus recalled:

> The sight of this mighty airborne armada had unsuspected and unforeseen consequences on the German side. For the men of the 21. *Panzer Division*

A column of 105mm SP guns based on captured French armour. The industrialist and reserve artillery officer Major Becker oversaw such conversions that equipped 21st Panzer Division.

> and 716. *Infanterie Division*, this incoming flight was an immense demonstration of the Allied control of the air. Not a single German aeroplane contested the approach. All the grenadiers could do was lie on their backs and fire on the aircraft with their rifles. The lack of suitable means to defend against the incoming flight was shattering and had significant psychological effects. Many now realized that the war was lost.

Believing that the drop was behind them, the two *Kampfgruppen* promptly withdrew. For the 3rd Division it was a short and nervy night, expecting a renewal of the German counter-attack. A combination of late authorization of the release of the 12th *Hitlerjugend* SS Panzer Division, its misdirection and air interdiction had delayed the arrival of this powerful formation. Further away, the Panzer *Lehr* Division was still well to the south, but nonetheless, the 21st and the *Hitlerjugend* were ordered to attack on the 7th. However, there were further delays thanks to Allied fighter-bombers, and *Generalmajor* Feuchtinger stayed his hand and instead of attacking, deployed his division to defend Caen.

The Following Days

On D+1 the advance on Caen was to be resumed by the divisions of I Corps to secure their D Day objectives. On the right flank of the 3rd Division, 9 Brigade's battalions advanced from Périers-sur-le-Dan initially with little opposition, but when D Company of the 2nd Battalion, Royal Ulster Rifles (2 RUR) approached Cambes-en-Plaine they fought a brutal engagement with a battalion of Kurt 'Panzer' Meyer's 25 SS *Panzergrenadiers*. This regiment was the leading element of *Hitlerjugend* that had arrived during the night of 5/6 June. The RUR were beaten back with losses, but Rommel's drive to the sea was halted in this area as it was in front of the Canadians. Meanwhile, the advance on Lebisey was resumed by 185 Brigade, with an attack by 2nd Battalion, Warwickshire Regiment, but despite the assistance of the Norfolks the defence mounted by 21st Panzer Division, in contrast with the management of their counter-attack the previous evening, was masterly. Lebisey village and wood remained firmly in German hands until the fall of Caen.

The RUR's attack on Cambes was resumed on 9 June (D+3) with the full resources of the battalion and significant firepower, including the tanks of the East Riding Yeomanry. With the help of 1st Battalion King's Own Scottish Borderers (1 KOSB), Cambes was taken as dusk fell, and the SS outposts deployed there were driven back to their main position just a couple of hundred yards south of the village. The 3rd Division could make no more progress, and it was clear that the Germans, having deployed two panzer divisions around Caen, intended to hold the city. At the same time, it was equally clear that, at this stage of the build-up, the Second British Army lacked sufficient combat power to take their now well defended objective. Consequently, the main effort for the time being was transferred west from I Corps to XXX Corps, which was fighting south of Bayeux to get through Tilly-sur-Seulles and Panzer *Lehr*, towards Villers Bocage.

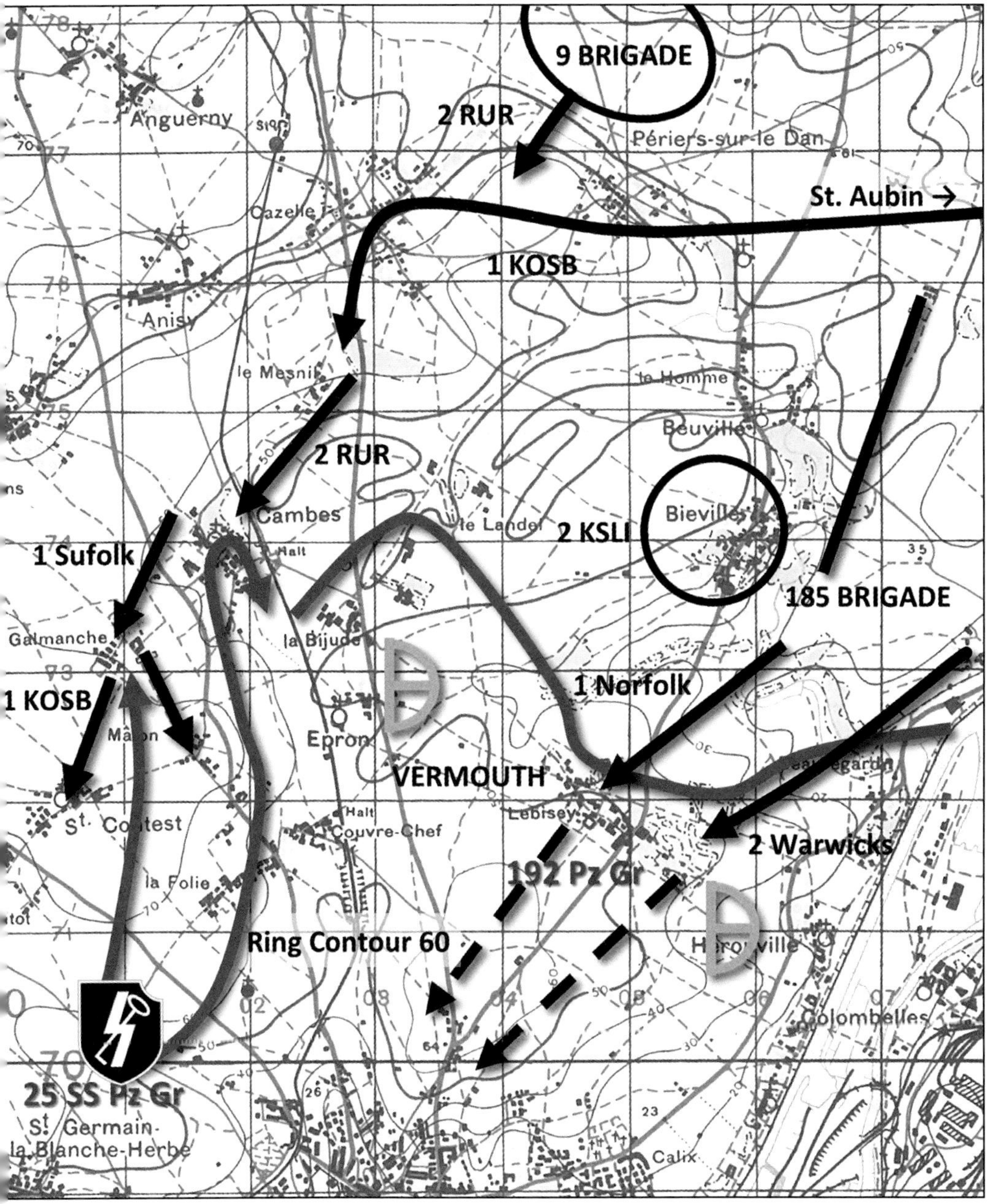

3rd Division's plans for the advance on Caen during D+1 and the arrival of I and II Battalions of 25 SS *Panzergrenadier* Regiment.

'The End of the First Phase'

'Caen is the key to Cherbourg.' [Montgomery to Bradley, 11 June 1944]

The failure to take Caen in the first few days of the invasion was just the first of several changes of aspiration forced on the Allies by the German reinforcement of Lower Normandy in the spring of 1944. The US VII Corps was also meeting stronger resistance than expected and was making slow progress in its advance north up the Cotentin Peninsula to capture the port city of Cherbourg. Given the scale of fighting and the enemy's success in 'roping off the lodgement', resources for the planned simultaneous drives south into Brittany and towards Falaise were lacking. Commander Edwards noted:

> There is always that critical period in an amphibious assault, when the first waves have begun to tire. If the follow-up and the build-up are not quick and sufficient the critical period will be prolonged and become a great danger to the whole enterprise. The military ideal is for the follow-up troops to be in position to attack 'through' the assault waves as soon as the latter begin to slow down through fatigue or expenditure of supplies. But like other military ideals in amphibious operations, this is only possible of attainment if the maritime component is perfect in every detail.
>
> The existence of such a critical period was, of course, well known to the German General Staff.[6]

In the Second Army's area, by 11 June the counter-attacks such as they were, to the north of Caen and more particularly to the west of the city by the 12th *Hitler-jugend* and Panzer *Lehr* divisions, had all failed. The Germans had, however, succeeded in containing I Corps' drive on Caen and to the south. General Dempsey had been discussing a switch of I Corps operations to take Caen to the east of the Orne as the situation north of the city was 'a bit messy'. General Montgomery, however had other ideas that he outlined in a signal to Major General Simpson, Deputy Director of Military Operations at the War Office:

> The Germans are doing everything they can to hold on to CAEN. I have decided not to have a lot of casualties by butting up against the place; so I have ordered Second Army to keep up a good pressure at CAEN, and to make its main effort towards VILLERS BOCAGE and EVRECY and thence S.E. towards FALAISE.

Consequently, General Dempsey's attention now lay with XXX Corps to the west. Their focus was on driving south from Bayeux towards Point 213 overlooking Villers Bocage, where they had been due to form an armoured brigade-sized patrol base on the evening of D Day. While I Corps had been attempting to secure Caen, 50th Infantry and 7th Armoured divisions were already fighting a protracted battle to get south through the bocage country via Tilly-sur-Seulles. This started as a battle with the elite 130th Panzer *Lehr* Division, which was attempting to drive north to Bayeux on the same axis.[7]

As predicted by General Montgomery, the Germans were prepared to fight to hold Caen and its access to the more open country south to Falaise, and from there the routes east to the River Seine and south-east to Paris. Hitler insisted on this until well after military logic indicted that his divisions should withdraw to more defensible positions out of range of naval gunfire.

Generals Sir Miles Dempsey and Montgomery. With I Corps halted before Caen by the German intent to hold the city, and the airborne lodgement being considered too small to exploit, Dempsey, lacking resources for two concurrent battles, transferred his main effort to the west.

Naval Gunfire Support

The low priority that the Royal Navy had afforded to naval gunfire support was revealed by the Dieppe Raid in August 1942, when the destroyers underperformed through a combination of inadequate manning and training and the lack of an effective bombardment round. By 1944, with better equipment and experience of supporting landings in North Africa, Sicily and Italy, performance was greatly improved, as was that of air OPs.

Forward Observation and Bombardment Units consisted of parties of Royal Artillery officers who were already trained as FOOs and became Forward Officers Bombardment (FOB). They were supported by two RN telegraphists and a signalman. The officers attended courses, initially at the Royal Naval Gunnery School at Whale Island, Portsmouth, and later at the Bombardment School in Scotland, where they were taught how to observe and adjust naval gunfire.

For D Day across the five bombardment forces there was a total of eighty-four ships (battleships, monitors and cruisers) and twenty-seven landing craft gun (LC(G)). Aboard every ship was a Bombardment Liaison Officer (BLO), whose task was to interpret for the naval gunners the requirements of an engagement in support of the army, passed to them by the FOBs. Eight FOBs supported the 3rd Division (landing H+20 and H+30), six parachute trained FOBs, the 6th Airborne Division and four, the commandos of 1 SS Brigade.

An FOB, his signaller and morse code telegraphist encoding a request for fire in support of I Corps.

Most shoots were initially by observed or map-predicted fire, but once FOBs were successfully across the beach and inland they passed fire control orders to their ships of the Bombardment Force. Fire on targets in excess of 12 miles inland for cruisers and 17 miles for battleships was observed by Seafire aircraft, which until temporary airfields were opened operated from the UK. A Seafire AOP engagement of panzers moving across the area of Point 64 north of Caen is described thus:

> The Polish cruiser *Dragon* [5 × 150mm and 1 × 102mm guns] was engaging a battery, with air spotting, on 17th June and had just obtained two direct hits, when the pilot observed a column of tanks moving up from Caen to Lebisey. The ship quickly changed to this new target. After the third salvo, the pilot so

forgot his wireless procedure as to report the fourth 'so near one tank, it didn't matter'. The fifth was a 'direct hit on the forward end of one tank'. The sixth and seventh were in among the tanks, damaging several. The eighth was a near-miss and blew the tank bodily off the road. The ninth brought forth, 'Yippee! You've hit it on the cupola.' At this point the shoot ended as the aircraft was short of petrol.[8]

An FOB party photographed in the 3rd Division's area during 21/22 June 1944.

In the SWORD area for the period covered by this book, there was normally an anchor OP established in Ouistreham, in either the lighthouse, the church or the German fire control bunker. FOB parties travelled out from a base in the town to join formations due to receive naval gunfire support. Due to the fact that ships had to return to UK ports to rearm, and because of high levels of barrel wear thanks to the high velocities used, the number of engagements was strictly controlled. In the Eastern Task Force area battleships fired a total of 3,371 rounds during the campaign, but the cruisers fired 30,216. A high proportion of naval gunfire was counter-battery. FOB Captain Dawes recalled:

> There were requests that we should take on jobs that couldn't be done. Naval artillery is more like anti-tank guns than field or medium or even heavy artillery but the [naval] heavies were really WW1 static situation artillery. Naval guns are of high muzzle velocity, like anti-tank guns and of course both are designed for a specific purpose. Most targets were map targets, ground was undulating. Naval guns can paste a forward slope but cannot hit the reverse

> slope because of the flat trajectory, and of course there's always the danger of friendly fire casualties (quite common, sad to say), but with the long range of naval guns harassing fire onto backward areas was very important.

A member of the 12th *Hitlerjugend* SS Panzer Division described coming across the aftermath of a naval fire strike:

> The enemy had virtually cut to pieces units … with heavy artillery. The SPWs [Hanomag half-tracks] and equipment had been ripped apart and next to them lay pieces of our comrades. Others hung from the trees. A dreadful silence covered all.[9]

The 16-inch guns of HMS *Nelson* in action off the coast of Normandy.

On 14 June the *Hitlerjugend* suffered a significant loss to naval gunfire when its divisional commander SS *Brigadeführer* Fritz Witt was killed in a strike on his headquarters in the western suburbs of Caen. *Sturmbannführer* Hubert Meyer wrote:

> The headquarters had been bracketed by naval artillery and then hit. Our chief SS *Brigadeführer* Witt and the staff went to take cover in the shelters in the garden. He was the last into the shelter and was hit in the head and killed instantly by shrapnel from a naval shell that detonated in the trees.

It is no wonder that German commanders repeatedly requested to be allowed to withdraw beyond the range of naval artillery.

The adjustment of fire by bracketing indicates that this was observed indirect fire, in this case with an air observation post adjusting the ship's fire. It is possible that the headquarters could have been within range of a cruiser's guns, with this sector being supported by HMS *Frobisher* (7.5″), *Mauritius*, *Arethusa*, *Dragon* and *Danae* (all 6″), but it is much more likely to have been hit by 15-inch or 16-inch shells. These would have easily been within range – and more importantly, within accurate range. Allowing for the cruisers being a mile or two offshore, the 6-inch would have been at max range and less than accurate. Thus, the shells probably came from the battleships HMS *Nelson* (16″) or *Ramillies* (15″), or the monitor *Roberts* (15″). The latter returned to Portsmouth at some point on 14 June, but a matelot's memoir records that HMS *Ramillies* fired twenty five rounds of 15-inch on 14 June 'at some German camp'.

At a critical moment during Operation CHARNWOOD, Royal Navy Telegraphist Penny, using a manpack No. 68 Wireless Set, successfully called for fire from HMS *Rodney* at a range of almost 18 miles, although admittedly, this was from the high ground of Point 64 with line of sight to the bombardment line out to sea.[10]

Most FOBs deployed in jeeps, but those attached to formation headquarters with a primarily command and control function were mounted in half-tracks.

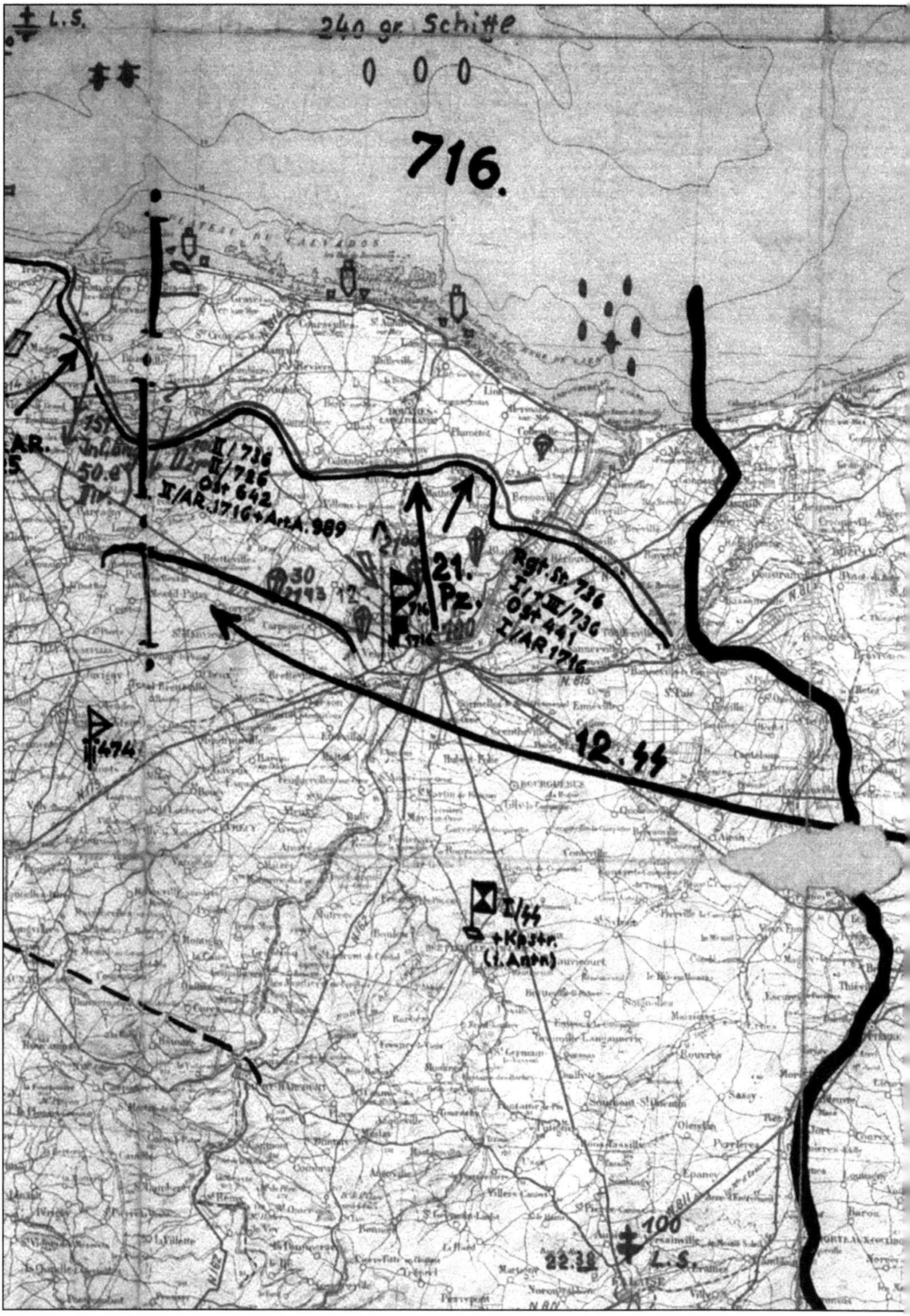

An extract from a map produced by C-in-C West's Headquarters showing the situation as seen by his staff on the evening of D Day.

Chapter Two

The Long June into July

With the focus of operation having been transferred further west, the role of I Corps, having effectively drawn the 21st Panzer and *Hitlerjugend* divisions to the area of Caen, was now to fix them in place. This would be achieved through continual activity, which would be a combination of local enterprises and operations mounted in support of attacks elsewhere on the army group front. The aim of capturing Caen was very much still alive, but for the time being resources did not permit another all-out attempt to take the city, as explained in the War Office report:

> This was a period from the Allied point of view of building up of resources to secure the lodgement area in a race against the enemy effort to bring in reserves and to launch a major counter-attack to thrust them back to the sea. On the left sector of the front, after the initial failure to capture Caen, resources did not permit a major offensive and operations were restricted primarily to active defence. On the right sector 30 Corps have begun to make efforts to deepen the lodgement area in the direction of Villers Bocage.[1]

'Active defence' for the 3rd Division meant maintaining pressure on the enemy by day and night and taking every opportunity to launch limited attacks to gain ground and/or advantage. It had been stressed in revised orders that 'should Caen not be captured on D Day and the defences prove to be strongly organised, direct frontal assaults which might prove costly should not be undertaken without reference to I Corps.'

In Defence

The 3rd Division was deployed with all three brigades in the line, usually with two battalions up and a third in reserve providing a 'firm base' and getting what rest it could. On the left, 185 Brigade covered the ground west from Canal de Caen; 8 Brigade was deployed facing Lebisey in the centre; and 9 Brigade overlooked open ground on the right towards 3rd Canadian Division's positions. This period of defence, as for other divisions holding the line, was a very difficult time for the 3rd Division, as the RUR's history notes:

> The governing factor in life at Cambes was, however, the intensity of the Boche shelling and mortaring; this was eternally imprinted upon the minds of those who survived until July 3rd, the day we left Cambes. During the period we lost between three and five men killed or wounded each day from

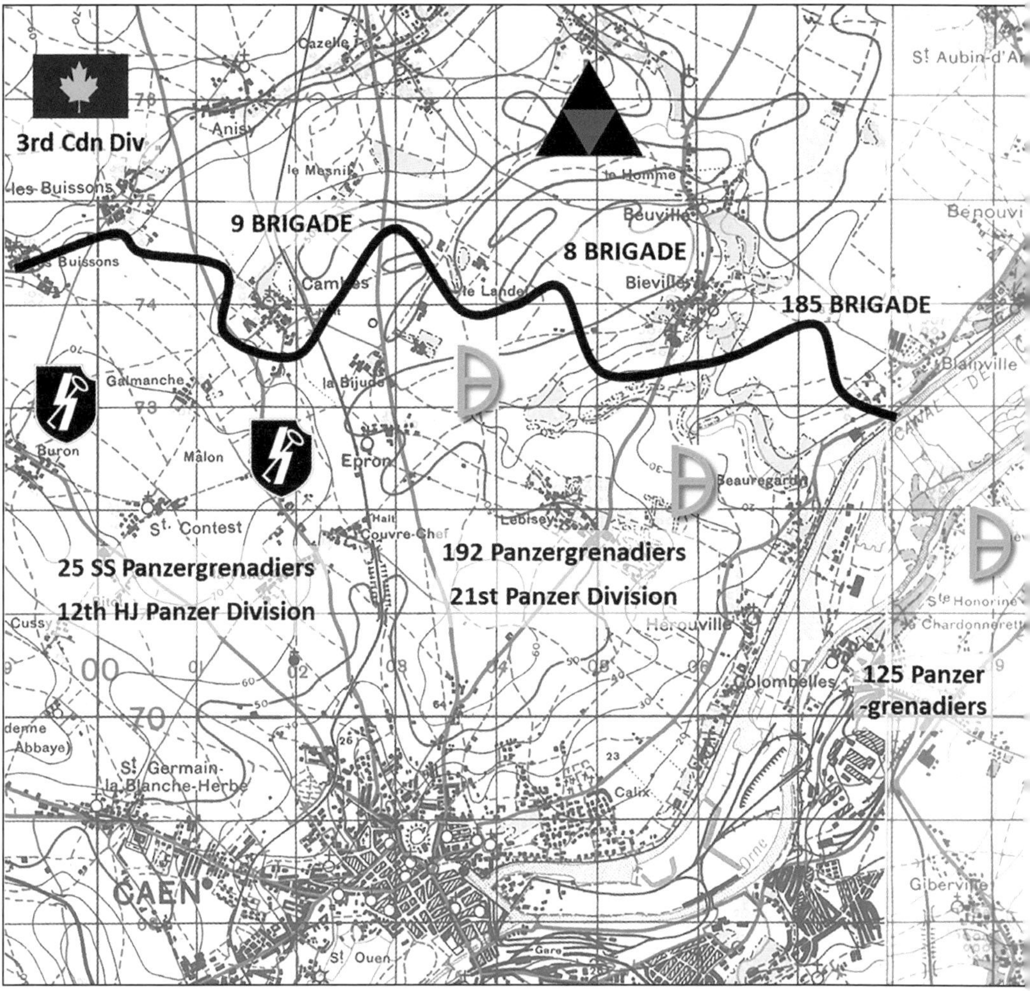

The 3rd Division's deployment, along with that of the 21st Panzer Division and 25 SS *Panzer-grenadiers*, following the 9 June attacks.

> shellfire. The Boche was adroit enough to select times when he could rely upon people leaving their slit trenches for one reason or another. He had the main road past the Church, the Chateau, and the area of Battalion Headquarters exactly ranged, while among the forward Companies it seems certain that he was able by some means to carry out observed shooting.[2]

The shelling was not all incoming, as the Suffolk's historian recorded:

> The Battalion established an observation post line just forward of Le Mesnil Wood. From there the gunners and the mortars made the most of their orders to hit the enemy as hard and as often as possible. Certainly, the amount of shelling passing overhead on to enemy positions was substantial and heartening. German reports have shown how devastating the shelling was and how often attacks and counter-attacks were broken up before they could make any progress. There were a number of tall trees in the forward

> edge of the Battalion position and the tops could often be seen to be swaying with the slipstream of shells passing over them. On at least one occasion a shell touched the top of a tree causing an air burst with consequent casualties below.

The battalions quickly learnt that 'routine in defence' had to be anything but routine, and that the periodic night-time reliefs-in-place had to be conducted in absolute silence, with protective patrols deployed in no-man's-land.

Producing obstacles to slow and shape an enemy attack was a key part of defensive activity, but to produce a barbed-wire obstacle worthy of the name, in close contact with the enemy, was almost impossible even at night. Not so mine-laying, which could be done with minimal noise while lying down. The RUR's history notes:

> As one means of strengthening our positions, mines were laid on an extensive scale. Long belts of anti-tank mines bridged the gap between ourselves, the Canadians on the right and 8th Brigade on our left. Additionally, our own Pioneer platoon under Lt Shimmin covered our own front, working always by night, since they were within speaking distance of the Boche. Anti-personnel mines were laid around the level crossing as a precaution against infiltration by Boche patrols down the avenue [of trees from the south-east].

A CANLOAN officer who joined with 2 Middlesex (Machine Gun) as a replacement after D Day, Lieutenant Fendick, described No. 1 Platoon s activities when he took over the platoon near Le Mesnil:[3]

> They were dug in, in the long, narrow, treed hedgerow which Pat [A Company's commander] had pointed out as we passed that afternoon. It was only a few yards wide but extended out about 100 yards from a farm complex into the wheat fields.
>
> One section (2 Vickers guns) of the platoon, in the right of the hedgerow tip, had Defensive Fire (DF) tasks extending across open fields for about 2–3,000 yards, covering the front and back of Cambes Wood, and enfilading across the front of a Canadian battalion of 3 Cdn Div to the west. The other section was pointed south and east, covering the front of Cambes Wood, which was about 800 yards beyond our hedge, and left (east) towards La Londe.
>
> During my first night with them in action it rained steadily, and we were also mortared several times during the night. I couldn't make up my mind whether to keep to the discomfort of a water-filled slit trench, but in some cover from the mortars, or get out under a tree where it was still wet but not so muddy, and chance the bombs. In fact I did both from time to time and neither was restful. Making the rounds to the guns throughout the night gave some relief from personal discomfort.
>
> I was pleased to find that I was not going to panic when under fire; one never knew until the first time how one would react. I found that concern for

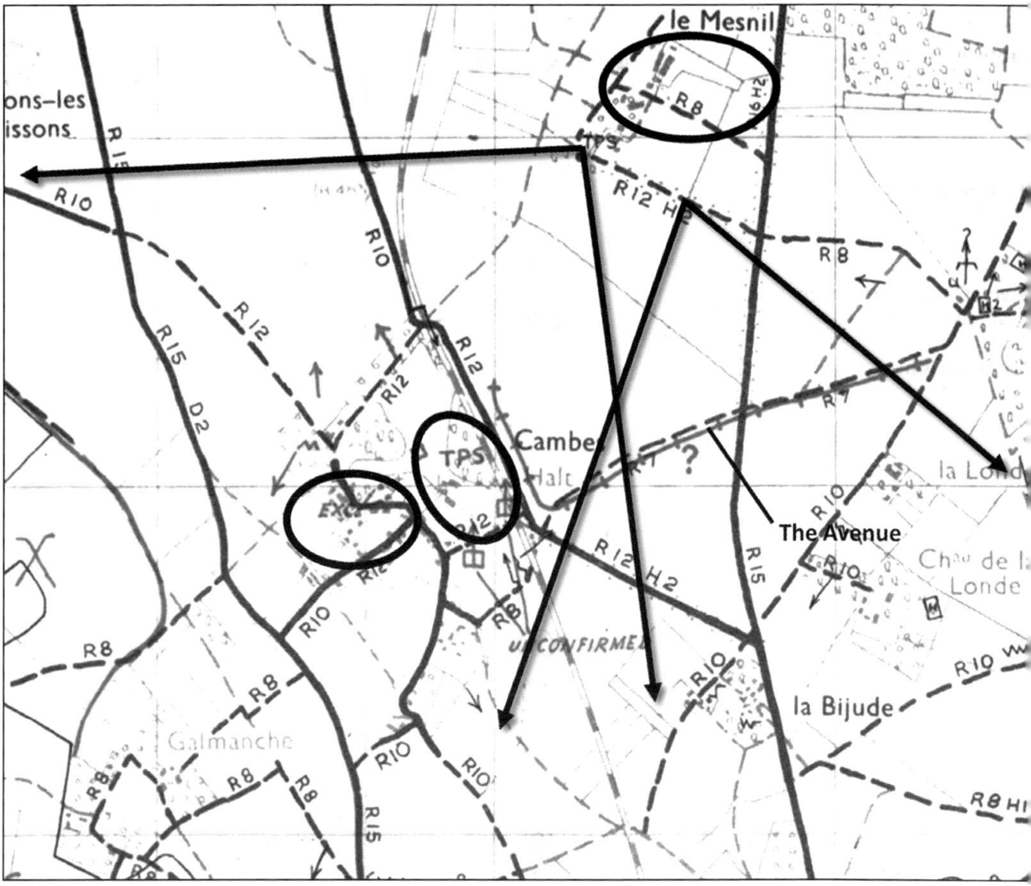

The arcs of fire of the Vickers machine guns of No. 1 Platoon, 2 Middlesex.

Machine-gunners of the Middlesex Regiment manning the 3rd Division's Vickers during pre-D Day training..

the men, and the checking which was always necessary, served to help keep one's mind off the personal danger. It was not so easy for the men, who had less responsibility to distract their minds from their own situation, so the NCOs and I had to keep this in our minds' eye at all times.

Also, if any example was needed, I learned very quickly from my Cockneys never to show trepidation, or even display signs of excitement, although there were many episodes which generated great nervous tension. They usually behaved as though it was all a peace-time exercise and few ever got jumpy, so as Platoon Commander I didn't dare display alarm or excitement, even if at times I felt very much like it. Their coolness and professionalism was a wonderful example which was of great benefit to me. Perhaps it was mutual.

Apart from sporadic shelling or mortaring, this position was usually quiet. And while we could see the odd Jerry movement (which we reported), they were a fairly long way off on the high ground, and our orders were not to engage unless called on for our DF (defensive fire) tasks; the restrictions on ammunition expenditure were still in effect. In this area too, our patrols usually dominated No-Man's-Land, so we were not bothered much by enemy patrols. But all our defensive positions were in widely scattered clusters, with open gaps between, so we had to stay very alert at all times.[4]

Despite the best efforts of the Royal Navy's Bombardment Squadrons operating in sea area TROUT to the east of SWORD, German batteries out to the east were not entirely suppressed, and the beach and divisional area were regularly shelled as well.

On the eastern flank there remained for a long time the necessity for bombardments other than those giving 'deep support' to our troops far inland. The batteries east of the River Orne and the big gun batteries at Le Havre were forever coming to life and having to be neutralised anew. This could not always be done, particularly in the case of the German mobile batteries east of the River Orne, where the contours of the land were such that they militated against accurate fire from low trajectory naval guns. The result was that the anchorage in the SWORD area had to be abandoned as it was considered that ships lying there would be exposed to unjustifiable risk from enemy shell fire.

The Germans also produced one or two other most annoying innovations. One of the most infuriating of these was a heavy gun on a railway truck mounting. The Germans used to keep this gun in a railway tunnel behind Houlgate, east of the Orne. At intervals they used to trundle it out, fire a round or two into our anchorage, and trundle it back again into the shelter of the tunnel just before our retaliatory shells arrived. This infernal jack-in-the-box was more annoying than harmful, but it was not silenced until our troops had cleared the enemy from the area.[5]

An infantry commander and his radio operator. The No. 18 Set was both cumbersome and fragile, a combination, along with its low power, that meant infantry communications, especially when moving, were invariably poor.

It was not only the naval anchorage off SWORD Beach that had to be abandoned, but also the Beach Maintenance Area and the logistic infrastructure that was being developed a little further inland.

> Owing to enemy shelling to the EAST from behind the River ORNE the PETER beaches were gradually developed in the hope that these would be out of accurate gun range. It had been hoped that OUISTREHAM which had been captured on D Day with the locks virtually intact would be operated by 101 Beach Sub Area and would have compensated for the limited capacity of the beaches but this never materialised as the port area was under constant shell fire from enemy positions on the EAST of the CAEN canal. On D+2 disaster nearly overtook the maintenance build up in this area as a

> stick of bombs hit one of the four sector stores dumps and 100,000 gallons of petrol and 400 tons of ammunition were lost. A new site was immediately reconnoitred for ammunition and petrol and the latter was brought in on a high priority from a cased petrol carrier lying in the anchorage. In actual fact, enemy interference with the unloading over this sector continued throughout this phase. In spite of the great gallantry and hard work displayed by all ranks which resulted in as high a daily average weight of stores per beach group being brought in as any other beach group achieved in the beach-head, the SWORD beaches were abandoned on 12 July.[6]

One of the guilty parties was known as the *Batterie de Tournebride* or the Houlgate Battery, almost 8 miles east of the Orne. This consisted of five 155mm guns and was considered a serious threat to the landing, so much so that it was initially

The Beach Maintenance Areas inland from SWORD (BMA MOON) were consistently shelled following D Day.

planned to be taken by No. 4 Commando in Operation FROG during D Day. However, two factors, the increasing numbers of enemy troops around Caen and the RAF and Royal Navy being confident that they could destroy the battery, led to the operation being cancelled. However, the bomber strike on the night of 5/6 June did little damage to the battery, and it remained the D Day target of the monitor HMS *Roberts*. The Houlgate Battery and the other guns to the east came into action periodically but they proved very difficult to knock out.

> The Houlgate Battery was under constant fire from bombarding ships. On 13th June *Nelson* engaged the target, with aircraft spotting, and out of seventeen salvoes fired, four fell within 100 yards, two within 50 yards, two within 10–15 yards and one was a direct hit. Next day the battery was engaged twice. Three direct hits resulted in the first shoot and in the second eight broadsides were reported as hits and a fire started. On 17th June the battery was still in action and *Ramillies* had eight direct hits on it. The aircraft reported: 'Battery all craters, hell of a mess – two guns buried in dirt, another gun drooping, piece chipped off second gun.'[7]

Despite optimistic reports such as these, the Germans only finally abandoned the Houlgate Battery at the end of June, moving the guns back to positions inland.

The German Perspective

With all three of the 3rd Division's brigades in a defensive line, they were faced by 192 *Panzergrenadiers* of the 21st Panzer Division and a battalion of the *Hitlerjugend* Panzer Division, some of the most effective German troops in Normandy. On 3rd Division's western boundary, *Obersturmführer* Havemeister, a platoon commander the II/25 SS *Panzergrenadiers*, prepared defences around the hamlet of Galmanche, all the while subject to Allied artillery fire:

> We were able to take turns digging by day and night. We cleared fields of fire by cutting down the crops during the night. We also laid Teller mines at the edges of the fields, with wires running from the mines to the bunkers.[8] The company headquarters section dug a narrow trench on the side of the manor away from the enemy. They blew a hole into the foundation wall and set up the company headquarters in the coal cellar. Although the young soldiers thought that the defences were finally complete, they later dug trenches connecting the platoons. In the other cellars … rooms were prepared for the wounded, for the storage of supplies and ammunition, and [as] temporary shelters for artillery observers and prisoners.
>
> To stop me bothering them, my young soldiers furnished my headquarters very comfortably. They covered the coal with mats from the chateau and brought down a Louis something-or-other chaise longue, which was covered with silk damask material …
>
> After repulsing two recce patrols and an unsuccessful enemy attack, we daily expected heavy fire and larger-scale operations. Instead, we enjoyed a

A Wespe 10.5cm le.FH 18/2 self-propelled gun mounted on a Panzer II chassis. These equipped four of the 12th *Hitlerjugend* Panzer Division's artillery batteries.

The 105mm M7 Priest, issued for D Day, remained in service with 3rd and 3rd Canadian divisions until after the fall of Caen, before being replaced by towed 25-pounders.

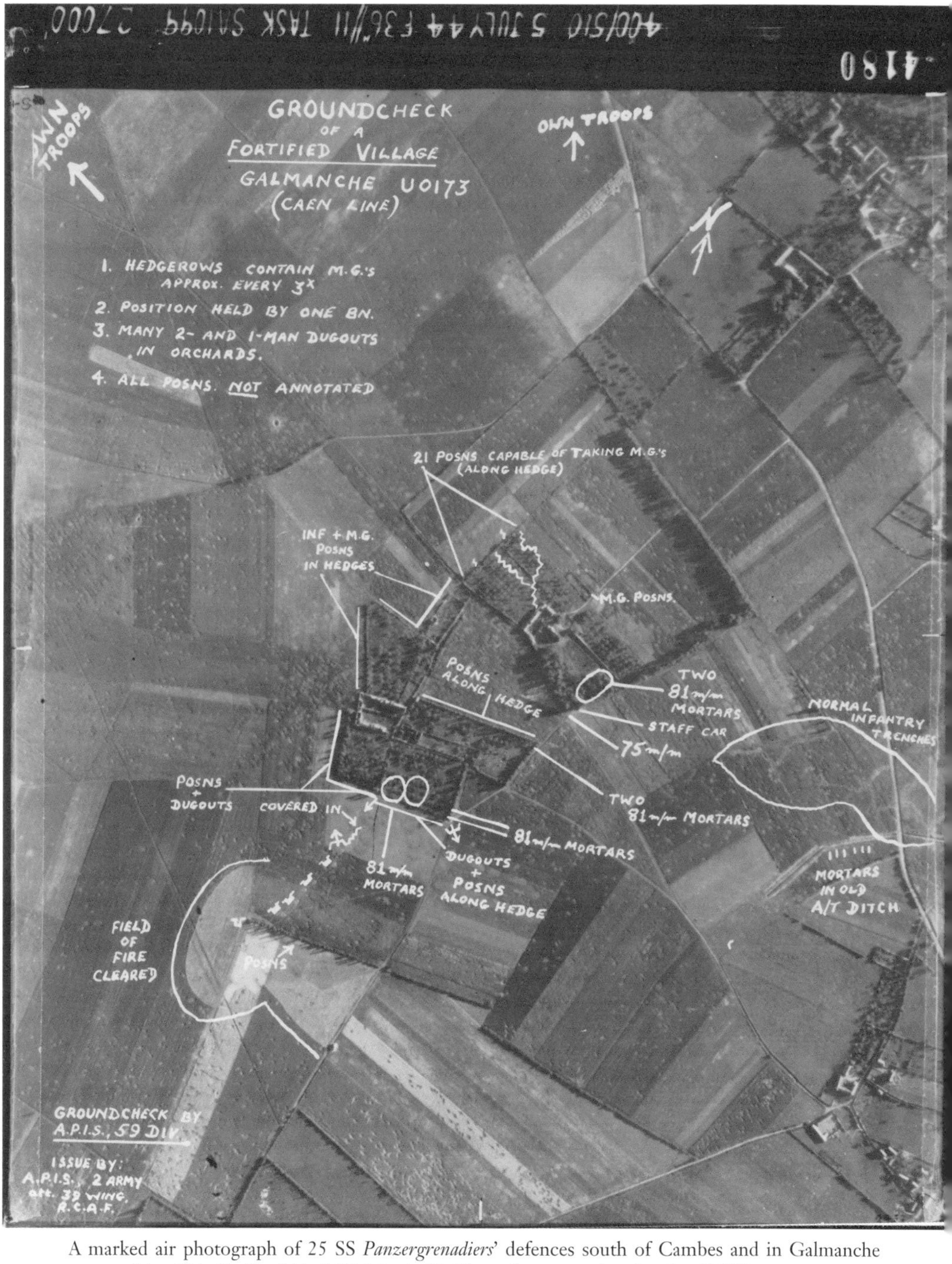

A marked air photograph of 25 SS *Panzergrenadiers*' defences south of Cambes and in Galmanche prepared by 59th (Staffordshire) Division's Air Photo Interpretation Section (APIS).

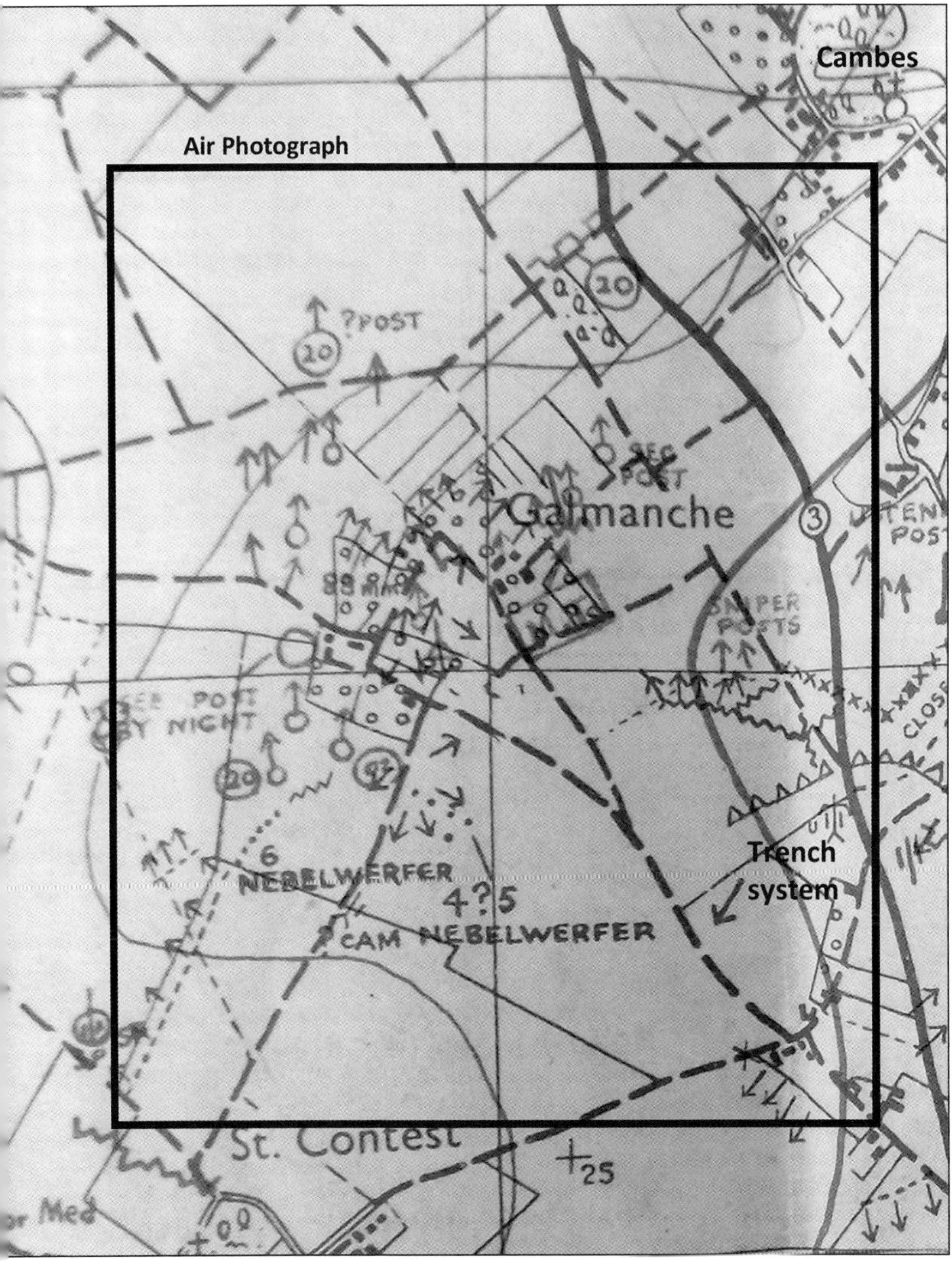

An extract of the defences overprint map for comparison.

> surprise visit from the rear by *Standartenführer* Kurt Meyer with a small entourage.[9] The Regimental commander was obviously satisfied that we had not dug our positions in close proximity to the buildings.[10]

The German defenders found themselves chronically short of combat supplies. As the invasion had been expected in the Pas de Calais, Army Group B's logistic bases were established east of the Seine in a position where combat supplies could be delivered to either Seventh or Fifteenth Army. As a result, supply columns faced a long journey to Normandy, including the crossing of the Seine, rendered difficult by the Transport Plan's air attacks, which seriously disrupted logistic traffic. Consequently, the *Hitlerjugend*'s logisticians, located in the forests of Grimbosq and Cinglais south of Caen, were more often than not short of supplies to send forward. They increasingly found themselves responsible for collecting supplies that had been brought round via the Chartres Gap, from the north of Paris. *Sturmmann* Decker of 25 SS *Panzergrenadiers* provides an insight into some of the practicalities of life for German infantrymen at the front during this phase of the Battle of Normandy:

> Disruption on the railways caused by Allied bombing and increased partisan activity meant supplies were no longer reaching the fighting troops at the front. As a result, we were given permission to enter French houses and to take whatever was necessary for personal use, such as clean underwear and so on, but nothing more. We were not allowed to take any more than was absolutely essential ... I can remember cutting up a bedsheet and wrapping the strips around my feet because I didn't have any socks. Fortunately, I had one chap in my mortar team who could always find food, so we never went hungry, as he always returned with a chicken, a duck, a rabbit, whatever he could find.
>
> One evening we came across an abandoned French farmhouse and went inside to have a look around and discovered a bed, which we hadn't seen for some time, so we thought we would have a couple of hours rest. Of course, we weren't allowed to take our clothes off, so, while some of the men made themselves comfortable on the floor, one of the lads and I jumped up and lay down on the bed. It wasn't long before we regretted our decision, as no sooner had we warmed up that we were bitten alive. The damned bed was full of fleas; no wonder it had been left behind. We ended up sleeping on the floor with the others, all of whom had a good laugh at our expense.
>
> Conditions in the field meant we were unable to wash or clean our uniforms regularly, and this led to many of us catching lice. The lice used to gather in the crotch of our trousers and drive us mad. When we had time, we would remove our trousers, turn them inside out and hold the crotch over a lighted candle. This was a horrendous job, but it killed most of the little blighters. When we were finally taken prisoner, one of the first things they did was to delouse us with DDT. They sprayed every nook and cranny; they had to.[11]

Sturmmann Karl-Heinz Decker.

If enduring German mortaring and shelling was a trial for the 3rd Division, the time spent in defence by 25 SS *Panzergrenadiers* north-west of Caen was marked by the presence of Allied fighter-bombers overhead as a matter of routine. *Sturmmann* Decker recalled:

> *Jabo* [slang term for Allied fighter-bombers] activity made it virtually impossible to move about during the daytime. We always moved at night. We moved almost every night to another position. It was horrendous in the daytime; you just couldn't move at all. I was walking by the edge of a field early one morning; there was a lot of enemy air activity. I was on my own, but even so these fighter-bombers came down after me! They attacked me,

> on my own! Let me tell you I jumped into the woods at the side of the field pretty damn quick. The sky was full of planes, all Allied. They shot at everything that moved.

It was not only fighter-bombers that Decker and his comrades had to cope with:

> I remember another incident that took place when we were dug in. We were in the woods. While one might think that this would be reasonably safe, that was not always the case. Enemy artillery would often fire into the woods at random, probing our positions. The shells would often explode in the treetops. This resulted in shrapnel flying all over the place. It was very dangerous; we had to be particularly careful, and if they thought we were in the woods they fired into them.

Change of Command

It is a fundamental part of a commander's job to leave his headquarters and visit his units to assess the situation and gauge his soldiers' morale. General Rennie, who frequently visited his formations in their front-line positions, went forward on 13 June to visit 9 Brigade's defences. Captain Beck, manning a Contact Detachment of the divisional Recce regiment, wrote: 'General Rennie arrives in Cambes from the hostile end, and his Jeep blows up on a mine. Short cuts suggested by Officers Commanding Field Ambulances are *out*.'[12] Having avoided being engaged by the Germans, General Rennie had been driven over one of the RUR's own mines, being badly shaken and suffering an injury to his arm when he was blown from the vehicle. Initially, the wound was thought to be slight, but the following day, he was evacuated from his headquarters to HMS *Largs* to rest. His injuries were, however, even more severe than first thought, and on 18 June he was evacuated to the UK to recuperate. In the meantime, Brigadier Cass took command of the 3rd Division, and with no prospect of General Rennie returning soon, Major General 'Bolo' Whistler took command of the division on 23 June. Another departure was Brigadier Smith, who handed over command of 185 Brigade to Brigadier Bols on 2 July.

Patrolling

The best-known example of a plunge in morale thanks to a protracted time spent in defence under seemingly constant shell fire is that of the 51st Highland Division.[13] The 3rd Division in very similar circumstances could also have suffered in the same way. One war diary described the effect enforced inactivity has on morale:

> The men become more and more like vegetables if forced to sit in one or two man slit trenches for long periods and this vegetable growth is encouraged by enemy shelling and mortaring from which there is little relief. This atmosphere is encountered most the further forward the troops are, being more noticeable in the forward infantry. Whatever the condition of affairs

Major General 'Bolo' Whistler took command of 3rd Division when General Rennie was injured.

> may be at the front, the administrative services in rear are always fully occupied carrying out their normal functions, and their daily tasks vary only in the degree of intensity occasioned by the battle further forward.

The 3rd Division took steps to 'counter boredom and maintain both morale and the fighting spirit of the forward infantry by dominating no-man's-land through ceaseless and vigorous patrolling'. As well as establishing dominance over the enemy, this also paid dividends in intelligence gained on the enemy's defences and fostered the soldierly virtues of alertness, self-confidence and aggression. All of the division's combat units record, in diaries, histories and reports, the value of patrol activity during this period.

In the 3rd Division's area, no-man's-land varied from a broad expanse of open ground between the villages and woods to just 150–250 yards between Cambes

The Cambes château was reduced to a ruin by artillery fire during a month in the front-line area.

and the German trenches. In the wider, more open areas, 1 Norfolk, in addition to patrolling, deployed a screen of battle outposts in cover 200 yards forward of their main position. This not only kept German patrols away but took a goodly haul of prisoners in the shape of disorientated enemy soldiers. Anywhere in no-man's-land, short, sharp encounters with the enemy were not unusual, and bloody hand-to-hand fighting often resulted. 2 RUR's battalion history describes how patrolling fitted in with other activities:

> We soon learnt that when the Boche chose to expose himself he did so with a purpose: it was to distract attention from the real strength with which he held the villages of La Bijude and Épron, Malon and Galmanche. Some picture of this strength could be gathered by scrupulous, tireless observation which noticed the change in colour of foliage where some natural camouflage on a tank or SP gun died, or some suspicious shape which had obtruded itself where previously there had been nothing. But information about the enemy was amplified and confirmed as always by patrols. Three listening posts were found each night on different parts of the front; and sorties further forward brought our men to within yards of the Boche so that such activities as feeding, mining, wiring and digging could be studied at close range.

Patrolling and close observation revealed that the enemy had, by 11 June, up to twenty-seven panzers positioned across the divisional front. In spite of this discovery, the panzers were so well dug in that the gunners could not make their positions untenable. On 8 Brigade's front it was discovered that I/192 *Panzergrenadiers* only occupied the Le Landel area with four men by day and reinforced it at night; so on the afternoon of 10 June, 1 South Lancs chased off the enemy and occupied the farms and houses of the hamlet unopposed, holding them from then on against minor enemy raids and counter-attacks.

The 59th (Staffordshire) Division

At the end of June, the final British infantry division arrived in Normandy and joined I Corps and was inserted between the 3rd British and 3rd Canadian Division. This was the 59th (Staffordshire) Division's first operational deployment, and they were deemed to be well trained; but as Lieutenant Fendick of the 3rd Division's machine-gun battalion recalled, they still needed to understand battlefield realities:

> The [platoon] HQ area was well within view, and shelling and mortaring range, of Jerry, so we were always careful and we were well dug in with overhead cover. We never allowed smoke to show during daylight, or lights or fires after dark. Early on, the chaps had learned from a nasty experience with a night air attack, during which Jerry dropped 'butterfly bombs', little ones which flutter down and sit on the ground, exploding at random later or if disturbed.
>
> One afternoon, a battalion of a follow-up Div, which had just landed, moved into the field just across the track from us, proceeded to erect groundsheet shelters all over the place, and showed no signs of digging in. During the evening, many small fires were lit, for the traditional 'brew-up'. Several of us strolled over, and pointed out tactfully that their area was well in view of Jerry and his unpleasantness, but the newcomers were very haughty and superior, and seemed to resent any suggestions from us. So we retired to our own field, and took pains to get well under cover. The inevitable soon happened and continued sporadically all night.
>
> In the morning, although they were still there, there wasn't a sign to be seen of the new battalion; they must have spent the night digging. We didn't bother to go and ask them if they'd had a good night.

Although the tanks of 27 Armoured Brigade withdrew at night to leaguer, squadrons from two of the regiments were normally forward during daylight hours, often sniping at panzers that had been identified in the enemy-held woods and villages and more often than not being sniped back. The 17-pounder of the Sherman Firefly proved to be particularly effective, coming forward firing and pulling back before the enemy responded. The arrival of the tanks was, however, not universally popular, as recalled by Lieutenant Fendick:

> A troop of four Sherman tanks of our supporting 27th Independent Armd Bdc pulled up against the outside of our hedgerow and swung their guns

A Sherman Firefly with its distinctive long barrel camouflaged to make it less obvious as a prime target to German anti-tank gunners.

> almost over our heads. I went to their Troop Comd and asked him to go elsewhere, as if he fired he was sure to bring counter-fire down on us. He said he'd been sent up to engage a suspected Jerry tank on the far slope and wouldn't be staying, 'and anyway, mortars don't bother us.' I pointed out that we *did* have to stay, and mortars *did* bother us, but his mind was made up.
>
> His tanks duly fired a few rounds each and then the crews got out for a smoke before leaving. Within moments we heard the familiar distant thump as the Jerry mortars fired, and we dived into our holes while their bombs were in the air. The tank crews scrambled into their tanks and buttoned down their hatches, but the Troop Comd had been standing talking to me and was too far from his tank. I'm afraid I rather rubbed in his remark about mortars not bothering him, as he huddled beside me in my slit while we endured 5 or 10 minutes of accurate stonking.

The gunners and 2 Middlesex varied their routine shoots by 'crash actions' and 'mortar runs' into forward areas; these were harassing shoots followed by rapid withdrawals before the Germans could respond. Such activities helped to keep all concerned on their toes during this waiting period. Unlike his cavalryman acquaintance, Lieutenant Fendick was careful not to draw enemy fire onto fellow infantrymen's positions during his machine-gun sallies out from reserve:

> From there we went out daily to various uninhabited spots (where the enemy retaliation to our fire wouldn't be a hazard to dug-in Infantry positions) and

> carried out harassing shoots. These were 'shoot and scoot' operations. Sometimes our shoot would be timed to coincide with a shoot on the same target by our 4.2-inch mortars, or artillery.
>
> We'd be given a target, and the number of belts to be fired, usually no more than two or three minutes of Indirect Fire. I would park the platoon under cover, on carriers, while I went forward and found a suitable gun line. While I was working out the fire control problem, my DR (Murley) would go back and bring up the gun carriers. They would roar up as fast as possible, the sections would pile out with guns, tripods, ammo etc., and the carriers would tear off back into concealment.
>
> I would indicate the gun line, the guns would be mounted and laid very quickly (we were often in enemy view), get the prescribed belts away and then the only order I'd give was 'GO'. The carriers dashed forward, the guns were thrown in, often not even dismounted, and we got the hell out of it as fast as possible.
>
> If we were lucky, we finished the shoot and were away before Jerry had time to locate us and get his mortars on to us. His location and counter-fire drills were usually very fast and accurate, so if we were too long in action or he was quick, we finished and went out of action through whatever he chose to throw at us.

With their emphasis on accuracy rather than speed, German artillery and mortars were normally slower in engaging a target, but in a static period where every inch of ground was known to command posts this disadvantage was lowered. The number of calculations necessary was much reduced, and response to call for fire was quicker.

Replacement of Panzer Divisions by Infantry

On 13 June, with fears still rife of further Allied landings, thanks to FORTITUDE and FUSAG's presence on German strategic maps, while leaving the Fifteenth Army intact, OKW gave orders for four infantry divisions to march from the Mediterranean and Atlantic coasts of southern France. The plan was for the 271, 272, 276 and 277 divisions to relieve the panzer divisions facing the British in Normandy. They would then be withdrawn and reconstituted for expected action with the Fifteenth Army in the Pas de Calais. With 2nd *Das Reich* SS Panzer Division already making the same painful journey, it was already apparent that marches north across France would be slow. Therefore, on 16 June the 16th *Luftwaffe Feld* Division was ordered to make the journey from Noordwijk aan Zee on the coast of Holland, via Paris, to replace the part of the 21st Panzer Division deployed to the north of Caen. This division was always planned to be moved to confront a landing but, probably thanks to FORTITUDE, had left a cadre behind to man the coastal defences and join the division later.[14]

In the event, the leading elements of the 16th only arrived on 26 June, and such were the difficulties of strategic movement under the shadow of Allied air power that it was not until 5 July that the division was largely complete in Normandy. The final divisional units only arrived after the fall of Caen on 9 July. Meanwhile, the first elements of the badly delayed divisions from the South of France arrived in Normandy during the first week of July, while the remainder straggled in over the following ten days, having been subject to interdiction by the air forces, the SAS and the Resistance.

16th *Luftwaffe Feld* Division

With the continued expansion of the Wehrmacht to meet the demands of the Eastern Front and to garrison captured territories, there was growing pressure to free up manpower for the Army. *Reichsmarschall* Göring, head of the Luftwaffe, was obliged to provide surplus manpower from his pool of ground crews, and in September 1942 he issued a call for volunteers to form *Luftwaffe Feld* divisions. By May 1943 no fewer than twenty divisions had been raised, but at Göring's insistence they remained under Luftwaffe command. They generally consisted of 12,500 men and were organized and equipped along the lines of an ordinary infantry division, but like the *Fallschirmjäger* they wore Luftwaffe uniforms and insignia.

Despite the generally high standard of Luftwaffe recruits, these divisions' lack of military depth or experience of combat meant that their performance and reputation in battle were poor. When these formations suffered significant casualties they tended to be subsumed into the Army or used as a sacrificial defensive layer, rear-area garrisons or support troops. Those that remained, such as the 16th *Luftwaffe Feld* Division, were eventually absorbed by the Army in November 1943 but retained their Luftwaffe title.

Generalleutnant Sievers' 16th *Luftwaffe Feld* Division, being one of the junior formations, was raised in the third *Welle* (wave) during December 1942 with two three-battalion infantry regiments, a *Panzerjäger Abteilung*, an artillery regiment and a pioneer battalion. In February the following year they moved to the Holland as garrison troops and to man coastal defences.

Having been transferred to the Army, the 16th was reorganized into a *Jäger* (light) division as follows:

31 *Jäger* Regiment – three battalions
32 *Jäger* Regiment – two battalions
46 *Jäger* Regiment – two battalions
16 Fusilier *Abteilung* with three companies and one machine-gun company
16 *Panzerjäger Abteilung* – one a/tk company Pak 38 & 40, one AA company (20mm)
1016 *Sturmgeschütz* Battery (2 × StuG III)
16 Artillery Regiment (two battalions – one 76mm and one heavy 122mm Russian guns)
16 Pioneer *Abteilung* with two companies.[15]
A total of 9,354 men on arrival in Normandy with the division.

By 1944 the soldiers of *Luftwaffe Feld* divisions wore a mixture of Luftwaffe and army uniform as available.

Air Support

At close quarters with the enemy on a 'quiet sector' there were few calls on Second Tactical Airforce, which was anyway busy with calls from XXX Corps further west. That is not to say that Allied aircraft did not materially help I Corps. One of the tasks that Brigadier Belchem, BGS (Ops) of 21st Army Group, had was to deal with 'the issues of smoothing out the procedure for requesting RAF support' – which were convoluted in the early days of the campaign. When he noticed a pattern of enemy activity that could be exploited by air attack he used the personal contacts that he had developed in the Western Desert to good effect:

> I recall the occasion when I discovered that the Germans in Normandy were confining their movements (e.g. of replenishment convoys and reinforcements) to the secondary roads. From our photographs it was possible to discern the main traffic routes, though sometimes it was not easy to follow them on our British maps of Normandy. It occurred to me to get a French Michelin map of the area: first class main roads are in red on a Michelin map, and second-class roads are in yellow. The pattern of German movements observed by us was, in virtually all cases, on yellow roads. From this point,

B-26 Marauders bombing a road and rail crossing south-east of Caen.

we pin-pointed the main bottlenecks on yellow routes leading to the rear areas of the enemy's known positions, where delivery by night of ammunition, stores and rations was probably made.[16]

[Air Vice-Marshal] Kingston [McCloughry] then requested the RAF to arrange bombing raids at these bottlenecks, as late in the day as possible. He also arranged fighter-bomber sorties to the same bottlenecks at first light the following morning. The plan proved successful because the fighter-bombers found heavy traffic congestion at the target areas, which were chosen where reversing the night convoys would be most difficult, and finding alternative routes in order to by-pass the cratered area would involve long detours.[17]

Build-up Control (BUCO)

The assault corps, with their respective naval forces, were responsible for the organization and embarking of troops on the pre-loaded shipping for the D Day landing and the immediate follow-up. This was difficult enough, but, to reiterate, as Commander Edwards RN wrote:

> There is always that critical period in an amphibious assault, when the first waves have begun to tire. If the follow-up and the build-up is not quick and sufficient the critical period will be prolonged and become a great danger to the whole enterprise. The military ideal is for the follow-up troops to be in position to attack 'through' the assault waves as soon as the latter begin to slow down through fatigue or expenditure of supplies. But like other military ideals in amphibious operations, this is only possible of attainment if the maritime component is perfect in every detail.[18]

It had always been realized that achieving a rapid build-up in Normandy was one of the most difficult components of Operation OVERLORD. To deliver troops to Normandy, 21st Army Group Build-Up Control Organisation was evolved as a tri-service organization, with officers from both the British and US armies. It was organized as a main headquarters, subordinate headquarters at the embarkation ports (*aka* 'tentacles') and a series of 'Little BUCOs' on the beaches in Normandy.

Headquarters BUCO assembled at Combined Headquarters, Fort Southwick, near Portsmouth on 24 April, taking over the preliminary planning that had been undertaken across 21st Army Group since January. Following OVERLORD's initial phase, BUCO assumed complete responsibility for the build-up, exercising command through MOVCO (Movement Control Organisation) and TURNCO (Turn Round Control Organisation). The former issued orders for movement from assembly areas to the marshalling areas, and the latter co-ordinated the turn-round of all types of cross-Channel shipping.

BUCO maintained a desired 'build-up priority table', listing all formations and units in the order in which they were required in Normandy. It was always understood that the armies would request changes in priority to meet the tactical situation. This entailed much re-planning to break units down into 'serials' of vehicles and men that matched the capacity of returning landing craft and ships.

The number of landing craft of different types disabled on the beaches was an immediate challenge for BUCO staff.

The loss of 296 assorted landing craft servicing Second Army, sunk, damaged or broken down, was the immediate challenge to BUCO, and when combined with poor weather, this had produced by 12 June a cumulative delay of 48 hours to the planned build-up. An example of a significant change of priority was the 'phasing back' of two armoured division in favour of infantry divisions during July.

BUCO remained in being for the duration, with amendments to staffing levels as the campaign developed and the number of units and formations leaving the UK was reduced. Many members of BUCO subsequently found themselves posted to various functions in the Lines of Communication as the armies advanced east across France and into Belgium.

The Storm

During the period 19–22 June (D+13 to +16) a north-easterly storm caught the Allies by surprise. Without the protection of the Cotentin Peninsula, which gave some shelter from the normal south-westerlies, the storm caused havoc, greatly reducing the build-up of troops and the in-load of supplies, destroying the US Mulberry harbour and severely damaging that of the British. During Exercise THUNDERCLAP in early April, Montgomery had briefed his army group's general officers in these terms:

> Should there be a serious and unexpected break in the weather before D+14, this will have a serious effect on both forces. Plans for emergency maintenance have been made but this will not cover a prolonged spell.[19]

Despite being towards the end of Montgomery's identified window of vulnerability, the build-up of stocks in the maintenance areas was by this time running three to four days behind schedule. An example of the storm's impact is that 25-pounder ammunition, even at the lower army group rates of consumption, was reduced to a dangerously low two days' supply. This led one logistician to comment that it was just as well the Germans did not choose the cover of the storm to mount an offensive.[20]

Not only were stocks run down as in-load failed to keep up with consumption, but operations were curtailed. XXX Corps' attack south of Bayeux culminated with the capture of Tilly-sur-Seulles and joined I Corps in standing on the defensive for the best part of a week. In addition, the 43rd Wessex Division (VIII Corps), whose entry into the build-up system was already delayed, found itself split, with some of its advance parties and leading units ashore and others in shipping off the beaches or still in the marshalling areas back in the UK.

The impact of the storm on offensive operations was to delay the next series of attacks. With XXX Corps to the west having failed at Villers Bocage (Operation PERCH), and culminating with the capture of Tilly-sur-Seulles and in the bocage to the west, the renewed attacks were to focus on Caen, as explained in Montgomery's directive M 505 of 18 June:

> The Allies have not quite achieved all their objectives, but the situation is satisfactory since they have gained a firm foothold on the Continent. They

The north-easterly storm that raged between 19 and 22 June all but halted the build-up of men, equipment and ammunition and badly damaged the Mulberry harbours.

> must not allow themselves to be hemmed in by the enemy within territory already occupied. Immediate objectives: Cherbourg and Caen.[21]

The plan detailed in Montgomery's directive M 502 had specified a D Day of 22 June for his next offensive, Operation EPSOM, but in the event this was delayed until stocks of combat supplies had arrived and build-up formations were complete.[22] Montgomery signalled to his Chief of Staff at Main Headquarters:

> 20 June 1944, 2015 hours.
> TOPSEC (.) Personal for Chief of Staff from General Montgomery (.) The continued rough weather has put us now 5 days behind in our planned build

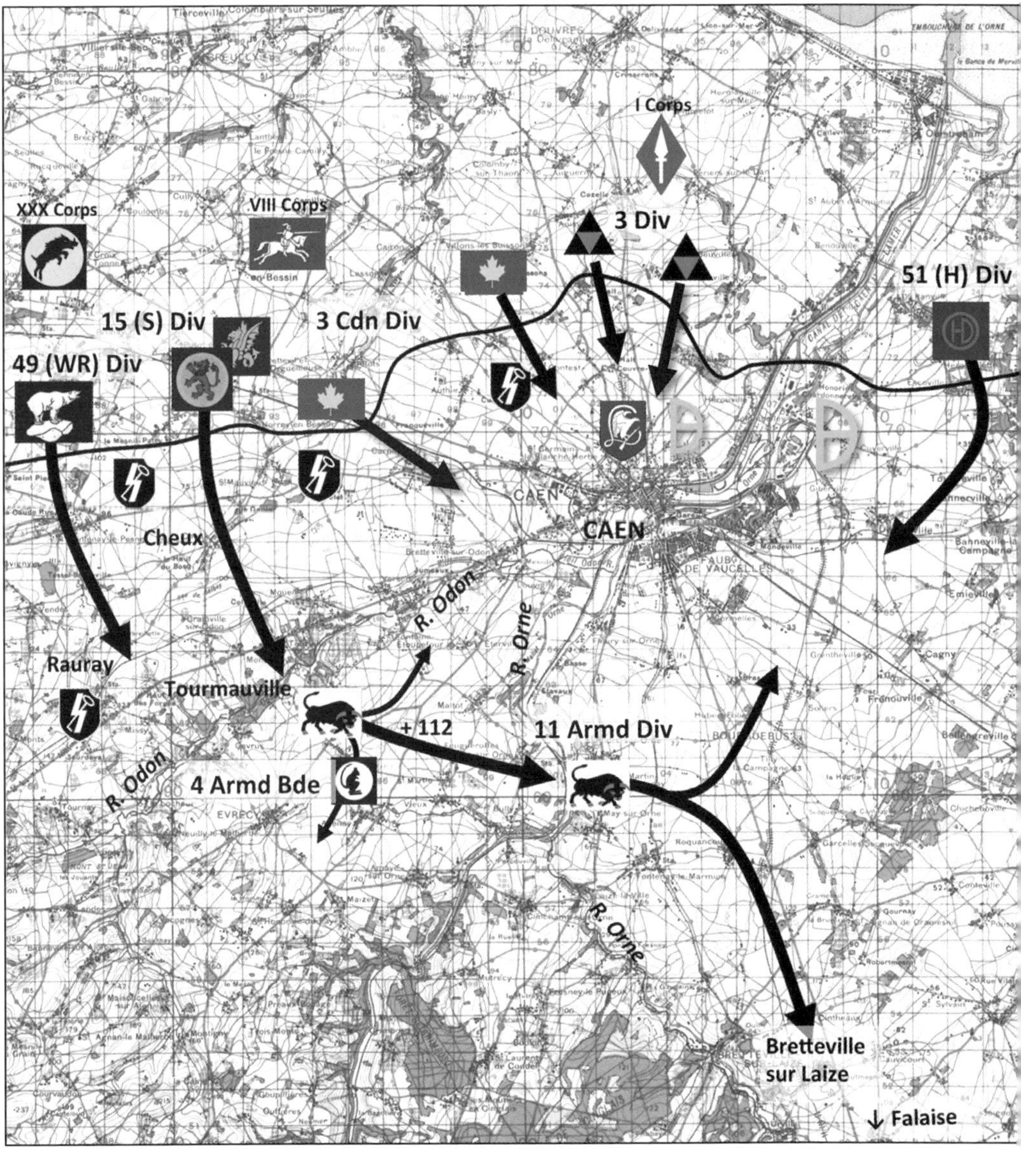

Operation EPSOM, the centrepiece of the next offensives, and its supporting operations around Caen.

The B-52 medium bombers of the RAF's 2nd Tactical Air Force flew preplanned mission from UK airfields during the Normandy Campaign.

up (.) Essential portions of 15 Div. and 43 Div. and essential artillery ammunition waiting at anchor to be unloaded (.) Given calm weather for unloading tomorrow and Thursday will deliver blitz attack of 8 Corps on Sunday 25 June and that is now the earliest date (.) Each further day of bad weather will mean a further postponement of one day (.)[23]

Air Attacks on the Mézidon Railway Target

The attacks on the Mézidon area 13 miles south-east of Caen provide an example of air action to reduce enemy re-supply and reinforcement of their troops facing I Corps' front. The railway junction and marshalling yard at Mézidon-Canon, on the Caen–Rouen–Paris lines, were attacked by the RAF Second Tactical Air Force's Hurricanes of 247 Squadron in the fighter-bomber role at last light on 16 June 1944. The following night, the attack was repeated by twenty-four Boston bombers of the Free French Air Force (FFAF) 342 (Lorraine) and 88 (Hong Kong) squadrons. The nearby bridges over the River Dives were also regularly attacked to block or create choke points on a key logistic re-supply route.

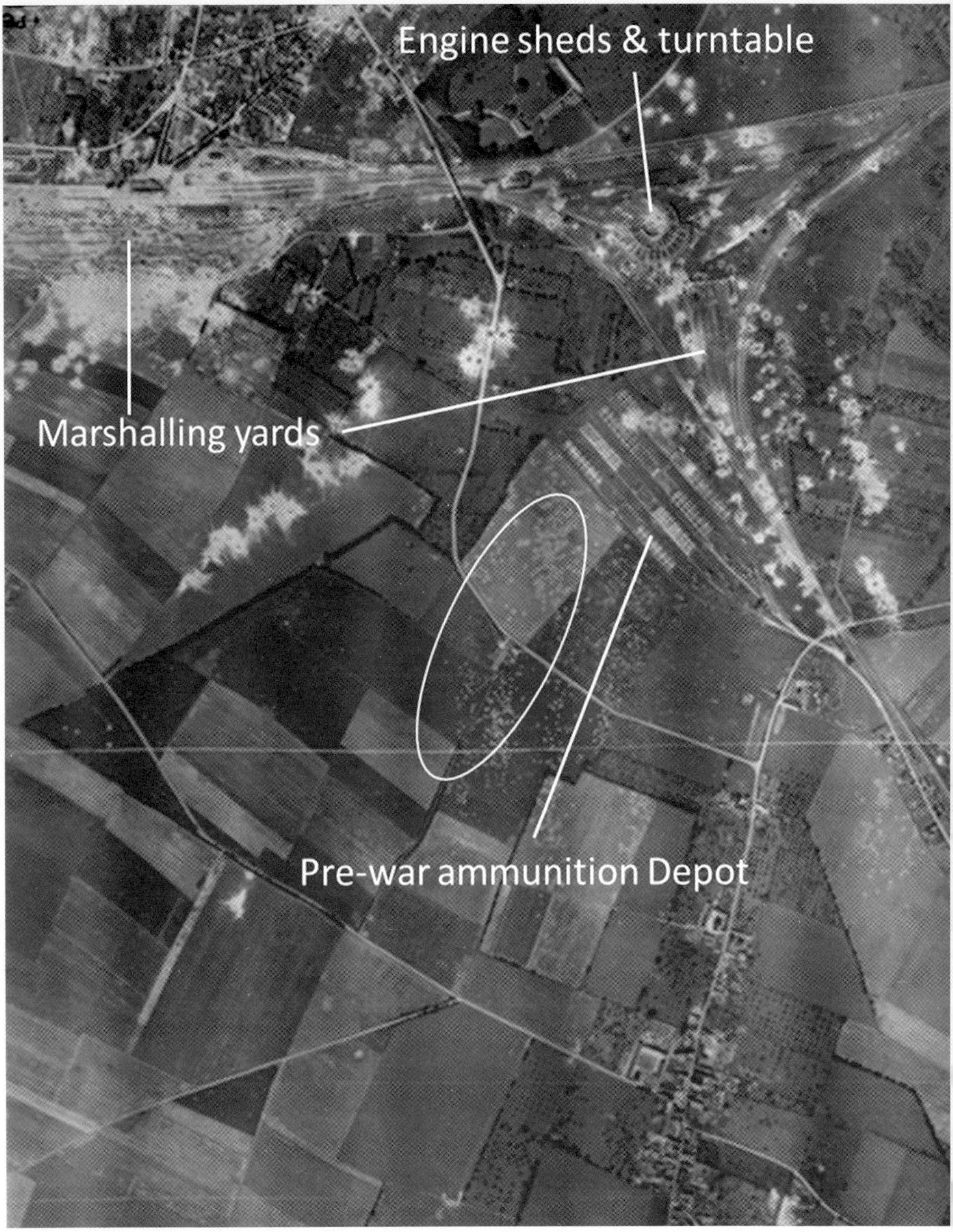

One of the air photographs taken after the Mézidon raids in order to assess the level of bomb damage to the railway marshalling yards and junction.

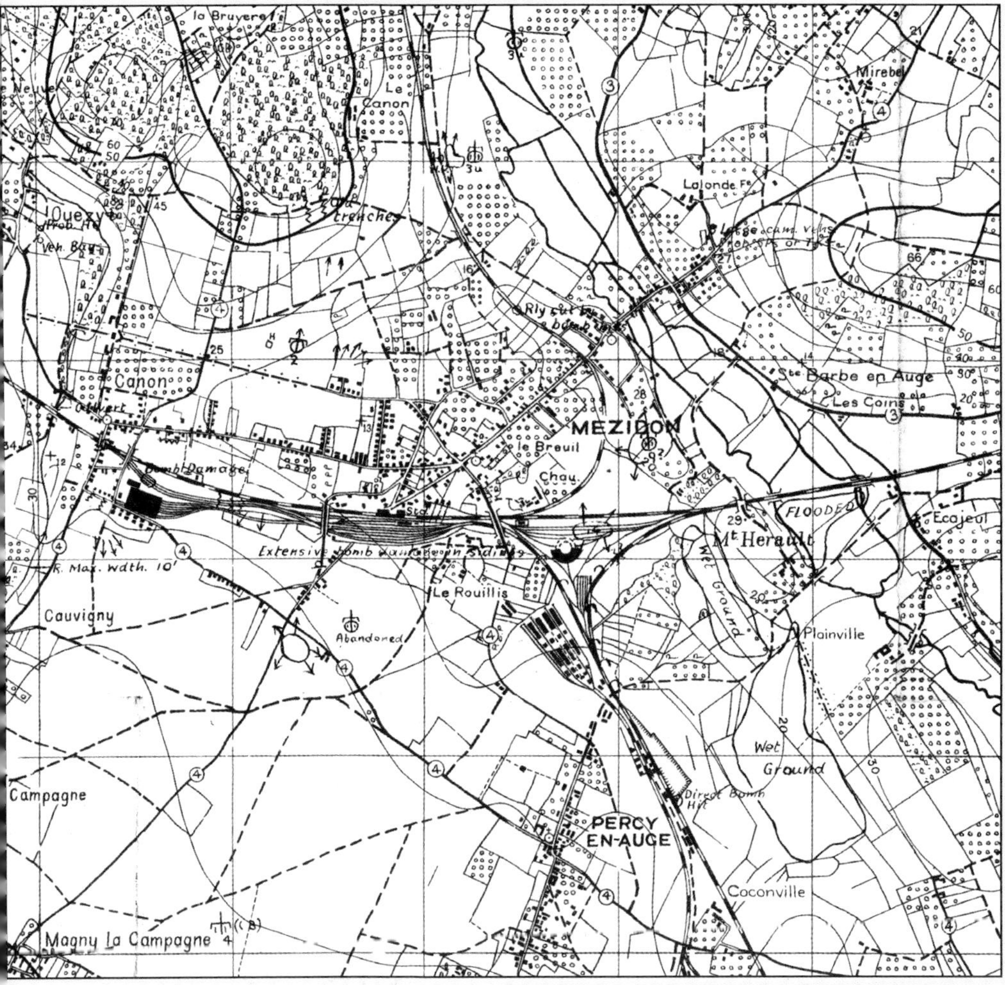

The same area as portrayed on the 1:25,000 map of the day.

Close Air Support

Air Marshal Conningham's Desert Air Force in North Africa played a significant part in the Eighth Army's victories, but in the close country of Normandy, fighter-bombers struggled to identify well-camouflaged targets. Consequently, a series of local initiatives were soon established by the RAF and army formations to address the issue of attacking enemy targets in the battle area. These evolved from small beginnings to a system that was formalised in 1944.

On D Day and the immediate aftermath, the bomb line was established safely to the south of Caen, where the fighter-bombers were highly effective in interdicting

A cannon armed Typhoon with D Day stripes.

the *Hitlerjugend* and further west *Panzer Lehr* as they rushed north to deliver Rommel's counter-attacks. That the Germans were unable to achieve this in any meaningful way was a significant victory for Second Tactical Airforce (2 TAF). However, once the Germans successfully 'roped off' the Allied beachhead and the armies were at close quarters to each other, the existing system struggled. Calling for support via RAF liaison officers at divisional and corps level, through Air Support Signals Unit's (ASSU) tentacles, proved to be slow and far less effective. What was needed was a system that enabled fighter-bombers to identify and promptly attack enemy targets just hundreds of yards from friendly forces without fratricide.

Despite tensions between 2 TAF and the army, local initiatives produced a system of Forward Control Posts that delegated control down to the RAF at corps level and Visual Control Posts (VCPs) at brigade level. It was practice for requests for CAS to be passed through 2 TAF to the airfields, but once airborne and on their way, the strike would be handed over to a Visual Control Point (VCP) or 'contact car' forward of the tentacle to direct the attacking aircraft onto the target. The centralised system was also increasingly short-cut at RAF group or even wing level to provide a quicker response from the cab ranks of circling aircraft or fighter-bombers at cockpit readiness, in order to provide a timely response.[24]

RAF Regiment armoured cars were amongst those pressed into use as contact cars for VCPs.

The classic photo of an RAF pilot and an officer from Second Army at work.

The contact cars being in the forward area were mounted in a variety of armoured vehicles that could accommodate the appropriate radios, normally White Scout Cars, half-tracks, larger armoured cars and even tanks, which were often on loan for specific operations. Additional vehicles and equipment for more permanent but still unofficial solutions were usually procurable thanks to relaxed wartime accounting.

The contact car would be crewed by an army officer, often Royal Artillery, who would take and interpret the army's requirement, a signaller or two and importantly a fighter-bomber pilot. This would normally be an experience officer who was at the end of a tour of duty or being otherwise rested. He would be able to empathise (sometimes a familiar voice) with the pilot and direct him to the target using language and terminology readily understood in the aircraft moving at several hundred miles an hour.

It must be stressed that this system took the whole Normandy campaign to fully develop and that a large proportion of 2 TAF's sorties remained attacking. In addition, there were of course occasions when wholesale enemy movement such as during the Mortain Counter-Attack and at Falaise, meant contact cars were not required.

With Hitler ordering the 'roping off of the Allied beachhead', there was far less space available in Normandy for the advanced airfields that were being demanded by air commanders. However, with barely a threat from Luftwaffe fighters, 2 TAF's fighter-bombers could be prioritised for deployment to Normandy.

Approximately 20,000 men of the Royal Engineer and RAF airfield construction groups worked to establish the seventeen British Temporary airfields in Normandy by the time of the breakout.

Chapter Three

Château de la Londe

Delayed by the storm and its aftermath, Operation EPSOM, the next attempt to capture Caen, was to begin on 25 June with 49th Division's Operation MARTLET, a preliminary attack on the Raury Spur. VIII Corps' main EPSOM attack, designed to envelop Caen via the west, began the following day (see map, page 46). A feature of General Montgomery's operational art were the supporting operations launched all along the Second Army's front, designed to 'unbalance the enemy'. This involved two main elements: attacks on enemy positions both before and during the main event which were designed to keep the enemy guessing as to Montgomery's intent; and the drawing away of enemy reinforcements. The attacks in support of EPSOM, including those by General Crocker's I Corps, were not only designed to 'unbalance' the Germans but also had a substantial tactical aim – to gain ground.

In order for I Corps to play its part in Montgomery's plan, General Crocker was to take the enemy position at Château de la Londe, in order that his divisions would be able to exploit EPSOM's planned envelopment of Caen. During the night of 21/22 June, the 3rd Division was to launch an attack on the 21st Panzer Division's defences at the château, which was some 500 yards south of the woods surrounding the hamlet of Le Landel at the tip of a salient held by 8 Brigade.

Between Le Landel and the château stood the well-defended farm of La Londe (see map overleaf), which was held by strong outposts of 192 *Panzergrenadiers*.[1] In addition to the farm and château, Major Vierzig's II/192 held the villages of La Bijude and Épron, each with a rifle company and support weapons. Salients are always vulnerable, but in this case the defenders benefited from overlapping arcs of defensive fire, with I/25 SS *Panzergrenadiers* to the west and on the opposite flank their I/192 *Panzergrenadiers*. The château itself was held by 5 Company supported by the Panzer IVs of 6 Company/II Panzer Battalion.

The attack on La Londe farm and the château was to be carried out by 1 South Lancs, who relieved 2 East Yorks in the front line during the afternoon of 21 June. They immediately made their presence felt by firing 263 3-inch mortar bombs into enemy positions in the adjacent hamlet of La Bijude. Early on, the 22nd South Lancs' battle procedure was well under way, with Lieutenant Colonel Stone holding his orders at 1200 hours. The battalion's war diary recorded 'CO's 'O' Gp including reps of sp arms – Mx [Middlesex MG], Suffolk, 246 RE, 76 Fd Regt, 67 A Tk. Attack on CHATEAU de la LONDE outlined.'[2] After recces had been completed, confirmatory orders were issued at 1800 hours. With battle preparations completed and movement around Le Landel inevitable, the German were alert. The war diary continued:

> 2130 Sharp bout of shelling (about 45 HE). 1 killed, 7 wounded.
> 2300 Further bout of shelling, harassing coys as they deployed for attack. 16 casualties.
> 2330 C & B Coys moved off, frontal attack on LA LONDE, following through CHATEAU to line beyond.

The silent attack, without the customary bombardment or the sound of tanks moving forward, caught the Germans by surprise, and the La Londe farm complex was overrun. Lieutenant Jones recalled:

> As I remember it, we formed up just before midnight and moved across what I think was a cornfield in open order. We had not gone very far before

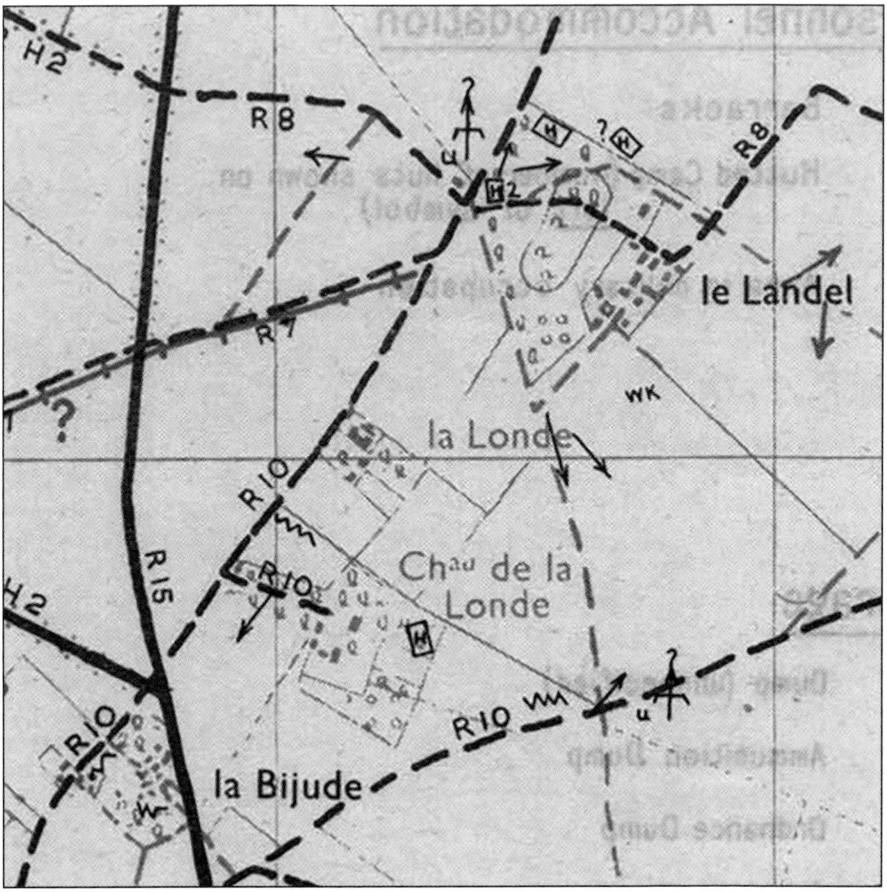

An extract from the defences map showing Le Landel, La Londe farm and the château, plus the adjacent hamlet of La Bijude.

> sporadic artillery fire started dropping amongst us. However, although there were a few casualties, we kept on moving forward and it was not until we entered the wood at the far end of the field that we came under enfiladed machine gun tracer fire from what appeared to be at least two or three weapon positions deep in the wood.
>
> At the time I was very near to the Company Commander, Captain Murison, and on seeing me he ordered me to collect the Bren gunners of the Company and engage the German positions. Although it was extremely dark with much shooting, I managed to get most of them to my position, and allotted two or three to each weapon pit. Eventually, after a hectic exchange of fire and using the tracer as a guide, we silenced the positions. The Company by then had well infiltrated the wood and we overran their positions. Some of the *Panzergrenadiers* were wounded, some [were] captured and the rest fled. I remember thinking we must have taken them by surprise after all. We then moved forward to the hedgerow which faced the Chateau and proceeded to dig in in what was a shallow ditch. For the next hour or so we were subjected to some not very heavy mortar fire, and as I remember, we all thought that reinforcements would arrive, including anti-tank guns and armoured vehicles, for this had been the case in previous attacks.[3]

B Company reached the edge of the farm's gardens and drove the German outposts back. Looking south less than 100 yards were the hedges around the château, to which the Germans had withdrawn. On the left, however, C Company had been taken in the flank by enfilade machine-gun fire 'causing some disorganization in darkness'. Major Vierzig ordered the II/192 into an immediate response. Although this was described as 'a weak counter-attack' it seems to have forced 'most of C Company to withdraw', as they were reported as being back with the rest of the battalion at 0445 hours.

In the meantime, A Company had been sent forward to help B Company to consolidate around the farm and swing left to clear the area left by C Company's withdrawal. 'B Coy took 3 prisoners including an FOO who relinquished marked maps of arty plan intact, and supplied useful information.' At 0500 hours, however, the war diary records, 'Heavy mortaring of A and B Coys. Smoke screen put down on flanks by enemy, and sharp counter-attack put in.' This attack by panzers and a handful of German pioneers supported by tanks was successful.

> Vierzig ordered his orderly officer, Second Lieutenant Lotze, 'You'll have to put things right, Lotze. But because of the uncertainty of the situation I can't spare you more than ten men.' Lotze was not exactly enthusiastic, but since the penetration was believed to be only in platoon strength he thought that with one sergeant and ten men, whom he presently picked from the headquarters company and 220th Panzer Pioneer Battalion, he might manage it.
>
> They set out at first light. Cover on the left was provided by Sergeant Dietsch with a machine-pistol, on the right by Lance Corporal Moller with

> a machine gun. They worked their way forward right up to the trench occupied by the Tommies. Lotze intended to do the job in the traditional infantry way: leap up, yell wildly, open fire, and down into the trench. And then enfilade with the machine gun.[4]

Without an effective anti-tank defence, B Company was overwhelmed and had been clearly taken by surprise by the yelling, firing and explosion of hand grenades. Corporal Penter of B Company described the enemy attack:

> As I recall they were using a lot of airburst shells. Worse was yet to come. After what seemed an eternity and when we were still trying to burrow into the earth, we heard the dreaded sound of tank engines immediately before us. They were also now using smoke on each side of our positions. Our Canadian Platoon Commander and Sgt Horan ordered us to engage the flitting shapes we could now see coming through the wood in the glare of the bursting shells. This we did with great gusto, but it was to no avail. By now the tanks, some of which I think were Panthers, were rearing up over the hedge, some actually falling on the sections in the ditch. Also their *Panzergrenadiers* had broken through the smoke and were coming round the back of us.
>
> It was by now chaos, and we were standing up trying to take them on as we were completely surrounded, armoured vehicles at both flanks and enemy infantry front and back. I well remember we engaged what appeared to be a German Platoon coming swiftly towards us, our lads were dropping like flies.

The South Lancs war diary records that 'Enemy tanks (approx 6) supported by inf broke into B Coy posns, causing heavy casualties. Remainder of Coy withdrew through A Coy to LE LANDEL.' One survivor remembers seeing Panzer IVs performing neutral turns on top of the German trenches, now occupied by B Company, in an attempt to grind the British infantrymen into the ground.

The badges worn by 1 S Lancs. The single red infantry bar below the divisional sign (right) was for the battalions of 8 Brigade. The badge worn by 9 Brigade battalions had two bars.

A survivor commented that 'For some reason unknown our own anti-tank guns were not in position and the German panzers swanned over the position machine-gunning and throwing hand grenades into slit trenches.' B Company soldiers were soon surrendering to the German attackers.

> Half a dozen [British] were lying in the trench dead or wounded, and the others were standing up with their hands above their heads. Lotze grabbed the British lieutenant round whose neck the whistle dangled. 'How many men?' he asked him. 'Eighty-four,' the officer replied. He made the lieutenant stand beside him and, gesturing with his pistol, made him understand that if any of his men tried anything it would be the end of him, the lieutenant. The British officer nodded. He ordered his men to fall in, and in marching order they went off along the road to German headquarters. Major Vierzig's eyes nearly popped out when he saw the procession approaching.

Corporal Penter was numbered amongst the wounded:

> All of a sudden, I felt as though I had been hit in the face with a sledgehammer and I was thrown across Sgt Horan, who seemed to be hit at the same time. I felt 'this is it', as I was choking with blood and bone in my throat, and I could not see through my left eye ... I owe my life to a L/Cpl Ball, who cleared my throat and applied a shell dressing to the large wound in my face. Sgt Horan was now dead, as seemed to be most of our platoon, and the action was ended. Even at that time. I remember the Germans lining up the survivors to march away to captivity. I also recall them bringing up a truck and loading our dead into it. All the wounded including me were taken forward to their regimental aid post which was by the Chateau and we were treated with great respect. All around the Chateau were a considerable number of tanks hull down in soil bunkers. I was now quite sure the powers that be had underestimated the enemy strength, certainly considering we had no major anti-tank defence.

Lieutenant Edwards of 246 Field Company RE was lucky to survive:

> When the positions were first taken, I checked round the captured defences with one of the Battalion officers to see whether there were any engineering tasks, and then, promising to give a report on the overall situation to the Battalion Commander, I started to make my way back to Battalion H.Q. Just as I walked through a gateway in the high wall and towards the cornfield outside, there was heavy firing of automatic weapons and I had to crawl – then almost immediately a tremendous 'Stonk' came down and the whole area was pounded with mortars. I could also hear the sound of high velocity 88mm guns firing. I was stuck in the middle of the cornfield, straddled with mortar bursts, much too close for comfort. I managed to move very slowly by rolling, in between the bursts, from one smoking crater to the next, clinging hopefully to the old saying, 'Lightning never strikes the same place

A knocked-out Panzer IV.

> twice.' It must have taken me an hour to move about 500yds, and when at last I arrived at H.Q., very shaken and rather deaf, they listened to my report with some surprise.[5]

A report issued by II/192 *Panzergrenadiers* contains this passage: 'In this operation the enemy, including his dead, lost about one company. At 0700 hours the defensive position of 5th Company, 192nd was again in our hands.'

With most of B Company being taken prisoner, A Company managed to retain a toehold on the northern tip of the La Londe farm. This became a platoon outpost, but so difficult was it to hold that it was finally abandoned on the night of 25/26 June. The area remained tense, with regular exchanges of fire and German counter-attacks expected daily.

At the operational level, the failure to secure Château de la Londe on the night of 21/22 June meant that it would have to be taken as a preliminary objective before there could be any advance onto the high ground overlooking Caen. In the aftermath of the storm, levels of combat supplies needed to be built back up before the execution of plans to capture Caen became a practical proposition.

Operations MITTEN and ABERLOUR

It was originally intended to launch the next attack on Caen to the east of the Orne, but the restricted space available militated against this. I Corps, however, remained responsible for a reduced-scale attack to be launched in that area by

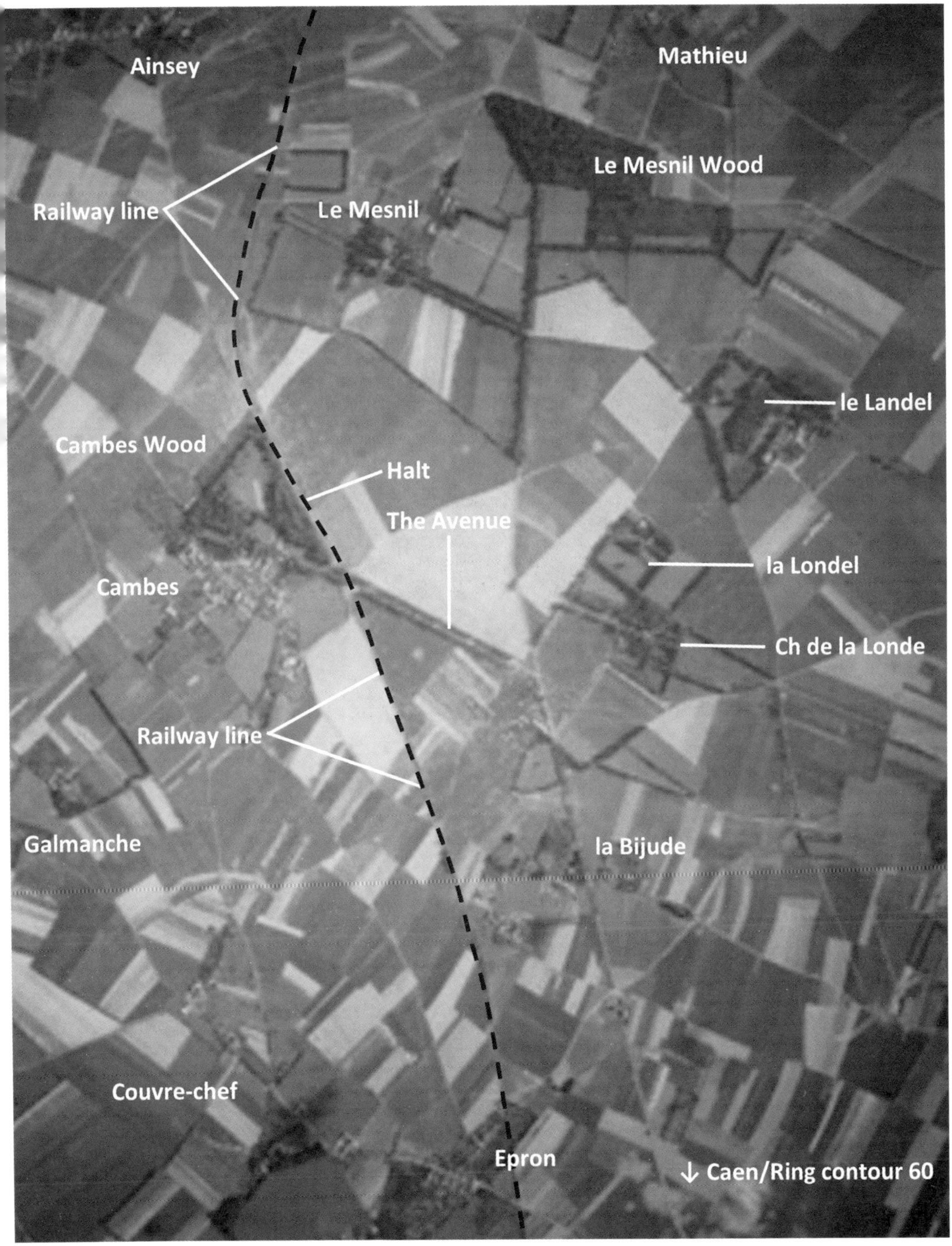

An aerial photograph of the 3rd Division's main battle area during late June 1944.

51st Highland Division and significant attacks to the north and west of Caen, Operations MITTEN and ABERLOUR.

With EPSOM underway, I Corps was to extend the pressure on the Germans to the east, in line with Montgomery's tactics, in order to prevent the movement of reserves from 25 SS *Panzergrenadiers*' or 21st Panzer Division's front to the support of their sister regiments, which were already facing the full weight of VIII Corps' attack. General Crocker's operational aims were to advance some 2 miles onto the ridge overlooking Caen. On the afternoon of 27 June, in Operation MITTEN, 8 Brigade of 3rd Division was to capture the Germans' forward bastion of Château de la Londe, which had resisted a previous attempt to take it, and Point 64, the high ground beyond. In phase two of the Corps plan this would be followed by an attack further west by the 3rd Canadian Division. In this phase, once the La Londe salient had been reduced and 8 Brigade was advancing, Brigadier Orr's 9 Brigade, and Brigadier Cunningham's 9 Canadian Brigade, were to launch Operation ABERLOUR, which was scheduled for 29 June.

The line held by the Germans, and I Corps' plans for MITTEN and ABERLOUR.

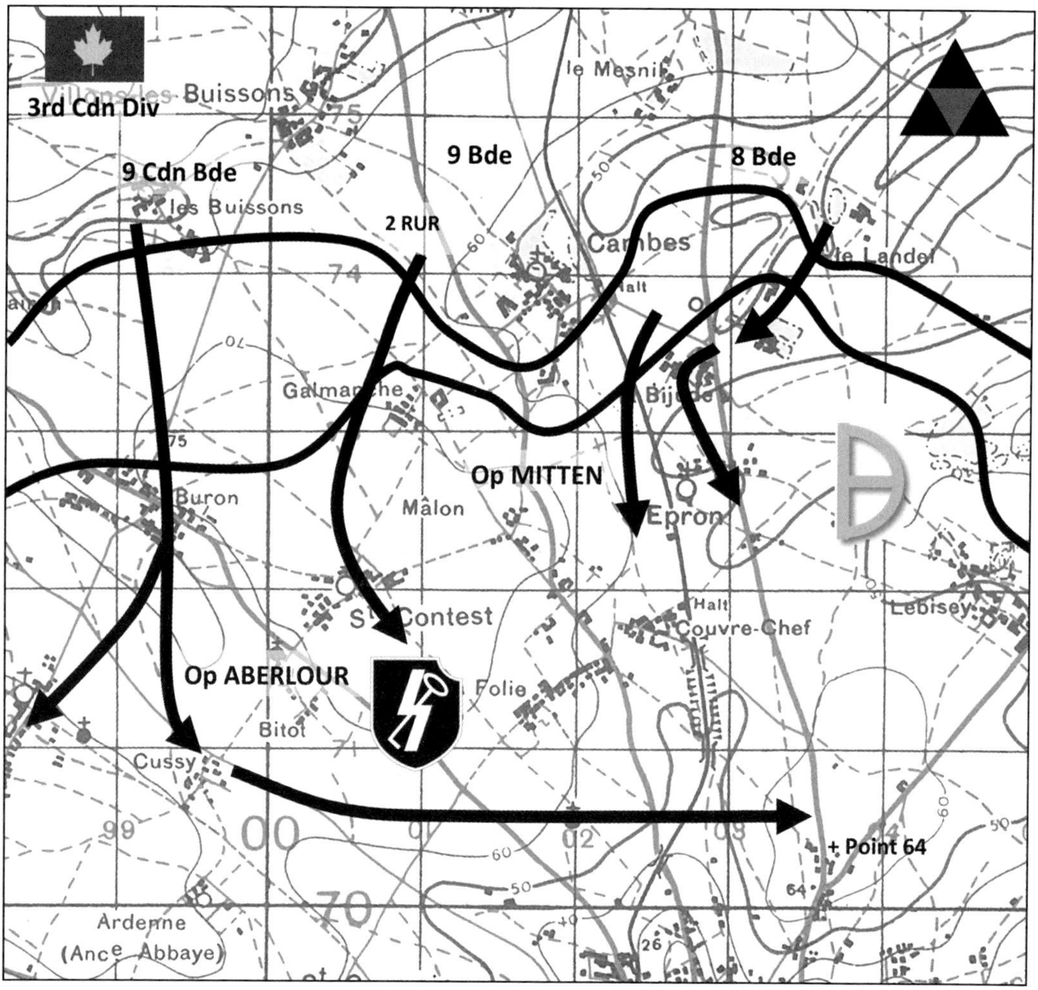

The brigade was to capture the villages of St Contest, Authie and Cussy, with their final objective being Point 64.

Sadly for 8 Brigade, British operational security had let them down. The German radio intercept platoons in the two divisions reported increased chatter over the air, including a statement by the British that they expected to be in Caen in the next twenty-four hours.[6] One regimental historian stated that the number of Germans the brigade had been told to expect at La Londe was based on faulty intelligence, namely:

> The information about the enemy was that the area between the Chateau and Galmanche South of Cambes including Épron was held by a very weak II Bn 192 Panzer Grenadier Regiment, with probably a weak company in La Bijude and the Chateau with another company in Épron and further south.

This assessment, plus the well-known presence of panzers, was substantially correct – until, that is, the Germans executed a reinforcement, probably prompted by the lapses in British OPSEC. The attrition of battle had taken its toll on the bayonet strength of 192 *Panzergrenadiers*, but on 26 June the leading elements of the as yet un-depleted ranks of the 16th *Luftwaffe Feld* Division were arriving and taking over the defences after a nine-day march on foot from Holland, principally by night. That the handover between a Luftwaffe *Jäger* regiment and the 192 *Panzergrenadiers* had taken place is confirmed by the eventual capture of a 37mm Pak 36 and two 50mm Pak 38, both of which were in the 16th's ORBAT but not 21st Panzer Division's.[7] However, reinforcing the Luftwaffe was a platoon of 21st's Pioneers and the tanks of Headquarters 22 Panzer Regiment.[8] Some of the panzers were dug in, mainly to the flanks, while others were deployed further back with a mobile counter-attack role.

The first phase of Operation MITTEN, the attack on Château de la Londe, was again to be delivered by 1 South Lancs. In the second phase 1 Suffolk was to advance 1,000 yards through 1 South Lancs and take La Bijude and Épron, while 2 East Yorks advanced on the brigade's right flank. Armoured support was provided by a squadron of the Staffordshire Yeomanry and specialist assault vehicles of 79th Armoured Division, including for the first time in support of the 3rd Division two troops of Churchill Crocodile flame-throwers.

The Churchill Crocodile

The Crocodile flame-throwing tank had been under development in various forms for most of the war, but following a demonstration organized by 79th Armoured Division fresh impetus was given to the project, and conversion kits for the Mark VII Churchill tank were rushed into production. 141 Regiment RAC (The Buffs) was hastily trained, in secrecy, in the use of the Crocodile for the invasion.[9] Of the two troops that landed on GOLD Beach, two vehicles got ashore and carried out their first flame action on D+1. The regiment's first substantial action

The Churchill Crocodile flame-thrower.

was in support of EPSOM and MITTEN, with two troops of B Squadron under command of 8 Brigade for the latter operation.

A flame gun replaced the Churchill's hull BESA machine gun, but the sighting mechanism for the BESA was retained. With a maximum range of 120 yards, and its fuel carried in a 6.4-ton two-wheeled armoured trailer, the flame-thrower was a fearsome weapon. The key element of the Crocodile system was the 400 gallons of flame fuel, known as 'FRAS' (Fuel Research Aluminium Stearate), a secret mixture of petrol, aluminium stearate and other chemicals which caused the gel mixture to stick to any surface it touched and burn continuously. A trailer-full provided enough fuel for bursts totalling eighty seconds. Trooper Joseph Ellis provides a simple description of the jelly-like fuel:

> The trailer contained 400 gallons of flame fuel. In simple terms, it was made of a mix of soap, petrol and rubber. The petrol burned, the soap spread, and the rubber stuck. The fuel was ignited as it left the nozzle and the burning petroleum jelly stuck to everything it touched. If it got on your clothes by accident and you tried to brush it off, it would stick to that as well. The only way to put it out was to roll you in something.

The composition of the flame fuel was such a closely guarded secret that crews in Normandy were under strict instructions to destroy their tanks rather than let them and their secrets fall into enemy hands.

The FRAS flame fuel tank was pressurized by five large gas cylinders. To bring the Crocodile into action took about thirty minutes, with fifteen minutes being required to bring the flame gun up to pressure, after which pressure fell steadily. An early lesson learnt in Normandy was the necessity of timely pressurization and the need to go straight into action before pressure leaked away.

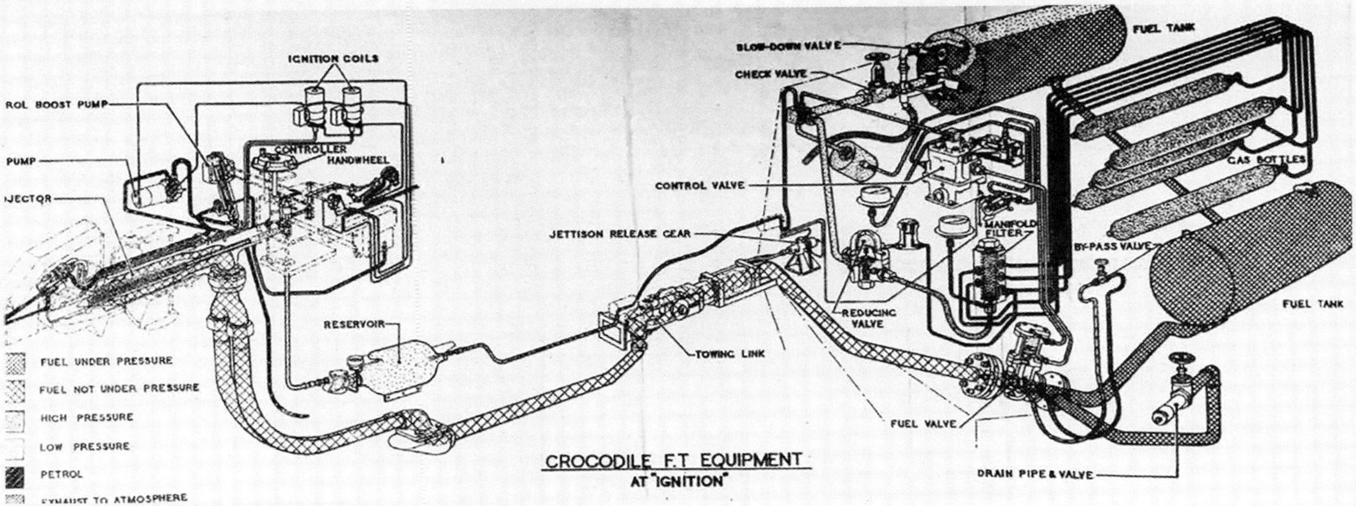

A diagram of the Crocodile's flame system, which consisted of three main elements, flame fuel and propellant gas, petrol to ignite the flame fuel and an electric system to provide the initiating spark.

The Crocodile's trailer was connected to the tank by an ingenious towing link, which allowed the tank to turn in any direction without overturning the trailer or interrupting the flow of gas and fuel. The link also included a micro switch, which gave the driver a warning, by way of red/green warning lights on his instrument panel, that he could turn no further. The flame fuel was carried from the trailer by a steel pipe that ran beneath the belly plate and into the hull through an opening originally designed for spent cartridge cases beneath the hull gunner's position.

Until late in the Normandy campaign, the trailer pipes, flame gun and ancillary equipment for Crocodile conversion were sent to 141 RAC for their REME fitters to install and test. Subsequently, however, all Mark VII Churchills came with the Crocodile's elbow joint, pipework and the tank end of the elbow joint pre-installed, leaving only the BESA to be replaced by a flame gun.

Some 800 Crocodile conversion kits and trailers were produced; of these, several regiments' worth were supplied to units in Italy and Burma during the autumn of 1944. A further 250 were held back in the UK for the invasion of Japan.

The elbow joint assembly at the rear between tank and trailer eventually became standard on every Churchill Mk VII built, making conversion to a Crocodile quick and easy.

Operation MITTEN – the First Attack

On this occasion, the battalions of 8 Brigade assembled around Le Landel for the attack, while a bombardment was fired by five field artillery regiments, the 4.2-inch mortars and machine guns of 2 Middlesex and the 3-inch mortar platoons of 9 and 185 Brigades. The air support allocated to MITTEN in a period of indifferent flying weather was limited, as Operation EPSOM was the Army's main effort. Similarly, virtually all the medium and heavy guns of the Army Groups' Royal Artillery were allocated to VIII Corps. As recorded by 1 South Lancs in their war diary at 1515 hours, 'C and D Coys start to form up, but heavy mortaring begun by enemy.' Worse, however, was to follow:

> Concentrated arty fire on LA LONDE, but mortaring on own posns still fierce, CO's advance OP mortared, communications by wireless and telephone cut. One bomb wrecked CO's slit trench. Lt Col STONE slightly wounded in left leg, but carried on from main CP.

The advance began at 1530 hours, with C Company left and D Company on the right (see air photograph overleaf). They immediately came under mortar and machine-gun fire, and the two troops of tanks were, according to the Staffordshire Yeomanry's history, 'soon coming under heavy fire. Lieutenant Sinclair's Sherman received a direct hit and was destroyed but all the crew escaped unhurt.' Lieutenant Jones of A Company noted:

> The enemy reacted violently and had obviously been reinforced ... Shelling and mortaring was intense and many casualties were suffered as we formed up. MG fire from the Chateau was withering. 'C' and 'D' Companies ... advanced directly across the open cornfield.

As in the earlier attack, enfilading fire from enemy positions on the more open left flank checked the advance. Despite the volume of fire support from field artillery, the Germans in well-prepared defences were not adequately suppressed by the bombardment:

> D Coy reached wood LA LONDE. C Coy pinned down on left flank, Major E.F. Johnson wounded. Heavy casualties in both companies.
> 1610 D Coy moved up to fwd edge of LA LONDE, came under fire from well-placed enemy MGs, deeply entrenched [in the château's park]. Unable to move fwd due to enfilade fire from left flank.

For the first phase of the attack one troop of three Crocodiles supported the South Lancs, with the other troop in reserve to support the subsequent attacks on the villages. The Crocodiles' role in the attack was to flame the northern edge of the château's park to assist the infantry's break-in. 'Heavy defensive fire was still falling, however, and the ground was swept by fire from dug-in tanks and concealed machine-guns which slowed the pace of the advance.' The Crocodiles advanced with the infantry, but according to the regimental war diary, 'Seeing his other two tks going too far right, Lieut RC Brooke made a dash himself for the correct objective and was knocked out by a 75mm A tk gun at 20 yards range. Lieut RC Brooke and gunner killed.' The Pak 40 responsible was 'prettily concealed behind an ornamental grille in a wall', and there were not only anti-tank guns but a significant number of panzers, well dug in around the park. The result was that while the Staffordshire Yeomanry had perforce to duel with the

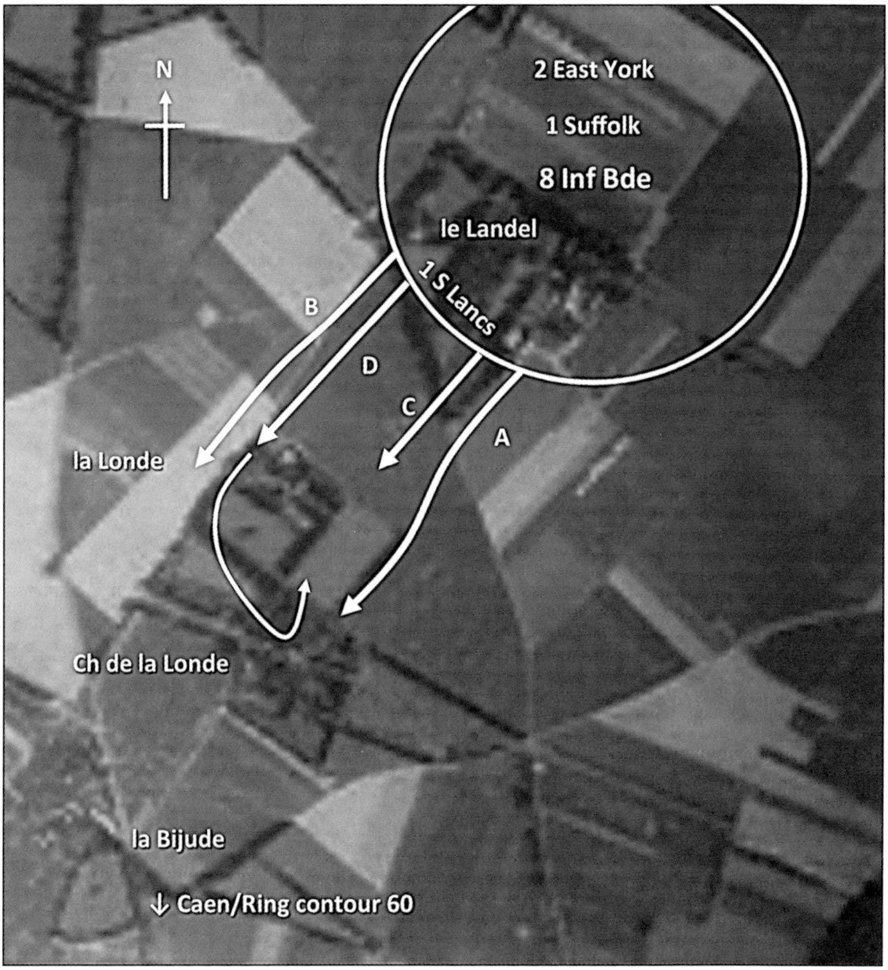

The attack by 8 Brigade on Château de la Londe on 27 June, spearheaded by 1 South Lancs.

enemy tanks, they were unable to provide meaningful support to 1 South Lancs or the Crocodiles.

With the defenders well prepared and the attackers lacking adequate close support, casualties in both infantry companies were heavy, and their frontal attacks ground to a halt. Consequently, A and B Companies were deployed to the flanks. Lieutenant Jones on the left fought alongside Lieutenant Brooke's Crocodile 'Spartan' and explained that they fared no better:

> I was ordered to lead with 8 Platoon. This I did, down both sides of a bank topped by a hedge, with a shallow ditch, which led directly towards the wall encircling the Chateau. My left hand section was supported by one of the Crocodiles. As we came within some 50 yards of this wall, a cluster of mortar

bombs straddled the hedge and the leading men of the left-hand section fell wounded or killed.

> We were also subjected to intense MG fire from both flanks and the front. Many men became casualties at once, others took refuge in the ditch and crawled back ... We were in a shallow ditch, blocked a few yards ahead by the bloated corpse of a cow, whilst the hedge-junction to our rear was continually raked by machine-gun fire.
>
> At the same moment the turret of the Crocodile was blown off at almost point-blank range and the tank and the trailer went up in a great sheet of flame as the flamethrower's fuel ignited. Most of the platoon became casualties and I found myself with two members of my platoon in the shelter of a ditch, cut off from the rest of the company. Any movement on our part drew intense MG fire from close range. One of the men with me was shot and died within seconds. A bullet struck the rifle of the other man and lodged across the barrel. We kept awaiting a fresh wave of our own troops, but none came.

Of the other two Crocodiles that had followed the Shermans, Captain Bailey the squadron 2iC concluded:

> The Sergeant's turret jammed and in the end both he and the Corporal were driven back by anti-tank gun fire, having accomplished precisely nothing at all. Two troops [of Crocodiles] in a frontal attack might well have pulled it off. But young Brooke was dead to prove that an assault must have a clear and simple plan with simple signals and infantry who are fresh and free to plan. The more Crocodiles the merrier – there was no doubt about that.[10]

Meanwhile, as planned, the Suffolks had left Mathieu at 1600 hours, followed by 2 East Yorks at 1630, and waited at Le Landel to pass through the South Lancs to their objectives astride the Épron road. Their attached Sapper officer, Lieutenant Edwards, recalled the wait:

> Some prisoners were seen being escorted back, a few wounded and shell-shocked soldiers passed back and an ambulance and jeep did sterling work time and time again picking up wounded despite the enemy fire. The sight of tanks withdrawing brought about realisation that the attack was not going well.

Back at Château de la Londe, unable to break through the German defences and the wall in the first rush, the Staffs Yeo claimed one 'kill'. The Shermans were, however, also forced back into cover, but the South Lancs continued to fight. The attack was reinforced by a sixteen M10s of 67 Anti-Tank Battery, but the remainder of the brigade remained waiting around Le Landel.

The M10s' role was to take on the panzers, which were well camouflaged and dug in, but with the tank-destroyers having to come forward into open fire positions they were vulnerable, and the firefight was distinctly one-sided. Brigadier Orr clearly saw that sending fresh infantry battalions into the enemy's killing area

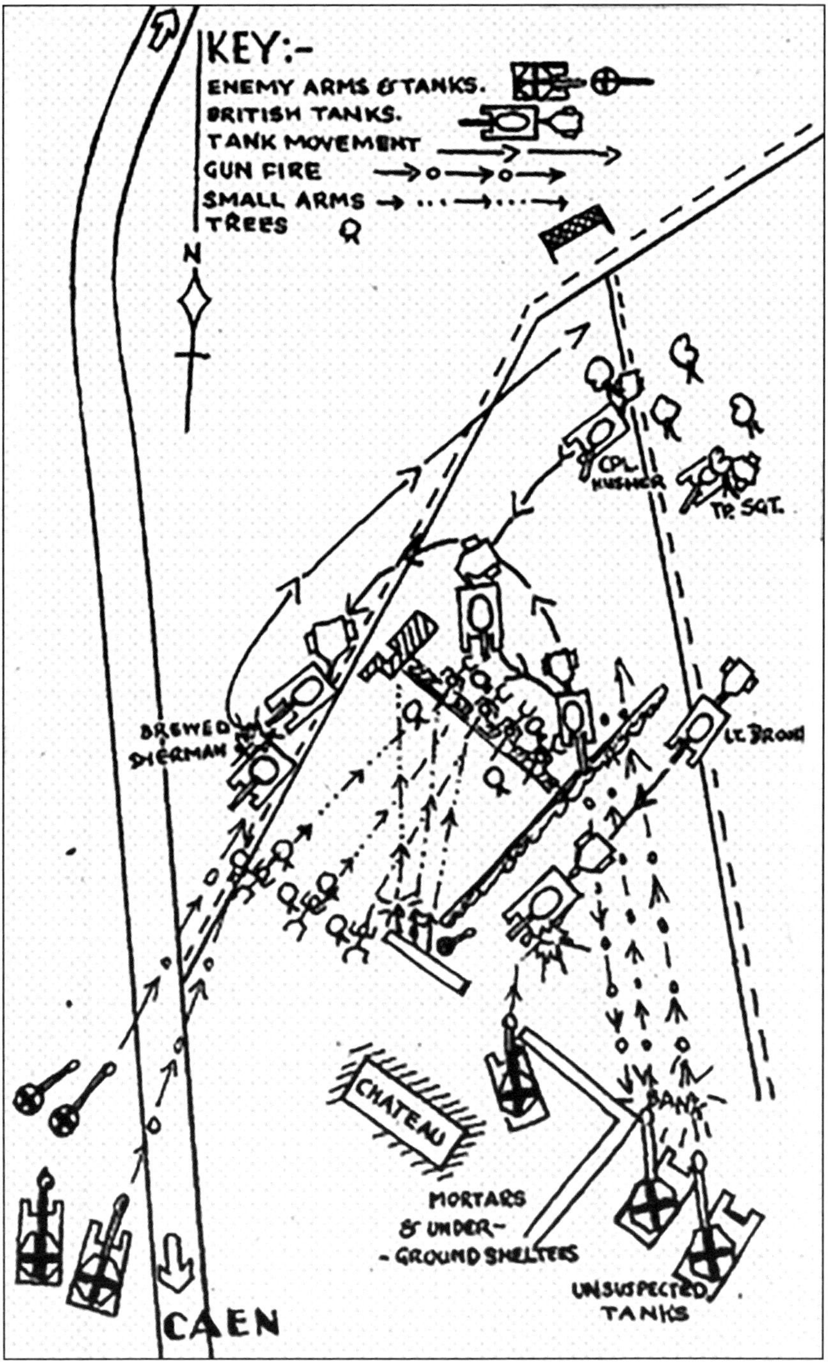

Captain Bailey's sketch map of the flame action at Château de la Londe.

would not help, hence the Suffolks and East Yorks sat under fire around Le Landel.

At 1845 hours the battle came to life again with a threat of an enemy counter-attack. The war diary recorded:

> Enemy tanks move up on right from LA BIJUDE, [M10] A Tk guns deploy. D Coy made progress on right, to line THRUSH halfway to objective CRANE, but sustained heavy casualties from mortar and MG fire and LE LANDEL heavily shelled at intervals.
> 1915 Two rocket firing Typhoons engaged tanks at LA BIJUDE.

Of this attack, or a similar one, an NCO signaller in C Squadron East Riding Yeomanry recalled in his personal diary: 'One of our Typhoons jettisoned his petrol tank, it came down like a train & landed right on top of a scout car, wrecking it. The whole place reeked of petrol & it's a wonder it did not catch fire.'

Meanwhile, D Company, with remarkable tenacity and better cover on the right, fought their way forward to the edge of the park, where the smaller cousin of the Crocodile came into play. Lieutenant Lacy's 16 Platoon was allocated a section of Wasp flame-throwing versions of the Universal Carrier:

> There wasn't a lot of hand-to-hand fighting, as far as I was concerned. At one stage, I was put in charge of the carrier platoon where we had three

The early version of the Wasp flame-throwing carrier.

> carriers with flamethrowers. These were particularly effective against snipers. If you had snipers in trees, the Bren gun carriers spurted forth flame and smoke ... it really got rid of them very quickly. They didn't hang about to find out how hot it was.
>
> We got as far as the chateau, into the chateau, there were no troops inside – all the usual drill about going in with grenades and so on was carried out – no enemy troops at all. But there was a telephone left hanging, and we wouldn't touch that with a bargepole, in case it was booby-trapped.[11]

Out on their own, D Company was heavily engaged by machine-gun fire, counter-attacked and driven back to La Londe, where they hung on amongst the trees on its southern edge.

By early evening, with the South Lancs having been fought to a standstill, Brigadier Orr ordered the suspension of the attack. As recorded by Lieutenant Jones, A Company was 'Under cover of darkness ... able to withdraw to the Le Landel position, where we learned that casualties throughout the Battalion had been very heavy including the CO, Lt-Col Jack Stone.'

The positions around Château de la Londe were clearly too strongly held by the reinforced Luftwaffe troops for a single infantry battalion and a squadron of tanks to capture and hold. With MITTEN and ABERLOUR having an important place in Second Army's plans, Major General Whistler was, however, not going to let matters rest and ordered 8 Brigade to renew the attack the following morning, 28 June.

Of the first attack the war diary of 141 Regiment RAC concluded, 'Failure. Bad plan – bad tie up with Inf. Far too few Crocodiles for large objective. Good job for a Sqn, which would have saved many Inf lives.' The process of understanding the capabilities of the Crocodile and how best to integrate it into operations was in its infancy, but by the end of the campaign flame-throwing tanks were in great demand; before the end of the war in Europe, three tank regiments had been converted to Crocodiles.

Private Wreford of 1 S Lancs recalled attempting to evacuate the battalion's wounded and becoming a casualty himself:

> We had been driven back in the morning. In the night you could hear the wounded crying out. We rescued as many as possible. At first light, I was in charge of a Bren gun with my pals. One was killed. We went forward, but a shell came over. We were blown into a ditch. My friend was on top of me, but I couldn't move him. He was dead.

Operation MITTEN – the Second Attack

Major General Whistler, with EPSOM making steady progress, reached the River Odon, needed to press on with Operation MITTEN. Consequently, he recast his plan for another attempt the following day. He ordered 9 Brigade to launch an attack on La Bijude from the ridge north of Cambes just before 8 Brigade's renewed attack on Château de la Londe, rather than in MITTEN's phase two as originally planned.[12] By doing this he aimed to draw German firepower and reserves away from the well defended château area and secure La Bijude.

At 2030 hours on 27 June, Brigadier Orr gave orders for 8 Brigade's renewed attack at first light the following morning, with an H Hour of 0425 hours. On the left, 1 Suffolk would advance with the benefit of the last of the darkness, with 2 East Yorks to their right. This time the tanks of two squadrons of the Staffordshire Yeomanry were to be in support of the infantry.[13]

Following the decision to call off the attack on the evening of 27 June, the Suffolks had returned to Mathieu and the East Yorks to Le Mesnil Wood. For commanders of all ranks involved in battle procedure there was no rest that night, and precious little for the soldiers before returning to FUPs at Le Landel. Captain Lummis recalled that 'Colonel Gough gave out his orders back in Mathieu in a barn by the light of two hurricane lamps . . . There was a heavy dew, and the troops were stiff and damp as they got ready to move forward before 4 o'clock. At about a hundred yards to the start line they lay down in the standing corn.' The Germans were alert and shelled the Le Landel area, inflicting casualties, including amongst the officers.

La Bijude

The part to be played in MITTEN by 2nd Royal Ulster Rifles (2 RUR) was originally to have been to attack St Contest once Château de la Londe and La Bijude were in the hands of 8 Brigade. The battalion's war diary recorded the process of re-planning:

> The [original] Battalion attack planned as part of a Brigade attack was based on the assumption that 8 Br Inf Bde should first capture the villages of LA BIJUDE and ÉPRON. They were, however, held up at an early objective – CHATEAU DE LA LONDE. In consequence our own attack, zeroed for the early morning, was indefinitely postponed. At 1200 hrs the plan was changed after a hurried conference between the Brigade Commander and the Commanding Officer. It was decided that B Company and a Squadron of the East Riding Yeomanry would launch an attack on LA BIJUDE. This attack can be described as a feeler with the hope that the enemy, hard pressed at CHATEAU DE LA LONDE, would be unable to resist a thrust on his left flank directed towards LA BIJUDE.

The attack was to be delivered by B Company, who were supported by C Squadron, the third of the ERY squadrons in action on 28 June. They formed up between Anisy and Cambes with the tanks prepared to lead, but the Germans were thoroughly alert and prepared, and the attack was doomed. The RUR's war diarist explained:

> The Squadron of the Yeomanry advanced to a ridge in front of our position and came under intense fire from M.Gs. and Anti-Tank guns firing from

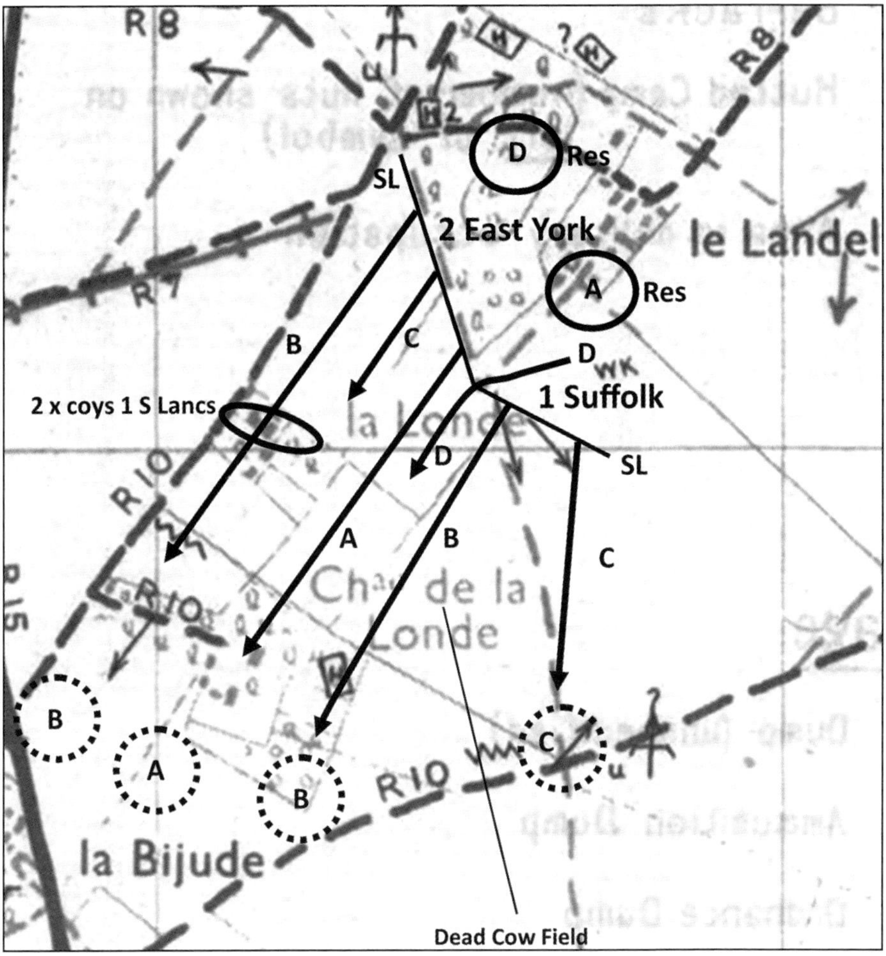

The second attack on Château de la Londe and La Bijude on 28 June 1944.

LA BIJUDE, MALON and CHATEAU itself. Against this punishing they could make no headway, though on three separate occasions they tried, with great gallantry, to push forward beyond the ridge. In consequence, B Company were pinned down on their start line, unable to advance.

Eventually the attack was called off. Casualties for the ERY were heavy, having two tanks destroyed and four out of action. Our own casualties were two men wounded by shrapnel.

Château de la Londe

With the assault companies of the Suffolks and East Yorks lying waiting in the corn, the bombardment of the château and its surrounding defences began at H–8 minutes. Private Harris of B Company 1 Suffolks recalled, 'The very ground

The view of the La Londe area from the centre of 8 Brigade's start line. The crop join marks the line of the long-since grubbed-out hedge used by the assaulting troops.

shuddered under the impact and the scene resembled a gigantic and terrible firework display, black smoke and fumes being wafted towards us as shell upon shell thundered down.' Promptly at H Hour, the soldiers of the brigade's leading companies crossed the start line into the gloom and started moving through the cornfields. Captain Lummis wrote:

> The noise was so great that words of command from officers could hardly be heard. Machine guns of the Middlesex joined in to add to the weight of fire. The enemy soon opened up with fire and shells started dropping our side of the barrage. Casualties started to mount and the cry of 'stretcher bearer' began to be heard. But the companies pressed on keeping as close as possible to our own barrage, occasionally having to wait for it to lift. They had been warned that with such a large amount of fire support there might be some which dropped short. With the noise and the smoke and the dust from the shelling in the faint light of early morning, it was difficult to see where one's own section was, let alone platoon.[14]

With greater numbers of men, despite heavy German fire thinning their ranks, the East Yorks reached the remains of the château wall and broke into the parkland, where a confused battle was fought. Meanwhile, the battalion's medics were searching the field, 'still under heavy shell fire and machine gun fire which made the attendance of casualties extremely difficult owing to the stretcher-bearers being unable to find the casualties in the standing corn.' Out in the open ground to the East Yorks' left, Private Lovewell of the Suffolks B Company recalled that the fields still contained killed and wounded from earlier attacks, and he passed the knocked-out Crocodile before going through the château's wall. Captain Lummis provides a sense of the confusion of battle for the Suffolks in the park:

> The one exception to the flat open cornfield was a hedge running through the centre of the Company's line of advance up to the wall surrounding the Chateau. With the heavy shelling, and now machine gunning and the poor visibility the Company continued advancing but became rather disorganized. Major McCaffrey soon lost his runner-wireless man and batman and with the bad light and noise found himself unable to control his company. He could see nothing of the two forward platoons and decided to take command of the reserve platoon following him. At one point in the middle of very heavy mortaring he found himself entirely alone. The reserve platoon No. 11 being now practically all casualties, he decided to move forward quickly and take control of the two platoons in front. He was out of touch with 10 Platoon who had moved up the hedgerow but looking back he was relieved to find Corporal Madden with about twenty men of 12 Platoon.

With B Company fighting their way through the left side of the park, Major McCaffrey came across a dug-in panzer. 'Corporal Madden stalked the tank and dropped two grenades through an open hatch only to realise that the tank had been abandoned.' Then four German infantrymen were seen emerging from some burning outbuildings, and 'without hesitation a Sten opened up and the figures crumpled up.' Out in the open fields to the left, C Company was suffering particularly heavy casualties, but by 0530 hours all four assault companies had reached their objectives. With the reorganization of the sections and redistribution of ammunition Major McCaffrey calmly shouted to B Company, 'God bless you, lads, now dig in as soon as you can, we may be counter-attacked at any moment' – and they were.

The Germans' immediate response was not long in coming. About six panzers advanced on the southern side of the château's park, falling mainly on the East Yorks' A Company and the Suffolks' B Company. Neither company's anti-tank defence was in place, as recalled by the East Yorks historian:

> Both 'A' and 'B' Coys reached their objectives and were consolidating their positions when a counter-attack by tanks and supported by infantry was put in on 'A' Coy's objective. An urgent call from 'A' Coy was received by Capt. Swinburne for anti-tank guns, just before his (wireless) set was put out of action. 'A' Coy was partially overrun and O.C. 'A' Coy was taken prisoner together with CSM Wakelin and a runner. Before their captors could get them away an artillery defensive barrage was called down, and in the resulting confusion, all made their escape.

Without 6-pounders or PIATs (those bringing them forward became casualties), the East Yorks had to let the panzers pass the cover or roll over the German trenches they occupied. The Suffolks were also in trouble.

> As the tanks came on, they held their fire … The remnants of B Company took the enemy infantry on and they went to ground about 50 yards away. The tanks were now aware of their presence and three remained shooting at

Soldiers of 2 RUR train with the infantry platoon's anti-tank weapon, the Projector Infantry Anti-Tank (PIAT). It was operated by a heavy spring and fired a shaped-charge warhead.

> them from the front with their machine guns while the other three moved round on their flank and took them in enfilade with both small arms and high explosive as they moved through the gate. In their incomplete slit trenches those that remained were in a bad way and were called upon by the enemy to surrender. Some of them started to do so and were followed by others.

In the confusion Major McCaffrey escaped, but

> suddenly seeing two tanks, he crossed to one of them to ask for fire support onto an intruder. A head rose from the turret, and each stared at the other in silence. The gun began to swing round, the British officer bolted, and though chased back to the position, managed to reach a slit-trench before being fired at.[15]

The Suffolks' B Company was overrun and most of the survivors were taken prisoner, but A Company of the East Yorks beat off the counter-attack, which then veered to the west and fell on B Company near the road. On the other flank the Suffolks' C Company also received the attention of enemy armour; in both cases PIATs were forward with the companies and knocked out Panzer IVs.

The Germans held the ground B Company 1 Suffolk had lost, but the remainder of the assault companies held on to their positions despite heavy losses. Behind them the château buildings, trees and undergrowth needed clearing in detail. To do this, the two supporting companies, D Company 1 Suffolk and C Company East Yorks, were moving up while the counter-attack was under way. They were engaged by snipers from the tree cover around the château, and worse, by five panzers that had driven around the chateau's park. These were, however, engaged by an M10 from the La Londe area, knocking one out with its second shot and driving the others back.

On reaching the park the two companies, eventually followed by the battalions' reserve companies, worked their way through the cover, with D Company of the Suffolks taking on the château itself. One platoon provided covering fire, while the other two dashed forward to break into the château building and clear it in detail. Germans found sheltering in the cellars were taken prisoner.

It was well into the morning before the Château de la Londe area could be considered secure, and all the while the two battalions were under vicious enemy shell and mortar fire as they dug in or turned enemy trenches. Without proper shelter, casualties continued to mount. Private Harris and a comrade emerged from cover after a particularly intense bombardment of their position to a horrific sight: 'Not a figure moved. All the twenty men or so who had lined the hedge lay in various attitudes, most with shovels in their lifeless hands.'

Many of the German prisoners were wounded and had to be evacuated, with some being hit for a second time by fire from their comrades.

> During the afternoon a very badly wounded German NCO made his way into D Company lines from La Bijude and asked for medical attention. His wounds were too serious and his condition too dazed for him to be of any

Château de la Londe after the battle.

Youthful *Panzergrenadiers* taken prisoner at Château de la Londe on 28 June 1944. Increasingly young soldiers were to be found across the Wehrmacht, not just in the *Hitlerjugend* Panzer Division.

> value for interrogation. Another prisoner, a wounded Pole, was only too willing to tell anything he knew. He was a member of 10 Company, 2 Bn, 192 Panzer Grenadier Regiment and had been one of the garrison of the Chateau. His company was no longer an effective unit having suffered heavy casualties from our shellfire. He was one of 20 Poles in that company.

Some 300 casualties were suffered by 8 Brigade on 28 June. When added to those from previous attacks, it is with some justification that 3rd Division referred to the Château de la Londe area as 'The bloodiest square mile in Normandy'.

In the aftermath of battle, Private Holdsworth of 2 East Yorks commented, 'We were pulled back out into some woods but were still in range. A war reporter came around, but we told him to bugger off – we weren't in the mood to talk and all a bit bomb happy'.

Having suffered such heavy casualties across the brigade for limited gains, pursuing subsequent phases of Operation MITTEN was not on, and General Whistler called off further attacks. The number of casualties in 8 Brigade was not the only factor being taken into consideration. By day three of Operation EPSOM, VIII Corps was making slow progress, and with the warning of the approach of II SS Panzer Corps, Operation ABERLOUR was cancelled.[16] The Germans, though they had lost the La Londe salient, held firm at La Bijude and would do so for another two weeks, until Operation CHARNWOOD and the fall of Caen.

Aftermath

On 29 June the East Yorks were pulled back into reserve at Cazelle (Mathieu), leaving the Suffolks to defend Château de la Londe, while the South Lancs remained at Le Landel. The brigade spent much of the afternoon reorganizing the companies, salvaging equipment and the all-too grim task of burying the dead.

In the day following the capture of the château, the situation remained tense. A measure of the expectation of a German counter-attack is afforded by Lieutenant Edwards. He and his troop of 246 Company RE were kept fully committed:

> For the next few days, the Company was busy laying about 2,000 A/Tk mines and all Platoons were employed throughout the night of June 30th without incident. Again in the first three nights of July, mine-laying continued each night in front of our forward positions along the Le Mesnil–Chateau de la Londe front. Ten rows of mines were laid to give two mines per yard in front, the fields were then fenced and carefully recorded. On rare occasions, we could enlist the help of Infantry as a protective screen when we were mine laying, but on all of the nights laying these mines in front of our infantry in the Le Mesnil–Chateau de la Londe front, and in no-man's-land! We were on our own and set up our own listening posts. Should any enemy movement occur, we would stop mine laying and get down into position ready to defend ourselves until it was quiet again. The amount of work that trained troops could do at night without detection (and right in front of the enemy) surprised me. On that particular minefield operation there were three Platoons, alongside one another in a long line, each field butting on to the other, and yet, I saw and heard nothing of the others although they came right up to my right-hand boundary.
>
> It was while we were on the mine laying operation on the night of the 2nd/3rd of July that we were caught out in the open. We had just completed mine laying shortly before first light and 3 Platoon were moving silently back along the approach route. I remained behind as usual with my bodyguard to complete the minefield record. As I finished my notes we began to feel an uneasy disquiet – the silence of the minutes before dawn. I decided to get back along the track, just at the moment that the enemy started to fire their automatic weapons in a wide sweep along their front, the tracers began to hit the ground behind us. In a flash we hurled ourselves into a side ditch as the bursts swept past and around us, at speed we were out on the track again to cover a few more yards before the next burst. We seemed to take such a long time to cover such a short distance.[17]

The majority of men in the battalions of 3rd Division had not seen action prior to D Day but could now be considered to be experienced battlefield soldiers. However, measured against the combat skills gained by units were the unexpectedly high casualties suffered by the division; even though these were largely replaced, the losses represented a serious drain of well-trained manpower.

Maschinengewehr 42 (MG 42) Rate of Fire

The German 'universal' machine guns of the Second World War are renowned for their prodigious rates of fire, with a cyclic rate being quoted as between 1,200 and 1,500 rounds per minute for the MG 42. Veterans' accounts liken the sound of German machine guns to a chainsaw and contrast it with the steadier rhythm of Allied weapons. As with most machine guns, however, the rate of fire for the MG 42 is theoretical due to overheating of barrels, and the real, practical rate is much lower.

In the light role within an infantry rifle *Gruppe* (section) the MG 42, crewed by three men, was usually used at a relatively short range with short bursts of three to five rounds being fired. When it first came into service, German manuals required the MG 42's barrels to be changed every 250 rounds, but the crew could reduce their rate of fire to lengthen the time before a replacement was necessary. The limited amount of ammunition carried by the *Gruppe* tended to reduce the rate of fire to reasonable levels. In the heavy machine-gun platoons, each of the four MG 42's had a crew of six. They were mounted on *Lafette 42* tripods, from which machine-gunners were trained to fire short bursts and bursts of 20–50 rounds as

An MG 42 in the light role loaded with a belt from a 300-round ammunition box or *Patronenkasten 41 für Maschinengewehr*.

needed. With the sustained fire from the guns in the medium role, barrel-changing was clearly a major part of keeping the weapon in action.

In both roles the No. 3 carried and changed the barrels using a quick-change mechanism and was issued with thick asbestos mitts to handle the hot, sometimes almost red-hot, barrel. Having been removed from the gun the barrel was placed in the *Laufschützer* barrel carrier, which helped it to cool, and a fresh barrel was fitted. According to German manuals it took ten minutes in normal conditions for barrels to cool for re-use. This time could be reduced, but with officially just two spare barrels, cumulative heating was an obvious danger.

The original requirement that the MG 42's barrel be changed every 250 rounds was reduced, as a result of wartime shortages of metals that led to less being used in the manufacture of special steels. In the case of the MG 42's barrels, the quantity of other metals was reduced during 1943 as follows:

Steel	10 kg	10 kg
Chrome	0.05 kg	0 kg
Nickel	0.045 kg	0 kg
Vanadium	0.045 kg	0 kg[18]

This final reduction to a pure carbon steel barrel reduced the overall strength of the barrel and made it less able to cope with the heat generated by sustained rapid fire, which would distort a barrel, rendering it useless. This led to manuals being amended, the number of rounds specified to be fired before a barrel change being reduced to 150 per minute.[19] An about face late in the war saw a chrome-coated barrel being introduced that was supposed to reduce overheating, but it did not make a significant difference.

The MG 42 in the medium or sustained fire role mounted on a Lafette 42 tripod.

Chapter Four

Operation WINDSOR

> Once it starts, I will continue to battle on the eastern flank until one of us cracks, and it will not be us ... If we can pull the enemy on to Second Army, it will make it easier for First Army when it attacks southwards.
>
> [Montgomery to Eisenhower, 25 June 1944]

The prompt capture of the Carpiquet airfield had been a feature of the invasion plan, but the 3rd Canadian Division had been prevented from reaching it by going over to the defensive on the afternoon of D Day as 21st Panzer Division prepared to counter-attack, and by the arrival the following day of 25 SS *Panzergrenadier* Regiment. The Canadians had fought a brutal battle with the *Hitlerjugend* over the course of four days, first as a meeting engagement and then as a mostly defensive action as the SS, reinforced by the arrival of the 26 *Panzergrenadiers*, tried to 'throw the Allies back into the sea'. For much of the time since 10 June, the 3rd Canadian Division had held a long front that almost exactly matched that of the *Hitlerjugend*, from Galmanche around the north-west of Caen and west along the line of the Caen–Bayeux railway to Brouay.

Possession of Carpiquet was regarded as a prerequisite for I Corps' capture of Caen, but in the shadow of EPSOM, not only was Operation ABERLOUR cancelled but also 8 Canadian Brigade's Operation OTTAWA. This was to have been launched from Authie and aimed to capture Carpiquet airfield, village and barracks. OTTAWA was recast and renamed WINDSOR, which would now be from Marcelet to the west, which was occupied by the recently arrived 32 Guards Armoured Brigade. The target date for this and Operation SHERWOOD, an attack on Lebisey, was 2 July, but with EPSOM's 'Scottish Corridor' still under pressure from II SS Panzer Corps' counter-attacks, the former was delayed and the latter cancelled.

The Carpiquet airfield, barracks and hangars, and the high ground between the airfield and Verson, if still in German hands, had wider significance to events around Caen. They overlooked the ground gained during EPSOM, as well as that on which future operations were planned by XII Corps on the western flank of the city, principally Operation JUPITER, the capture of Hill 112.[1]

In his directive M505, Montgomery gave his 'Plan in Outline':

> 7. To hold the maximum number of enemy divisions on our eastern flank between Caen and Villers Bocage, and to swing the western or right flank of the Army Group southwards and eastwards in a wide sweep so as to threaten the line of withdrawal of such enemy divisions to the south of

Paris. The bridges over the Seine between Paris and the sea have been destroyed by the Allied air forces and will be kept out of action; a strong Allied force established in the area Le Mans-Alençon would threaten seriously the enemy concentration in the Caen area and its 'get-away' south of Paris.

Second British Army

8. Tasks as follows:
   (a) To hold the main enemy forces in the area between Caen and Villers Bocage.
   (b) To have no set-backs.
   (c) To develop operations for the capture of Caen as opportunity offers – and the sooner the better.

General Montgomery and Lieutenant General Crocker pose for the camera.

The German Situation

By 1 July, largely thanks to FORTITUDE, only nineteen German divisions were in action in Normandy. This was a fraction of the thirty-seven enemy divisions that the Allied planners had estimated would be deployed to Normandy by the end of June. Most recently arrived, on 28 June, were the advanced elements of 1st SS Panzer Division (*Leibstandarte Adolf Hitler*), which had been fed piecemeal into action in support of the *Hitlerjugend*, who had been struggling to contain Operation EPSOM. To the north of Caen, the 16th *Luftwaffe Feld* Division was still arriving and taking over from the 21st Panzer Division, but the three infantry divisions from south and south-west France were still en route, leaving the panzer divisions still largely fixed holding ground. The 276th Division was the first of these to be inserted into the line at Hottot, to the south-east of Tilly-sur-Seulles, on 4 July.

Eisenhower wrote: 'Based on their belief that the Americans could only make very slow progress through the bocage country, the Germans had always regarded the landings near the Orne as chief danger in the area invaded so far and took steps to commit is strongest and most readily available reserves to that sector.' The Supreme Commander's report continued:

> Little was known of the strength or objectives of the American landings, and the operations in the Cotentin continued to be regarded simply as a diversionary effort which could easily be dealt with. This estimate of the situation dominated the enemy's policy, with fatal results, during the ensuing days.[2]

The biggest influence on the German conduct of the campaign was, however, the continuing belief that the main Allied assault was yet to come. Another major factor was Hitler's determination to 'rope off' the beachhead and launch counter-attacks to drive the Allies back into the sea. In his post-war Special Interrogation, von Rundstedt explained the effect of these factors to his questioner, who wrote:

> The inflexibility of operational direction which had so marked an effect on the enemy's first reaction to the assault continued thereafter to hamper his offensive activity against the bridgehead. Von Rundstedt's appreciation was that it was necessary to yield CAEN, and to withdraw to the South in order to form an infantry line behind the ORNE. The panzer divisions could thus be freed for a heavy attack against the Americans over the more favourable terrain to the west.[3]

Rommel, supported by *General der Panzertruppen* Geyr von Schweppenburg, who above all wanted his panzers out of the range of naval gunfire, had issued a report calling for a progressive withdrawal from the Caen salient. Both von Rundstedt and Rommel were summoned to the Führer Headquarters, where they put forward their alternative flexible concept of operations, but 'This proposal was refused. Not an inch of territory was to be given up.' Warning orders that Rommel had issued for a progressive withdrawal from the Caen salient were

General der Panzertruppen Geyr von Schweppenburg (left) and *Feldmarschall* Rommel (right).

cancelled on the evening of 1 July. After the war, von Rundstedt explained to his interrogator:

> Thus, with insufficient infantry to put in the line there remained little to do but cling desperately to each inch of ground while the Allies continued their feverish build-up in the beachhead. No division could be moved back without an explanation being sent to Hitler and every tactical change had to be ratified by Berlin. The conduct of the battle was no longer in Rundstedt's hands. Every decision was made by the Führer himself. 'I could have stood on my head,' remarked the Field Marshal, 'but I would still not have been able to budge a division if Hitler disagreed with my judgment.' There was no immediate plan or desire to retire to the Seine on Rundstedt's part, but once it was plain that there was no hope of obtaining the assistance of the divisions in Southern France it remained the only advisable thing to do, yet this suggestion was also rejected by Berlin.[4]

On 1 July von Rundstedt rang Berlin to report the failure of II SS Panzer Corps' attack on the 'Scottish Corridor'. As the news of the latest setback sunk in, *Feldmarschall* Keitel asked, 'What shall we do?' To this, von Rundstedt replied, 'Make peace, you fool! What else can you do?' and hung up.

Keitel reported this to a furious Hitler, and on 3 July *Feldmarschall* von Kluge arrived at the headquarters in Saint-Germain-en-Laye to take command in the

Feldmarschall von Kluge and his staff. Having visited formations at the front he found little to give him cause for amusement.

west, having been appointed over the head of Rommel. Von Rundstedt was presented with another award and officially 'retired' on grounds of 'failing health'. Von Kluge addressed his staff, brimming with confidence, but after three days of visiting formations in Normandy, the reality of the parlous situation became fully apparent to him.

General Geyr von Schweppenburg was labelled as a defeatist for sending a final message in an attempt to change minds in Berlin. His signal was forwarded by *Generalleutnant* Speidel without comment to OKW. It read:

> If the requested straightening of the front does not occur within a few days, the 9., 10., 12. SS-Pz.Divs. and the Pz-lehr-Div. will burn out to the extent that they will no longer be usable.
>
> We are here not talking about 'running away', but rather about a sensible and methodical removal from the fire of ships' artillery for which the men are helpless targets at the present.

Consequently, General Geyr von Schweppenburg lost his command of Panzer Group West, being replaced by General Ebberbach.

The Defences of Carpiquet

With the arrival of II SS Panzer Corps, and thanks to the grievous losses suffered by the *Hitlerjugend* in four weeks of fighting, the front now held by the division was greatly reduced, running from the original boundary on the railway north of Caen in an arc around the north-west of the city to the River Orne. Even so, *Kampfgruppen* from the *Leibstandarte* were needed to reinforce them and to hold Caen as ordered.

Carpiquet village and the airfield occupy a dominating bastion position covering the western approaches to Caen, and they afforded observation into the salient created by VIII Corps during EPSOM. The SS observers were now using these advantageous positions to the full, making life uncomfortable for the 43rd Wessex Division in the salient and inflicting a steady stream of casualties on them. For this reason, but also to remove an important outwork of Caen's defences, Carpiquet had to be taken.

Facing the 3rd Canadian Division in the Carpiquet area were *Sturmbannführer* Krause's I/26 SS *Panzergrenadiers*. Just four very under-strength companies totalling approximately 200 men held the village and the hangars to the north and south of the airfield. The airfield itself was an open killing area, so was not held but was dominated by five panzers of 6 Company in dug-in positions near the barracks; further back, in the outskirts of Caen, were the Panzer IVs of 9 Company, 12 SS Panzer Regiment. To the rear of the position were the 88mm Flak 36/37 guns of the divisional anti-aircraft battalion which could cover the eastern end of the airfield and the eastern exits from Carpiquet village. The 150mm guns of III/12 SS Artillery Regiment[5] and elements of 83 *Werfer* Regiment were in direct support, and much of I SS Panzer Corps' artillery was in range. The defenders had a company of about twelve Panthers held back as a counter-attacking force. Krause's battalion headquarters was located in one of the pre-invasion concrete bunkers near the southern hangars, from where they had a restricted view west, towards Marcelet. The Luftwaffe bunkers offered good protection from bombardment, but they were not fighting positions.

The defenders of Carpiquet were without a doubt a small force, with comparatively little artillery, to hold such a large and tactically important piece of ground. There was, however, high ground to either flank, and the Canadians' plan to drive a salient towards Caen would be enfiladed from both of these flanks by mutually supporting German defensive positions. In addition, it is clear from the war diary of I/12 SS Panzer Regiment that they were prepared for the Canadian attack:

> The *Abteilung* with three *Kompanien* was sent to provide defence for the airfield of Caen. The 2.*Kompanie* was deployed at the Venoix main road in the northern direction, the 4.*Kompanie* at the Venoix–St Germain [Saint-Germain-la-Blanche-Herbe] road in the western and north-western directions. The 1. and 2.*Kompanien* received heavy artillery fire.[6]

Sturmbannführer Krause, with his headquarters established deep in one of the Luftwaffe bunkers, was alerted to the imminence of the Canadian attack by patrols that reported increasing enemy activity during 2/3 July. The *Hitlerjugend*'s radio intelligence section also gathered a growing volume of Canadian radio chatter during the night of 3/4 July indicating an attack. Finally, an officer of the division who had been lying up in enemy-held territory since the first day of EPSOM took the opportunity provided by rain and Allied movement into assembly areas during the night of 3/4 July to exfiltrate to safety. He brought with

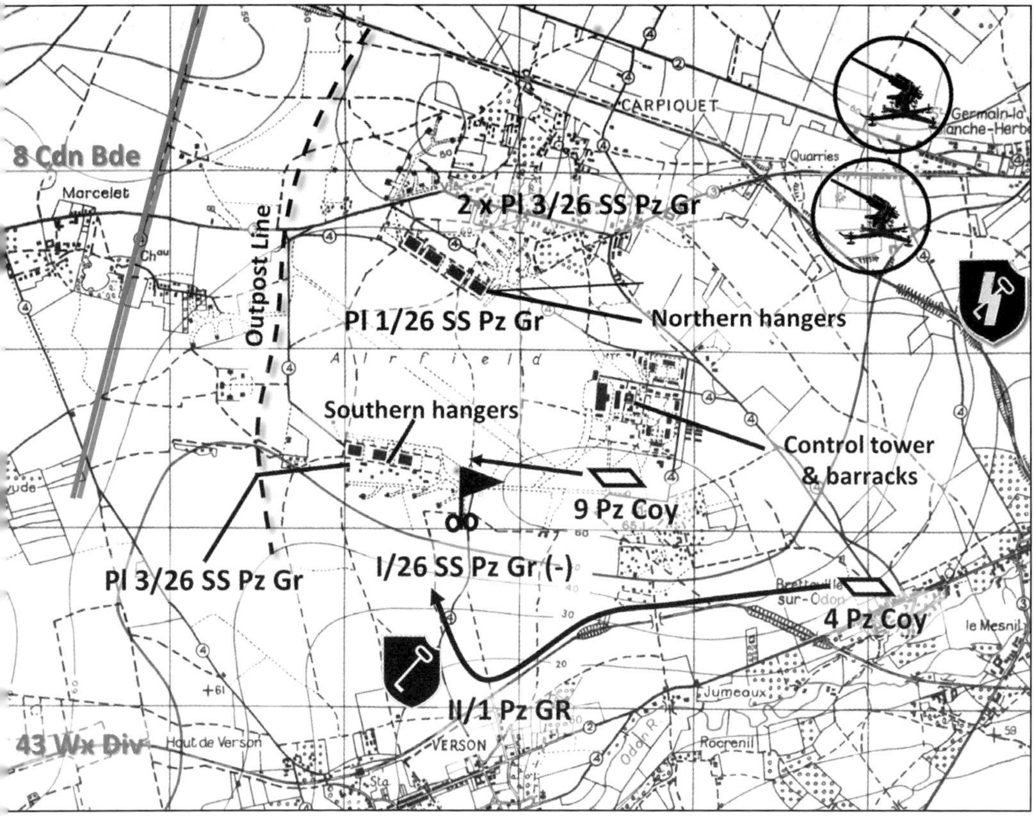

The thinly held defences of Carpiquet and the airfield.

him the location of enemy batteries and assembly areas, which were promptly shelled. *Sturmbannführer* Meyer wrote:

> In the early morning hours of 4 July, enemy radio traffic increased. The content of the messages indicated an impending attack. Based on previous experience, the Division calculated the start of the attack for 0600 hours. The wooded areas east and south-west of Marcelet were considered to be the assembly areas. In order to smash the assembly, or at least to inflict painful losses on the enemy, squeezed into a narrow space, two fire attacks by artillery and mortars carpeted these areas at approximately 0500 hours. The III. [heavy] *Abteilung* SS-*Panzer-artillerieregiment* 12 fired some ten salvos [approximately 220 shells] and the mortars fired two half-salvos. Ground observation of the target areas was not possible, but the enemy radio traffic indicated that the fire had been effective. A repetition of the fire attacks was not possible because of a lack of ammunition.[7]

The *Hitlerjugend* Radio Intelligence Section's intercepts were correct; the fire strikes were indeed effective, and but for the shortage of ammunition, the fire strike could have been more destructive. Artilleryman Herman Bull recalled:

> We opened fire, and after days of being rationed to a handful of rounds a day and only few shells per gun arriving to replace them, I was surprised at how

> much of our pile we fired, but when it was over I saw the *Scharführer* counting the remaining shells and shaking his head. We were worried because our pitiful pile of shells was nothing like what we supposed the Tommies had ready near their guns.[8]

Clearly with a degree of hindsight, the divisional commander *Standartenführer* Kurt Meyer explained the outline of his plan to defend the village:

> The defenders of Carpiquet no longer had any [towed Pak] anti-tank weapons, as they had been destroyed several days earlier. There were, however, minefields to the front of the village. The *Panzergrenadiers* were to tempt the enemy into the village and conduct a fighting withdrawal to the eastern edge, where the 88mm guns were in ambush positions.

Standartenführer Kurt 'Panzer' Meyer took over command of the *Hitlerjugend* Panzer Division when his predecessor Fritz Witt was killed by naval gunfire on 14 June. He is wearing a uniform of Italian camouflage cloth made up into a German pattern uniform.

Planning WINDSOR

Operation WINDSOR was not only launched from a different direction than planned for OTTAWA, but was also considerably beefed up as a result of the level of resistance by the *Hitlerjugend* during EPSOM. The Canadian report explained the importance of the Carpiquet area in plans being developed to take Caen:

> Any operation to deprive the enemy of this westerly sector of his perimeter before Caen would clearly have to be part of a larger undertaking to eliminate all his holdings, including the town [Caen] itself, north of the Odon. Such provision had been made in the planning. It was equally apparent that the Germans would defend their positions with as much energy as they had prepared them. It was decided, therefore, to mount the attack upon Carpiquet in greater strength than had previously been intended . . . as a prelude to larger operations to put on against Caen about 8 Jul.[9]

Brigadier Blackadder's 8 Canadian Infantry Brigade was reinforced by the tanks of the 10th Armoured Regiment (Fort Garry Horse), funnies from the 79th Armoured Division and the Royal Winnipeg Rifles from 7 Cdn Brigade. They were to be aided by feint and supporting attacks on WINDSOR's flanks: to the north by the tanks of the 27th Armoured Regiment (Sherbrooke Fusiliers) on Château de St Louet and the village of Gruchy, and on the right to the north of the Odon by the 43rd Wessex Division.

Fire support was lavish, starting with an air attack, followed by shelling from the nine 16-inch guns of HMS *Rodney* and the 15-inch guns of the monitor HMS *Roberts*. During 3 July *Rodney* alone fired fifteen broadsides, sending 135 shells each weighing 2,375lbs ploughing into the airfield's defences. For the attack itself there was the fire of the guns of 4 AGRA, a heavy artillery regiment, and eight medium, plus twelve field regiments, a total of nearly 600 guns. A creeping barrage fired by six of the field and two of the medium regiments would cover the advance. In addition, two squadrons of Typhoon fighter-bombers were on call.

The attack was to be in two phases. In phase one the objectives were Carpiquet village and the airfield's northern and southern hangars; in phase two, the control tower and the barrack area at the eastern end of the airfield were to be taken. The North Shore Regiment (NSR) on the left flank and Le Régiment de la Chaudière (centre right), were both supported by a squadron of tanks, and a half-platoon of sappers were to advance on the northern half of the village. The Chaudières had, in addition to the southern portion of the village, to secure the northern hangars. On the right, across the open runways of the airfield, the southern hangars were to be attacked simultaneously by the Royal Winnipeg Rifles, advancing from Marcelet. In phase two, the Queen's Own Rifles of Canada (QORC), which had initially been held in reserve, would carry out a passage of lines through the village and attack the barrack area from the eastern end of Carpiquet. H Hour was at 0500 hours on 4 July.

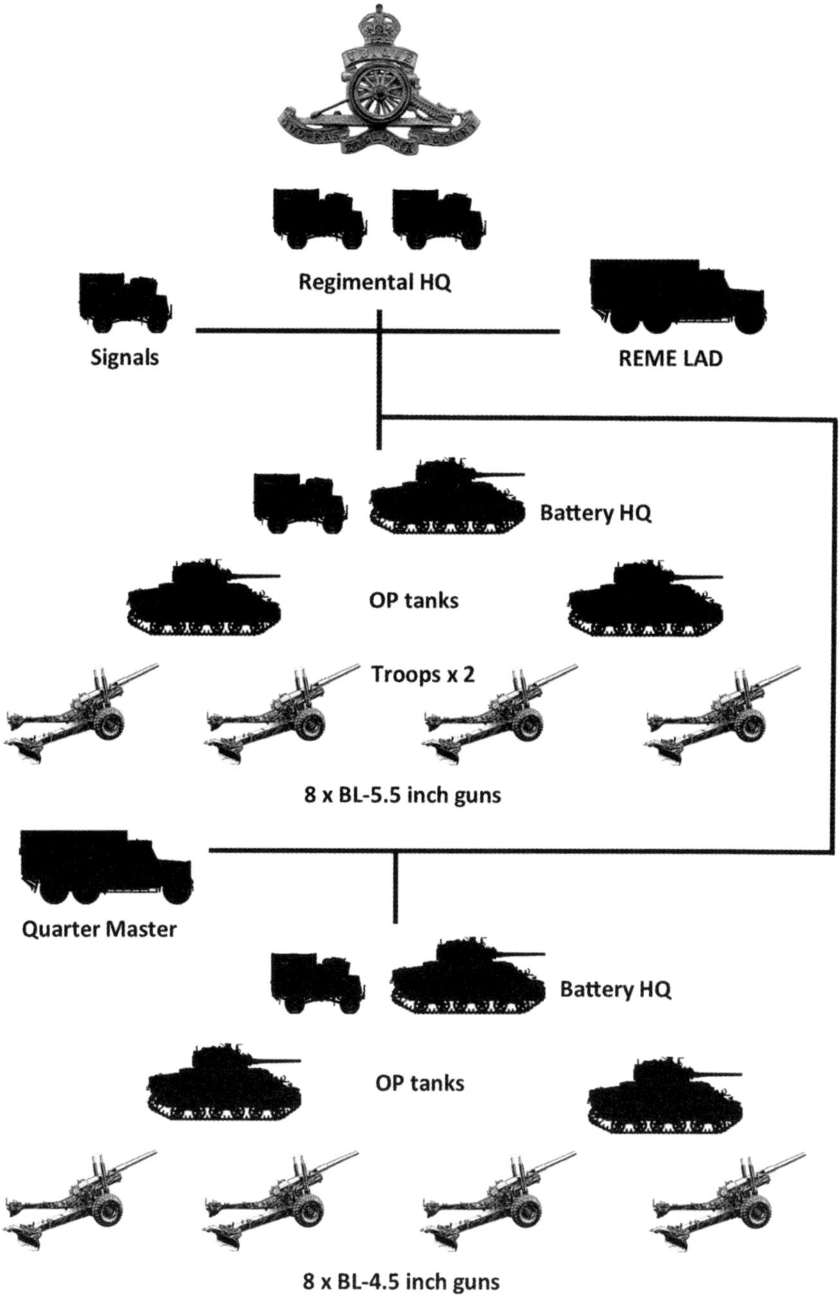

The organization of a medium regiment RA/RCA, including armoured observation post tanks, as found in the Army Groups Royal Artillery that supported offensive operations throughout the Normandy Campaign. Note: not all medium regiments had both 4.5 and 5.5-inch guns.

Three squadrons of assault armour were allocated to 8 Cdn Brigade. The Sherman flails of the 22nd Dragoons[10] were to beat their way through the minefields and, having broken into the position, the AVREs of 80 Assault Squadrons were to assist in reducing bunkers and defended buildings. The Crocodile flamethrowers of B Squadron 141 RAC were held in reserve, with two troops allocated to each flank. Captain Ryle of the half-squadron that was to follow behind the Royal Winnipegs complained that rather than sheltering behind the ridge at Marcelet in hull-down positions until needed, the Crocodiles were

> in the bright sunshine, naked as newborn babes ... fanned out in the flat cornfields and landing ground this side of Carpiquet. Where the mortars blossomed orange and the black plumes of earth shot skywards from the shells. Where the Messerschmitt played vulture overhead. They fanned out and waited tensely – a rendezvous with death.[11]

The Attack on Carpiquet

Operation WINDSOR began with a very heavy ten-minute bombardment, including continued naval gunfire. Major Gammon of D Company NSR recalled, 'At Zero hour the whole horizon in a semi-circle behind us became a blaze when the artillery opened up'; while Major Anderson of the same battalion's A Company noted that the 'quiet and peaceful countryside with dawn just breaking' was shattered, with the 'ground under us shaking from the bursts of shells'.[12]

The weight of fire was directed on strongpoints and the village, where the young SS *Panzergrenadier* defenders sheltered in concrete bunkers and deep dugouts, while out in the open, the Canadian soldiers of the three assault battalions

The Canadian OH map showing the plan for the attack on Carpiquet.

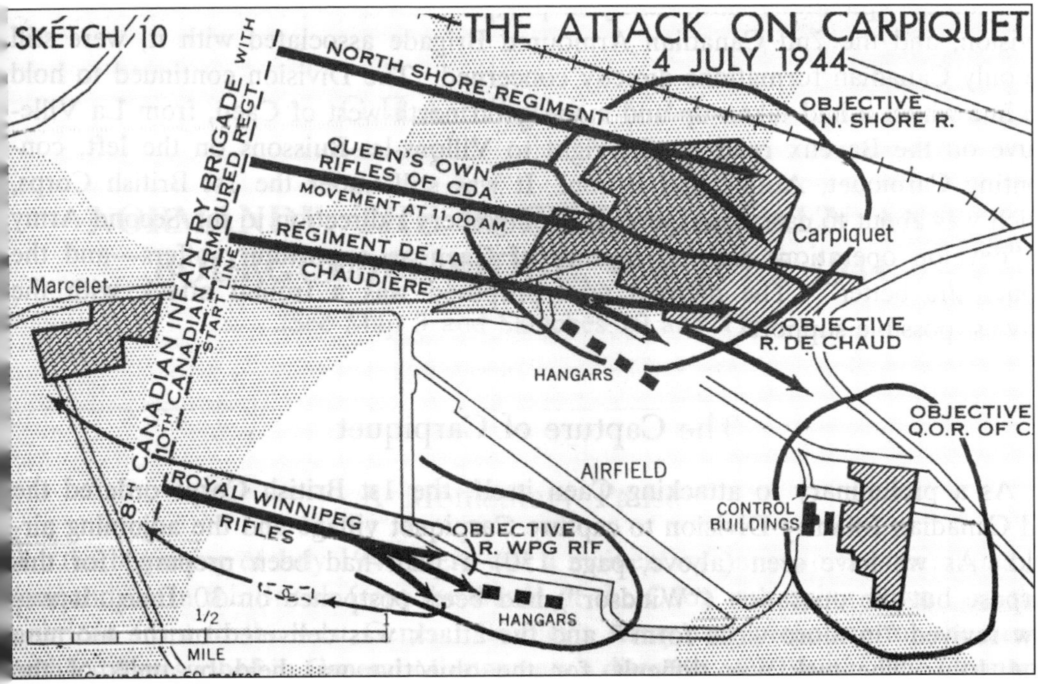

moved up to their start line. They were covered by the linear barrage that would creep forward at a rate of 100 yards every three minutes. This was, however, all too obvious to the defenders, and they put their shells down 200 yards behind the 'protective' wall of exploding shells, confident that they would then hit the Canadians in their FUP. This fire included *Nebelwerfer* rounds from 83 *Werfer* Regiment. Major Gammon wrote that 'The enemy counter-barrage was really coming down and a lot of my men were dead or wounded ... It looked for a while as if we would never get off the start line.' The problem was solved for the forward companies by 'getting under the barrage' and maintaining position between the enemy's shells and their own. The reserve companies, however, bore the brunt of the enemy shelling and mortaring. Lieutenant Richardson recalled that 'Within minutes of the opening salvoes the Moaning Minnies' [*Nebelwerfers*] crying for help began and we had no choice but to take it.' Of his 35-man-strong platoon only twenty-five men crossed the start line. Padre Hickey of the NSR went forward to B Company's FUP after the attack was under way and later recalled, 'Everywhere men lay dead or dying. I anointed about thirty right there.' A significant proportion of the casualties suffered during the operation were in the FUP and during the initial advance.[13]

83rd *Werfer* Regiment

The *Werfer* battalion of the *Hitlerjugend* did not serve in Normandy, thanks to a lack of equipment and vehicles. The *Leibstandarte* were similarly deficient when they arrived, as their battalion had only just been formed. To fill the capability gap 7 *Werfer* Brigade were deployed to join I SS Panzer Corps around Caen. Later, 8 *Werfer* Brigade came under command of II SS Panzer Corps further west. The balance of German forces on Second British Army's front is normally illustrated by the number of panzer divisions they faced, but the number of *Nebelwerfers*, along with the III Flak Corps, must also be taken into account.

Oberstleutnant Böhme's 83rd *Werfer* Regiment was raised in *Wehrkreise* [military district] IV during January 1944 as a part of 7 *Werfer* Brigade. They moved to northern France, from where they could be deployed to either of Rommel's armies, arriving in Normandy on 11 June from Beauvais, 100 miles east of Caen. Initially marching on 7 June in daylight, they suffered both manpower and equipment casualties from air attack, before reverting to night moves to complete their journey to join I SS Panzer Corps.

The 83rd Regiment consisted of three battalions, two with 15cm *Nebelwerfer* 41 launchers and one with the larger 21cm *Nebelwerfer* 42. In addition, there were two mobile batteries in the regiment's ORBAT, the 21st and 22nd batteries, which were both equipped with six of the ten-tube 15cm *Panzerwerfer* 42s mounted on Opel *Maultier* half-tracks (Sd.Kfz.4/1).

The *Nebelwerfer* ('fog' or 'smoke' mortar) was originally designed and produced in the mid-thirties to avoid the provisions of the Versailles Treaty limiting the number and type of weapons, including artillery, which the Germans could hold. The name *Nebelwerfer* was, of course, designed to obscure the true capability of the

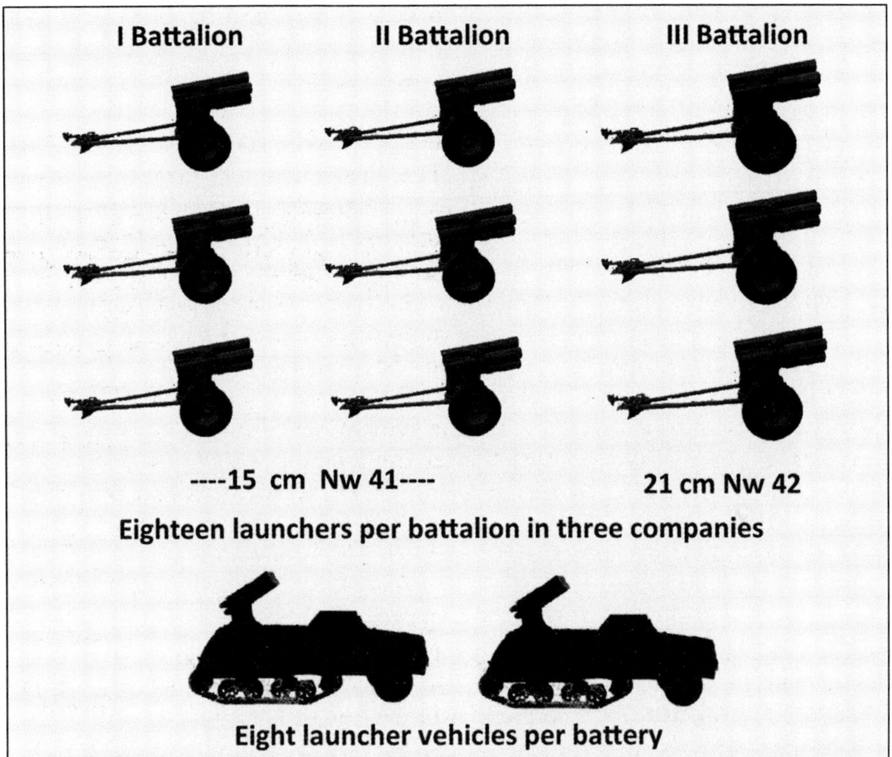

The organization of 83 *Werfer* Regiment. Rather than have mixed batteries as per establishment, both regiments in the brigade concentrated types in single battalions. The 84 *Werfer* Regiment organized its 30cm *Nebelwerfer* 42s in its III Battalion, as did 83 Regiment with its 21cm launchers.

system during League of Nations inspections. From the outset, however, the *Nebelwerfer*'s range of ammunition included not just smoke but high-explosive and chemical projectiles. The *Nebelwerfer*'s rockets were eventually produced in various calibres from 150mm to 320mm, for firing from a number of different types of launcher. Not having to survive the high muzzle velocities of artillery and mortars, the ammunition had relatively thin casing and consequently a large payload for its size. As was the case with mortars, the *Nebelwerfer* was quicker and cheaper to build than conventional artillery, an important factor in a wartime economy that was under severe pressure. Nearly 6,000 *Nebelwerfer* 41s were produced.

The six rounds of the 15cm *Nebelwerfer* were fired electrically in ten seconds; the book figure for a reload was two and a half minutes, but this could be reduced to ninety seconds by a well-drilled crew. Given the weapon's very obvious signature, careful siting in dead ground and concealment by a forward smokescreen were basic tactics. However, the best way of avoiding counter-battery fire by the British and Canadian artillery was a hasty redeployment to another pre-recced and surveyed position, which could be achieved in five minutes. A working figure for the range of the 15cm and 21cm *Nebelwerfer* is 7,000 yards, which in the case of

These scale drawings of the 15cm and the larger 21cm *Nebelwerfer* rounds illustrate the additional throw weight of the III/83 *Werfer* Regiment.

The six-tube 15cm Nebelwerfer 41 with its ammunition stacked alongside.

The five launch tubes of the larger 21cm *Nebelwerfer* 42 with its ammunition stored in wicker transit cases.

CHARNWOOD placed a high proportion of 83 Regiment's surviving launchers within range of I Corps' advance.

Unlike the 21cm *Nebelwerfer* round, the 15cm round had a nose cone which ensured that it detonated above the ground, delivering a significant splinter effect to add to the considerable HE blasts. On detonating, the splinters spread 13m to the front and 40m to either side.

The Panzer *Werfer* 42, with its ten launch tubes.

The launch signature, both on the ground and in the air, was considerable and gave rise to flying debris at the launch site.

Thanks to the rockets' built-in siren feature, *Nebelwerfers* were colourfully nicknamed 'moaning minnies' by the British and Canadians, 'screaming memes' by the Americans and the '*Heulende Kuh*' (howling cow) by the Germans.

Following the barrage were fifteen flail tanks of A Squadron 22nd Dragoons. Beating their way through the minefields and marking lanes with chalk dust at 1.5mph with the infantry a safe distance behind them, the squadron lost two Crabs. Only once they were well into the minefield would the Shermans of the Fort Garry Horse move forward into the gaps they created.

The Canadian report described the advance across 2,500 yards of very open terrain by the men of 8 Cdn Brigade on Carpiquet and the northern hangars:

> The infantry began to move forward hard behind the barrage at 0515 hours, to be followed 15 minutes later by the tank squadrons of the Fort Garry Horse. Our troops had some difficulty in keeping direction across the open fields through the smoke and dust raised by the shelling, and as they picked their interminable way amongst the tall, ripening wheat men fell in ones and twos, the places being marked by rifles stuck bayonet first into the ground to enable the stretcher-bearers to find them, until the sum of casualties caused by the enemy's fire reached sizeable proportions.

It is estimated that about a third of the defenders were deployed in an outpost line in the cornfields forward of the main German positions. However, overnight they were withdrawn by 100 yards in anticipation of the attack and were consequently largely missed by the first stage of the fire plan. When the creeping bombardment passed over them about sixty SS *Panzergrenadiers* emerged from their dugouts into their trenches. Major Anderson recalled that his company 'flushed out or killed enemy who had stayed in the slit trenches until the last moment.' One of those in the outpost line was *Sturmmann* Wambach, who called for artillery fire with flares, as his radios had failed and telephone lines were cut by the artillery:

> As the enemy shellfire moved on, the leading tanks rolled towards us. I fired a green flare for our artillery, but I was seen by an enemy tank, which drove up and did a neutral turn over my trench in an attempt to crush me. I was partly buried and surrounded by enemy tanks, some of which were burning. Then the infantry came and shouted, 'Hands up SS bastard!' They pulled me out of the earth and tied me up and hit me in the face and body with their rifle butts. I was tied to a post in the open where German shells were landing and left there for hours before I was taken to the rear.

Very little quarter was given by either the Canadians or the *Hitlerjugend*, thanks to the bitter mutual recrimination concerning war crimes, and a brutality that was at its height a month into the campaign. *Sturmmann* Wambach, however, was lucky and survived capture.

The leading companies of the NSR and the Chaudières reported reaching the western edge of their objectives at 0625 hours. It had taken over an hour to cover 2,500 yards, largely due to the time taken to breach the minefields, fight through the outpost line and overcome confusion and misdirection amidst the smoke and dust. However, the NSR, having taken cover behind a stone wall just outside the western edge of the village, the artillery blasted Carpiquet for twenty minutes, during which time there were a number of tree bursts amongst the surrounding poplars, causing a mix of shell splinters and splintered branches to rain down on the waiting infantrymen. Major Anderson recalled:

> I am sure that at some time during the attack every man felt he could not go on. Men were being killed or wounded on all sides and the advance seemed

The view east along the D9 to Carpiquet. This was 8 Brigade's axis of advance.

> pointless as well as hopeless. I never realized until the attack at Carpiquet how far discipline, pride of unit and, above all, pride in oneself and family can carry a man even when each step forward meant possible death.

The experience of the Chaudières in the centre was quite different, according to their war diary:

> Objectives were captured without much difficulty. The enemy was solidly organized. Its infantry positions constituted trenches offering almost perfect camouflage and much protection against our fire. The Boche also had at his disposal many machine gun nests and concrete sites whose reinforced walls

A map of Operation WINDSOR taken from the Canadian report.

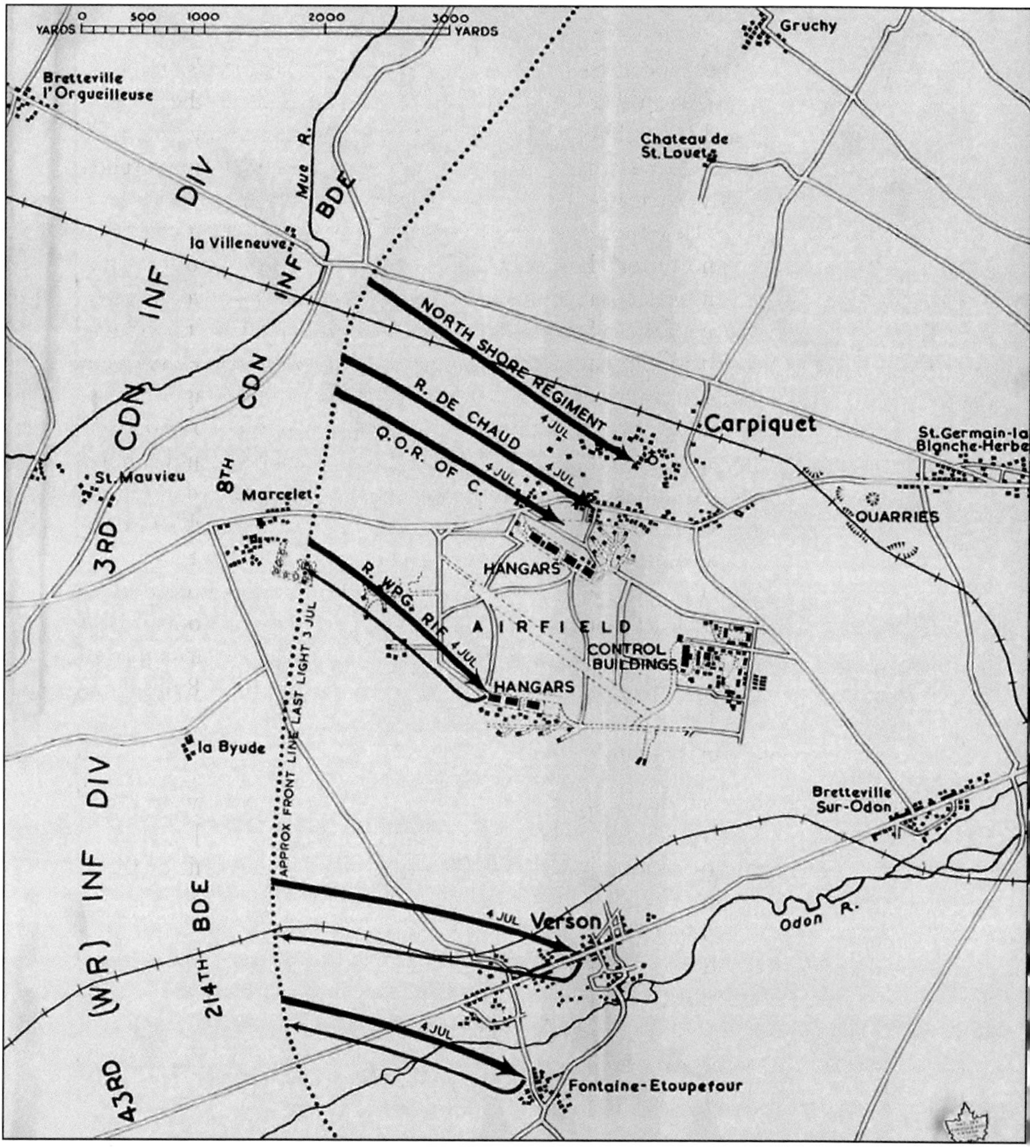

> were a minimum of 6 feet thick, and the roof was supported by solid pieces of steel. We needed the support of Crocodiles (assault tanks equipped with flamethrowers) to clear these almost impregnable positions.[14]

As 8 Brigade approached its objectives, the Crocodiles and AVREs were called into action, and a troop of 141 RAC supported the Chaudières' attack on the approaches to the northern hangars. Lieutenant Henderson's 6 Troop successfully flamed a pair of bunkers with a single Crocodile in a 'small action with no [own] casualties'. The Canadians reported:

> There was obvious employment here for Crocodiles, '*chars d'assault de lance de flammes*' [tanks with flame-throwers], with which the French-Canadians entered into an effective collaboration in flushing these 'quasi-impregnable' positions of the SS.

Next in action were the Crocodiles of 10 Troop, supporting the NSR's attack on Carpiquet village itself. However, thanks to bombing and shelling the ground was badly cratered, and Lieutenant Mason, having crossed the railway line, possibly to outflank the village, became 'hopelessly bogged. Sergeant Vernon ditched his tank and could only extricate himself by jettisoning the trailer.'[15]

Most accounts of the clearance of the village and the northern hangars describe it as being 'confused and bitter'. It was no doubt confused thanks to disorientation and casualties amongst commanders, but *Standartenführer* Meyer's stated intent and the testimony of the NSR make it plain that the majority of the SS had withdrawn. Those of 3rd Company that remained or had been left behind were overwhelmed by Canadian numbers. CSM Johnson recalled a final eager charge into the village, 'but the Jerry there had beat it.' Nonetheless, the two battalions cleared their way through the village and the hangars, with the tanks and funnies blasting their way into buildings with their 'flying dustbin' petard demolition rounds, and flaming points of resistance. On the left, Lieutenant Beck's Crocodiles were in action successfully flaming SS infantry positions dug into the railway embankment north of the village. Meanwhile, with Carpiquet being cleared by the infantry, some of the Fort Garry Horse's tanks were covering the outskirts of the village in order to cut off the German retreat. However, as the tanks moved forward to envelop the village, they came under fire from the 88mm guns deployed in depth and were driven back. Meanwhile, the Crocodiles were still clearing the railway embankment:

> A nearby Sherman suddenly spied a nest of Germans in a quarry by the Caen–Bayeux road, which said monstrosities [*Hitlerjugend* infantry] showed unmistakable signs of vicious life now that our infantry on the tail of the barrage had swept on. The Sherman asked [Captain] Nigel [Ryle] to 'fix em' ... There were no infantry so Beck with 7 Troop just went in without support. He poked his own nose in the quarry and gave them hell, burning some and flushing more as target practice for the other tanks.

A Crocodile of 141 Regiment RAC flaming.

But then the squadron's war diary recounts:

> Lieut Beck unfortunately went right into the Quarry and could not extricate his tank. An AP shot pierced the link and set the trailer on fire, whereupon the crew were evacuated from the tank by another tank from the Tp. Casualties: One Offr (Lieut Beck) and a gunner badly burned.[16]

The Attack on the Southern Hangars

The attack on the southern hangars began at 0530 hours, with A and D Coys leading, supported by B and C Coys. Despite the same heavy bombardment, the Winnipegs were in even greater trouble than the NSR and Chaudières, thanks to the presence on high ground to their right of a supporting *Leibstandarte* position that the Canadians believed should have been cleared by the 43rd Wessex

Division. This was an example of poor liaison across the corps boundary. The Wessex Division had, as ordered, mounted extensive patrols into the area of Version and Fontaine-Étoupefour and occupied the latter until after WINDSOR. The high ground had never been on their list of objectives. The Winnipegs' war diary described the results of their attack:

> A and D Coys suffered heavy casualties from the time they crossed the start line, until they neared their objectives, from enemy mortar fire. Enemy MGs opened up from the hangars. A Coy reached their objective 100 yds east of the hangars but D Coy was held up by enemy wire obstacles and fire. B Coy was sent fwd to assist D Coy and by 0900 hrs the two coys had reached the first hangar.[17]

The Canadian Military HQ report, with additional information from other sources, adds:

> Their advance was rendered the more hazardous by its deviation southward from the direction of the barrage and by the fact that in the initial stages the armoured squadron allotted to the battalion was to be held as the only reserve of armour for the action. The squadron had already been assisting with its guns, but the plight of the infantry demanded more active intervention. On an appeal from the commanding officer, Lt-Col John Meldram, one troop of tanks was committed to the battle.

A battalion war diarist, clearly unimpressed with the level of armoured support and having an unreasonable expectation of the Crocodiles, noted that this amounted to 'Two Sherman tks and four flame throwing Churchills (Crocodiles) [that] were sent to get the enemy out of their pillboxes in the hangars. The tks suffered some losses and left and the Crocodiles proved useless.' The Canadian report continued: 'Despite the two rifle companies succeeding in reaching the first of the southern hangars, the enemy was so strongly posted that neither tanks nor Crocodiles availed to drive him out of his resistant and ingenious pillboxes.' Unless scoring a direct hit on an aperture, even the heaviest naval shells had little effect on the 6ft-thick reinforced concrete, nor did the Crocodiles against sealed bunkers.

These were the positions held by a platoon of 3rd Company forward of and around the southern hangars. *Sturmbannführer* Krause's headquarters was at the eastern end of the hangars. Even though the barrage on an identified strongpoint was 'crushing', *Oberscharführer* Wohlgemuth reported:

> I sheltered in one of the bunkers, but the shelling was so heavy that pieces of concrete were dropping off the roof. When it stopped, I went out to repel the enemy; two of our mortarmen were dead and our artillery observation officer had a large shell splinter stuck in his back. The enemy infantry attacked in groups, and we fired away but we only stopped them when they reached the first hangar.

Sturmbannführer Krause pictured following promotion and award of the Knight's Cross. He earned the German Cross in Gold (below, left) for his part in the fighting during July and was awarded the Knight's Cross (below, right) for his delaying actions during the Canadian advance to Falaise in August 1944.

Lieutenant Henderson's troop of Crocodiles had been ordered forward to assist the Winnipeg Rifles:

> The infantry were held up just short of a bunker the other [north] side of the St Mauvieu [Marcelet]–Caen road. Mike bowled over with his troop, had a chat with the infantry captain some 50 yards away from the bunker. He decided that he could only get his own Croc on to it and went in giving the hot squirt for all he was worth. Whoever was in there didn't stand one earthly – ammunition went up inside and the whole thing was a blazing conflagration for hours.

The next call came to help clear the SS defenders from the southern hangars.

> Another urgent call came over for flame on a hangar some 500 yards to the S.W. of this bunker and Sydney slipped the leash on Peter [Sander, 9 Troop] to go bull-headed for the object of his disaffection, giving everything he had the whole way, 75mm, Besa, flame, his own revolver and a vocabulary as voluble as it was extensive ... The rest of the Squadron forgot the battle and turned in their cupolas to watch this fire-raising display by Peter and Sgt Decent – Sgt Decent of course was not to be outdone in ferocity, not even by Peter. Not satisfied with brewing it up from the front they brewed it up on both sides – by the fortune of heaven they did not go round the back where, all unknown then, there lurked a dirty 88.

The Winnipegs and their scant supporting armour overran most of the enemy platoon dug in to the west of the hangars and set about clearing the bunkers. Grenades and HE rounds from tanks all proved futile, but Corporal McKenzie found a Sapper officer, Lieutenant Yates, who had a small beehive-shaped charge with which they blew one of the air vents. However, it took a much heavier General Wade charge to demolish the heavy steel door of the bunker, and out came the Germans with their hands up.[18] With the Winnipegs having only a toehold on the enemy position, the panzers counter-attacked to aid Krause's men. Following some severe fighting around the westernmost trenches and bunkers and in the hangars, the Winnipeg Rifles B and D Companies were forced back and withdrew some 800 yards to the 'sparse cover of a small wood', with A and C soon following. The relief for Krause's young soldiers was short-lived, as the Allied artillery resumed its fire.

At 1600 hours the Canadians renewed their attack on the southern hangars supported by tanks and flame-throwers, this time penetrating I/26 *Panzergrenadiers'* defences. *Sturmbannführer* Krause ordered the survivors of the forward companies to pull back to the headquarters location and personally led a counter-attack to aid the withdrawal. On this occasion the panzers of 9th Company, by now heavily reinforced, attacked with the remaining Panthers of two companies, having already moved up under cover to the high ground to provide fire support from the south. *Unterscharführer* Richard Rudolph in one of the Panzer IVs took part in an advance from the high ground to the south and reached the hangars,

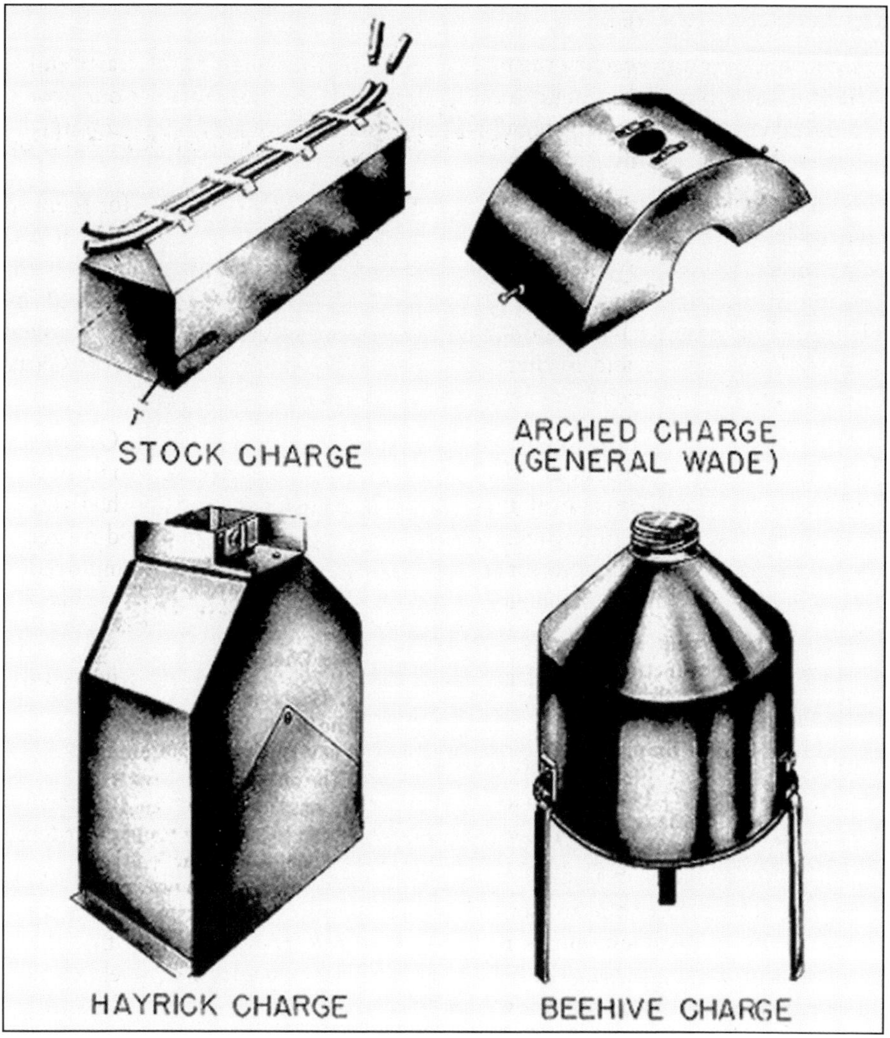

A diagram showing the range of shaped-charge munitions used by the British and Canadian Engineers who used the Munro Effect to focus explosive power.

knocking out six Shermans in the process and earning a Knight's Cross. The war diary of 12 SS Panzer Regiment reports:

> During the afternoon hours the 2. Kompanie, adjacent to the 9.Kompanie, was shifted northwards, in the direction of the aircraft hangars, as far as the 'Krause bunker'. The 1. Kompanie knocked out eight Shermans, the 2. Kompanie four Shermans. Three tanks (nos. 117, 228 and 237) [one lone Panther and two Panzer IVs] were damaged due to artillery hits and were towed to the repairs station.[19]

The Winnipegs reported:

> The fwd coys again reached the first hangars, but the enemy's aimed arty and mortar fire from high ground on our right made it impossible for our now reduced coys to hold this ground overnight, as we were now being counter-attacked by the enemy.

It soon became apparent that their numbers were now too depleted for them to hold their ground overnight. At 1800 hours the battalion reported that it was being forced to give way before a counter-attack by enemy tanks and was withdrawing westwards. Some three hours later, the battalion was ordered by 8 Brigade headquarters back behind the start line to Marcelet, 'for a night broken by patrolling, shelling and further casualties'. The war diary of the Fort Garry Horse noted that Marcelet was by no means pleasant:

> At 2130 hrs tonight B Sqn was withdrawn from its support of Queen's Own and put into harbour at 'MARCELET'. R.H.Q. had moved to its new location on the West side of the village. Probably never before had this Regiment taken such punishment from enemy mortars, artillery and rocket projection. On top of these three lethal weapons, the Germans employed 88mm guns firing H.E. airbursts. This type of weapon particularly disliked since high muzzle velocity, no warning sound is given.[20]

The 88mm gun firing HE was far more common and effective than in its anti-tank role.

The Second Phase

The Queen's Own Rifles of Canada (QORC) had flowed behind the advance of the rest of 8 Brigade towards the village as planned, but when they were ordered forward at 1000 hours they encountered pockets of resistance.

> But on approaching the western fringe of Carpiquet prior to forming up for the attack, the newcomers made the uncomfortable discovery that the enemy was still there. Some of his elements had evidently been left behind by the assaulting battalions and now remained to resist the approach of Q.O.R. of C. who found themselves obliged to pause and eliminate at least one strongpoint bypassed by R. de Chaud. As the enemy's concrete had been constructed to be impervious alike to the fire and flame of our tanks and the smoke and explosive charges of the sappers, the problem of persuading the terrified inmates to surrender could only be solved by introducing a sort of infernal sandwich made of grenades and petrol through the small, protected ventilators protruding above the roof. Only under such horrible provocation would the survivors give themselves up, for they had been told that the Canadians took no prisoners. A device of propaganda, throwing light upon both the reluctance of the troopers of 12 S.S. Pz Div to surrender and their preference for fighting to the last, and their savage and hysterical shooting of our own prisoners who had the misfortune to fall into their hands.

The Carpiquet hangars shredded by shell fire.

Clearing their entrance into the village took time, and it was not until 1050 hours that QORC were moving through it. However, the prospects of their being able to successfully advance on the control tower and barracks were darkened by reports of the misfortunes of the Winnipeg Rifles on the right flank. It subsequently became clear, with the southern hangars still in enemy hands, 'that QORC must remain among the now congested ruins of Carpiquet to await the outcome.' The battalion was soon digging in on the western edge of the village. Its war diarist concluded:

> Our attack postponed due to RWR being forced off their posn in the south hangars. The day is a very rough one with continual shell and mortar fire on our posns. At the moment we are in a very precarious situation with enemy on three sides of us. However a solid base is formed and will be held at all costs

The brigade staff had ordered defence stores to be brought up as soon as the village had been taken. These included barbed wire and mines, both anti-tank and anti-personnel, and under artillery fire the NSR and Chaudières laboured hard on their defences, knowing that a counter-attack would inevitably come. In addition, the tanks of the Fort Garry Horse were ordered to remain forward alongside some M10 tank destroyers, rather than going to the rear to leaguer. Two squadrons of Typhoon fighter-bombers remained on call until dusk, but *Standartenführer* Meyer wanted to stabilize his defences and had no intention of counter-attacking in daylight.

The casualties suffered by the infantry battalions in Operation WINDSOR were high. For the North Shore Regiment it was their 'worst day of the war'.

Unit	*Casualties*	*KIA*
The North Shore (New Brunswick) Regiment	132	46
The Royal Winnipeg Rifles	132	40
Le Régiment de la Chaudière	57	16
The Queen's Own Rifles of Canada	26	4
Fort Garry Horse	20	8
16th Field Company, RCE	10	3

Hitlerjugend soldiers captured in Carpiquet village.

The *Leibstandarte*'s Counter-Attack

During the evening of 4 July, the southern hangars and barrack area were attacked by forty-four Allied fighter-bombers; their targets were the seventeen panzers reported as 'dominating the airfield'. This air strike helped to cover the withdrawal of the Winnipeg Rifles from the southern hangars, and at the same time the QORC withdrew from their half-dug trenches to the west of Carpiquet to their original positions.

The *Hitlerjugend*'s loss of the northern part of the airfield and Carpiquet village was regarded as seriously compromising the defence of Caen and its bridges over the Orne. Consequently, Headquarters Seventh Army issued orders to the *Hitlerjugend* to recapture the area that night. The task was, however, passed to *Obersturmbannführer* Frey's 1st SS *Panzergrenadier* Regiment, which had now been joined after a torturous march from Belgium by most of its III Battalion and support companies.

During the evening, II Battalion, 1 SS *Panzergrenadiers* took over defence of the barrack area, from which they were able to bring fire down on the ruins of Carpiquet. This relieved the I and III battalions, plus ten Panthers, for the counter-attack. They waited until dark to avoid air attack and observation before

Obersturmbannführer Albert Frey, commander of 1st SS *Panzergrenadier* Regiment.

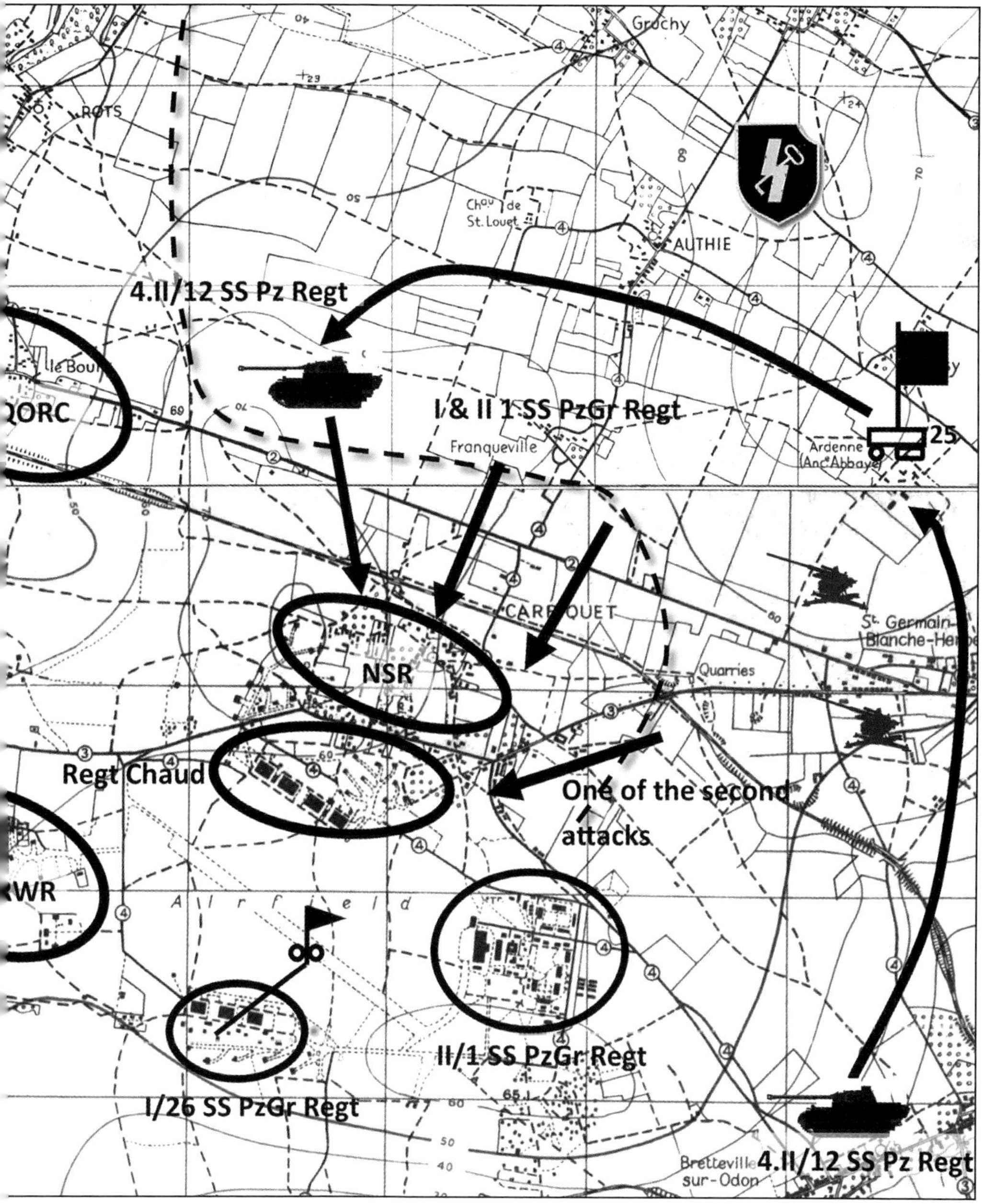

The attack of the 1 SS *Panzergrenadiers' Kampfgruppe* on Carpiquet during the night of 4/5 July 1944.

crossing the open ground towards the Caen–Bayeux road (N13), from where they would attack Carpiquet from the north. Grenadier Reiff, a recent replacement in 1 *Panzergrenadier* Regiment, recalled:

> We marched along the Orne and the Odon. The units marched spread out from one another. We moved through Venoix, the western part of Caen, and St-Germain-la-Blanche-Herbe. Later we marched along the road between

> Caen and Bayeux. In the late evening, we reached a point level with Carpiquet. It was from here we launched our attack down the slope onto the railway line between Caen and Bayeux.[21]

Obersturmführer Pohl commanding the Panthers of 4th Company, I/12 SS Panzer Regiment wrote:

> At 2230 hours the *Kompanie* received the order to attack Carpiquet from the north and support the attack and the penetration of the Grenadiers into the village. Around 2300 hours the *Kompanie* moved from the defended sector and coming through Caen reached the abbey [Ardenne] 2 km north of St Germain [-la-Blanche-Herbe]. A short briefing about the situation was held there for the tank commanders.

As a part of the German fire plan, the Canadians in the village were deluged with 28cm or 32cm *Wurfkörper Spreng* rockets, which the commander of the attached *Wehrmacht Nebelwerfer* Regiment 43 had found dumped and taken into use. The attack began in the early hours of 5 July, with the 400-yard advance from the start line to the railway completed without incident, as Grenadier Reiff of 2 Company recalled:

> The going was quiet as far as the railway embankment, where the signalman's house stood. As soon as we crossed the embankment, however, all hell broke loose. An exchange of fire occurred, but a short time later our machine guns failed. The replacement guns did not work either. On top of that, our fire seemed to be having no effect on the enemy.

Reiff recalled being ordered to return the fire with their rifles:

> If we were to follow the *Zugftihrer*'s orders, we had only a couple of choices. We had to make a rapid shift of position, either forward or to the left, using all available cover. For us inexperienced *Grenadiers*, that was very difficult in the night. It was also very difficult to move our wounded comrades from the embankment back to safety in the dark

The severely depleted companies of the NSR and Chaudières were waiting for them, and the *Panzergrenadiers*, despite their fire, moved on towards Carpiquet. Few made it, however. The attack from the German perspective is described in the account of *Obersturmführer* Pohl. The task of his Panthers was to provide fire support from the north in order to help the *Panzergrenadiers* into Carpiquet.

> The *Kompanie* attacked at 0200 hours, with the 1.*Zug* [platoon] on the left and the 2. *Zug* on the right. The rolling attack soon reached its aim, the Caen–Bretteville [L'Orgueilleuse] road 800 metres north of Carpiquet. Following three heavy fire strikes by the *Nebelwerfers* and the artillery, the Grenadiers launched the attack. The *Kompanie* supported this attack with the firepower of all of its guns [HE and machine guns]. The Grenadiers first reached the railway embankment, then the northern outskirts of Carpiquet.

Though suffering from mechanical issues and a shortage of replacements, the Panther was probably the most effective tank in Normandy.

> The enemy pulled itself together and responded with heavy machine-gun fire. After this, the enemy artillery covered the *Kompanie* positions in heavy fire. The *Kompanieführer* identified enemy artillery fire at a distance of 1,200 metres. By the order of the *Kompanieführer*, the fire of the 1.*Zug* destroyed six guns. The covered batteries that were unseen by the *Kompanie* repeated their fire with intensified force. Our Grenadiers suffered heavy losses and could not advance into Carpiquet on their own. The order of the *Abteilung* was then received: 'The *Kompanie* is to advance as far as the railway embankment!' The 2.*Zug* attacked the railway embankment with the fire support of the 1.*Zug*, and received heavy anti-tank gun fire. One enemy tank was knocked out and *Zug* and panzers no. 405, 415 and 426 received anti-tank gun hits although without effect. *Obersturmführer* Erich Pohl ordered the *Kompanie* to withdraw along the road to Caen.

The *Leibstandarte*'s *Panzergrenadiers* and their supporting *Hitlerjugend* panzers had been driven back by Canadian tanks and machine guns with losses. To make matters worse, III Battalion in the dark became the victims of their own artillery fire and they withdrew in haste to the limited cover of the railway line, where in turn, they were pinned down by Allied artillery fire.

Obersturmbannführer Frey was not prepared to give up but substituted II/Battalion for I/Battalion in the *Kampfgruppe*. He ordered *Obersturmbannführer* Weidenhaupt to renew the attack, which he did no fewer than five times, but the Canadians held their ground, with the NSR facing four of the five assaults. Of the attack from the east that fell on the Chaudières the battalion's war diary noted: 'The companies organized a solid defence in the south of the town of Carpiquet against the enemy. C Company is counter-attacked by German infantry and Panther tanks but repels the attack.' The war diary of 8 Cdn Brigade, however, makes it clear that this final attack well after dawn was the most successful of the SS counter-attacks:

> There were anxious minutes after 0725 hours when an attack on the south side of the village carried the enemy's infantry and tanks over a position held by a company of R. de Chaud. Self-propelled anti-tank guns and field artillery promptly engaged, and by 0810 hours the situation was restored.

The war diary of *Sturmbannführer* Jürgensen's I/12 Panzer Battalion's adds more detail:

> At dawn the armoured fighting vehicles were engaged in targeted fire by enemy anti-tank guns. This way panzer no. 418 was destroyed and *Untersturmführer* Günther Deutscher was not able to get out of the panzer and was killed in action. A number of other panzers received anti-tank gun hits although these had little effect. The disadvantageous, twisted position and the heavy enemy defence forced the panzers to retreat. They again occupied the previous defensive positions. Before the attack of the 4.*Kompanie*, the 1.*Kompanie*, commanded by *Hauptsturmführer* Kurt-Anton Berlin, carried out a distracting attack and destroyed five enemy tanks and two anti-tank guns. Furthermore, the 1.*Kompanie* captured fourteen Canadians who belonged to the French-Canadian de la Chaudiére Regiment. Panzer no. 138 from the 1.*Kompanie* was knocked out and burnt out.

The I/1SS *Panzergrenadiers* alone suffered seventy-six casualties, with a further twenty-one men missing. All that was left for Reiff to do was collect the wounded as best they could:

> During the day, the Canadians took it upon themselves to shoot from their advantageous position at everything which moved. One of our severely wounded comrades received a shot in his rear end. It cost him enormous amounts of energy to drag himself back to cover on the road. Thank God, there were medics on duty there, and they gave our comrades first aid. In the early morning, we crawled to the embankment and brought back some more wounded comrades

These attacks had, however, cost 8 Cdn Brigade had further heavy losses.

Carpiquet village remained securely held by the Canadians, who had occupied the *Panzergrenadiers*' defences, but the southern hangars, control tower and

One of the bunkers at Carpiquet airfield being used by the Canadians after the attack.

barracks remained in German hands until Operation CHARNWOOD. With enemy-held positions on both flanks, Carpiquet was a dangerous and uncomfortable salient for four days. The Chaudières described conditions in Carpiquet:

> The headquarters of the Bn were first established in a dugout built by the Germans. This dugout is very strong but attracts almost constant fire from the enemy. All afternoon and all night the Germans rained down a veritable deluge of artillery shells and mortar bombs on our positions. We then lost many men, dead and wounded.

The *véritable enfer* [hell] of continual shelling went on until the second day of the assault on Caen.

An extract from the four-sheet assembly of Lieutenant General Sir John Cocker's personal 1:50,000 map. To aid indirect bombardment fire, he has shaded the 60-foot contour of his map to help him understand the complexity of the ground he was to fight over in Normandy. He was probably copying a procedure he would have used in the First World War as an officer of the Machine Gun Corps.

Chapter Five

Operation CHARNWOOD: The Attack on Caen

With the US Army's advance underway and slowly gaining momentum south through the hedgerow country towards La Haye du Puis, at the operational level a distraction on the eastern flank of the Allied lodgement was needed. Therefore, Second Army was to intensify its operations to fix German troops, particularly the panzer divisions, away from General Bradley's army to the west. The capture of Caen would achieve this by reinforcing the threat of a breakout towards Falaise, as well as delivering much needed ground to complete the delayed build-up in the east, the deployment of the First Canadian Army and, of course, the prospect of more room for airfields. While the preliminary operations to capture Carpiquet were underway, I Corps, now numbering nearly 120,000 men, had been planning the assault on Caen with three divisions, supported by armoured brigades, with another armoured brigade in reserve.

Facing the Allies were just two German divisions. Of the now greatly weakened 12th *Hitlerjugend* Panzer Division the 25 SS *Panzergrenadiers* stood in the path of the 3rd Canadian Division and a brigade of 59th (Staffordshire) Division. To the *Hitlerjugend*'s right was 31 *Jäger* Regiment of the newly arrived 16th *Luftwaffe Feld* Division, which had only three days earlier finally relieved most of the 21st Panzer Division. They were to be attacked by another brigade of the 59th Division and the British 3rd Division.

The 1st SS *Panzergrenadier* Regiment, still under command of the *Hitlerjugend*, held the front from Éterville via the Carpiquet barracks north to Franceville, along with the remnants of 26 SS *Panzergrenadiers*. From there for 5 miles around the north-west of Caen 25 *Panzergrenadiers* held their now well-developed defensive positions. These defences extended as far east as the railway line that ran north from Caen and, with a belt of mines and anti-tank ditches, were over 2 miles deep. The railway line remained the divisional boundary between the *Hitlerjugend* and the 16th *Luftwaffe Feld* Division.

To the east beyond the railway, 16th *Luftwaffe Feld* Division was in similarly strong defensive positions on the ridges north of Caen, but as a single regiment they were backed up by half the remaining tanks of 21st Panzer Division and its artillery. Altogether, the German defences in depth represented a considerable challenge to Lieutenant General Sir John Crocker's I Corps. His deliberate attack on Caen was the Second Army's main effort. Having become aware of

Soldiers of the 16th *Luftwaffe Feld* Division in Normandy.

unusual enemy activity to their front, 9 Brigade ordered a raid on enemy positions. 33 Field Regiment RA's account provides the details:

> Our immediate front until now had been manned by 21 SS Pz Div, [who] appeared to be in the process of relief by 16 GAF Div. In order to secure an identification, a raid was staged by 1 KOSB during the night. This was supported by the regiment with some very close targets indeed to the tune of 1,750 rounds, which was sufficient indication that the shortage of ammunition, caused by the mid-June gales, had been more than made up.[1]

The King's Own Scottish Borderers' war diary entry for 4 July reads:

> 'C' Coy sent out raid to GALMANCHE. Party A was successful and overran an enemy platoon or section posn. Lieut Raines the officer commanding this party was killed. The party was rallied and brought back very ably by Cpl Cameron. No prisoners taken as enemy ran away but several enemy casualties claimed. Party B ran into what was at first thought to be a minefield and withdrew. Later it was thought that this was some form of warning device as the explosion on trip wires caused no casualties but MGs all along the GALMANCHE defences opened up.

The quality of the defenders facing the three Allied assault divisions differed markedly. The 16th *Luftwaffe Feld* Division was poor, General Feuchtinger commenting that 'this division was a waste of good men'; the SS soldiers of 25 *Panzergrenadiers*, though they had skirmished with the British and Canadians for a month, proved to be resolute in defence, having been spared the worst of the defensive fighting; but not so the remnants of Mohnke's 26 SS *Panzergrenadiers* now in the Carpiquet area. The latter had borne the brunt of post-D Day combat, had suffered very heavy casualties during Operation EPSOM and were now under command of the 1st SS *Panzergrenadier* Regiment.

The Second Army Intelligence Summary No. 33 provides a flavour of the defences that I Corps faced:

> The Germans had made good use of the passage of time to prepare these defences with great thoroughness. Farther to the west [they] could afford to rely to a greater extent on the nature of the ground, and displayed a highly professional skill in exploiting the close and wooded country so restrictive of manoeuvre. A few men, sometimes barely more than a section, working together with a tank or two, and posted securely in an orchard or hedgerow, could hold much larger numbers at bay; and while here and there more permanent works had been constructed amongst those obscure, deceptive undulations, the enemy's sense of terrain allowed him to deploy his troops to

The positions held by 25 SS *Panzergrenadiers* from the end of 9 June until Operation CHARNWOOD. Note that 4, 8 and 12 Companies were heavy weapons companies distributed around their battalion's positions and are not shown.

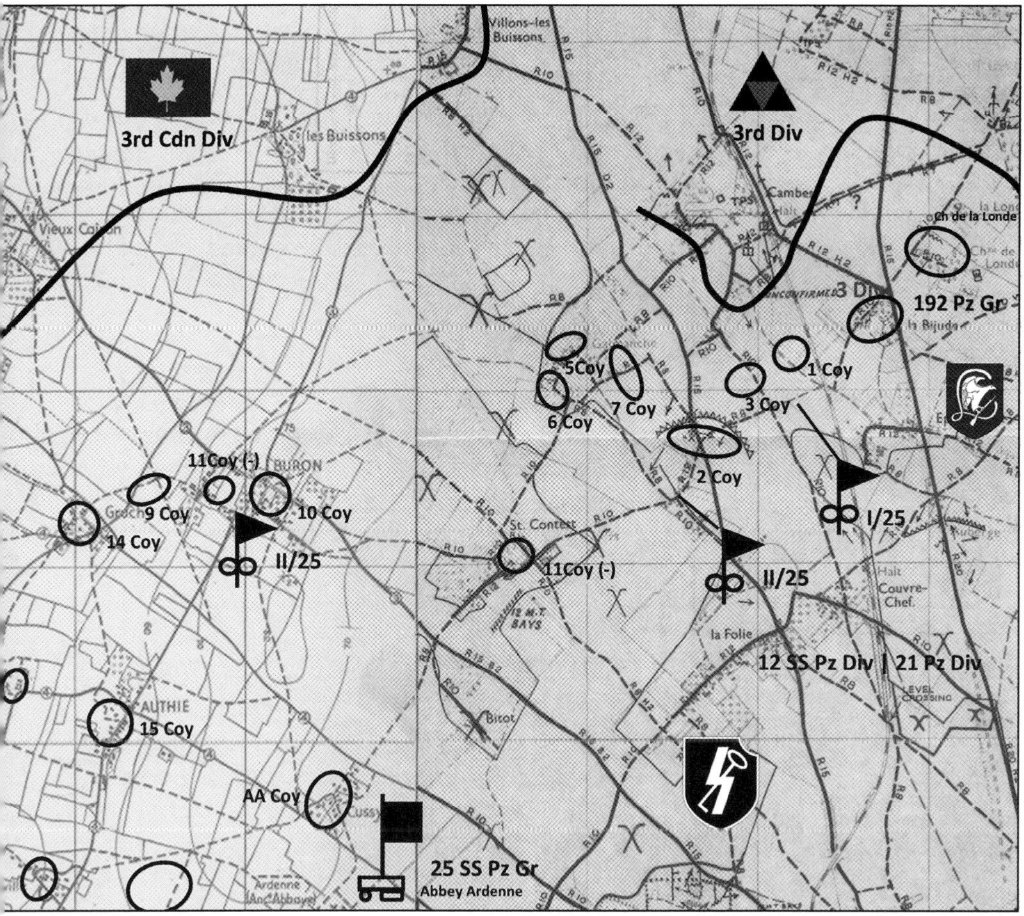

> excellent tactical advantage. Eastward, however, our Intelligence was aware that the enemy's urgent digging on both banks of the Odon might, if he were left alone, grow into more formidable obstacles rather than a thin, vicious line of weapon pits. But it was in the main sector of the front held by Second British Army before Caen that the enemy had betrayed further evidence of his set defensive purpose. During the past three weeks he had brought in an enormous number of guns of all types including flak, both light and heavy, self-propelled guns [and] *Nebelwerfers*, some of which our troops had already encountered in the defence of Carpiquet. Thus reinforced with a great weight of artillery, the enemy's perimeter through Franqueville, Gruchy, Buron, Galmanche, Cambes and the woods of Lebisey to the canal, threaded with several short sections of an anti-tank ditch and studded thickly with dug-in tanks, constituted a barrier of forbidding strength.[2]

From the armoured perspective, Captain Airey Neave commented: 'To add to our difficulties the Infantry have laid minefields in every possible direction which makes the natural limitations of movement even more restricted. They are all rather jungly and don't appear to know just where the minefields are either!'[3]

A key preparation for CHARNWOOD was conducted on the night of 5/6 July, when the newly arrived 59th Division was inserted into the line on a frontage of almost 4,000 yards; this necessitated a realignment of the by now well-established divisional boundaries. The 3rd Division gave up Château de la Londe and Cambes, and the Canadians' new boundary was moved to the west, leaving the sector of line facing Galmanche and La Bijude to the 59th Division.

The 59th Staffordshire Division

The division's shoulder flash.

The 59th Division was hastily formed in 1939 as a Second Line Territorial Army division, principally recruited from the West Midlands and the North-West. It had been based in the UK for the duration of the war so far, eventually transitioning from defence of the home base to training and selection for the Second Army. This development had not been easy or straightforward, as noted by Lieutenant Colonel Finlinson, one of the battle-experienced commanders who returned to the division from the Mediterranean:

> I went to the division as 2IC of 2/6 S STAFFS in August 1940 and at the time I thought they were perfectly awful. They were mostly territorials with

> a few regulars; their outlook on training, etc, was totally different to that of regulars. I was with them for two months, and then formed the divisional reconnaissance regiment which I had for two years, so that I saw a good deal of the training in the division.
>
> I then went away but came back to take command of the 2/6 S STAFFS in February 1944. It was obvious their standard was quite different from that in 1940 and that by this time they were well trained and working together. The spirit in the division was simply terrific and when we landed in NORMANDY about 26 June they were on the top of their form. Practically everyone in the battalion was inexperienced so far as active service was concerned as there was only a smattering of NCOs who had been in action before.[4]

In CHARNWOOD the 59th Division would have a very tough introduction to the realities of war.

The Decision to Bomb Caen

General Eisenhower remained increasingly concerned about 21st Army Group's lack of progress in terms of territory, and despite the reluctance of the bomber barons, he promised the full support of Allied bombers to Operation CHARNWOOD. Relations with the Army 'did not admit of easy solution. Whether the aircraft of Bomber Command should be diverted from their main strategic purpose to take part in a land battle involved considerations of high policy.'[5] However, Eisenhower got his way.[6]

The difference between striking the enemy's defences in a rural area and bombing targets in a city, in a friendly country, naturally made the strike on Caen controversial. However, in addition to shelling, bombing of the city by aircraft of Second Tactical Airforce was a routine feature of the campaign so far. These strikes had targeted re-supply and reinforcement routes across the Orne in and around the city that were used nightly by the Germans. A measure of the destruction meted out is afforded by an entry in I Corps' war diary as early as 15 June:

> About midnight a Frenchman who had gone into CAEN on relief work came in and stated that there were few enemy in the town, most having moved westward. The main bridges were down. The desolation was great.

The bombing of the bridges and the Vaculles area by thirty-six medium aircraft on 6 July was only the most recent strike on targets in Caen, which had been progressively abandoned by much of its population, with between 2,000 and 3,000 inhabitants having been killed since D Day. Many of the over 4,000 civilians who remained were sheltering in the Bon Sauveur hospital, the Abbaye de Saint-Etienne and the Lycée Malherbe; thanks to information passed via SOE, these were not bombed or shelled.

The bombing of Caen would take place on the evening of 7 June between 2139 and 2250 hours, four and a half hours before H Hour. This less than ideal

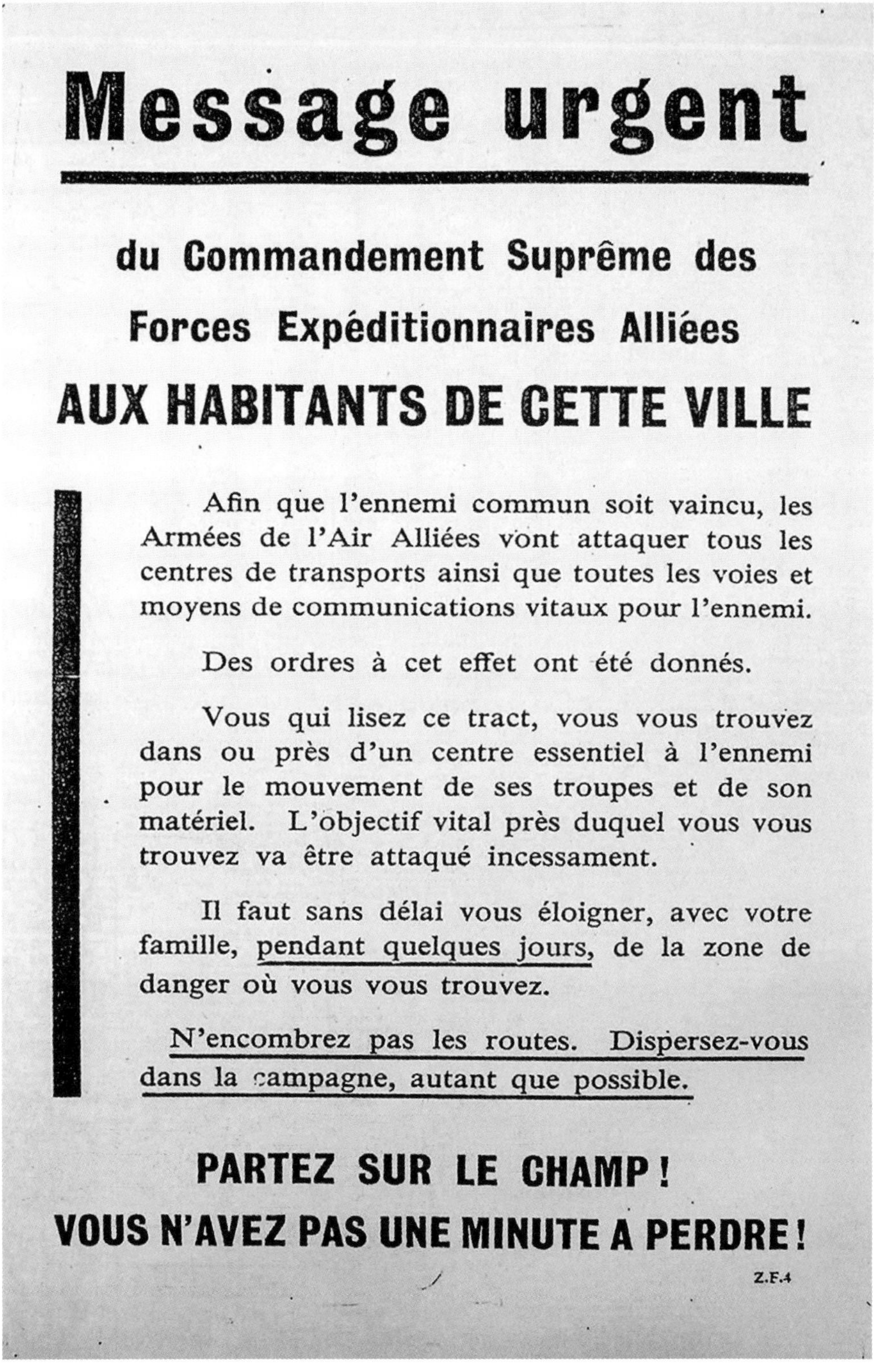

Message urgent

du Commandement Suprême des
Forces Expéditionnaires Alliées

AUX HABITANTS DE CETTE VILLE

Afin que l'ennemi commun soit vaincu, les Armées de l'Air Alliées vont attaquer tous les centres de transports ainsi que toutes les voies et moyens de communications vitaux pour l'ennemi.

Des ordres à cet effet ont été donnés.

Vous qui lisez ce tract, vous vous trouvez dans ou près d'un centre essentiel à l'ennemi pour le mouvement de ses troupes et de son matériel. L'objectif vital près duquel vous vous trouvez va être attaqué incessament.

Il faut sans délai vous éloigner, avec votre famille, pendant quelques jours, de la zone de danger où vous vous trouvez.

N'encombrez pas les routes. Dispersez-vous dans la campagne, autant que possible.

PARTEZ SUR LE CHAMP !

VOUS N'AVEZ PAS UNE MINUTE A PERDRE !

Z.F.4

Leaflets were dropped warning of imminent bombing.

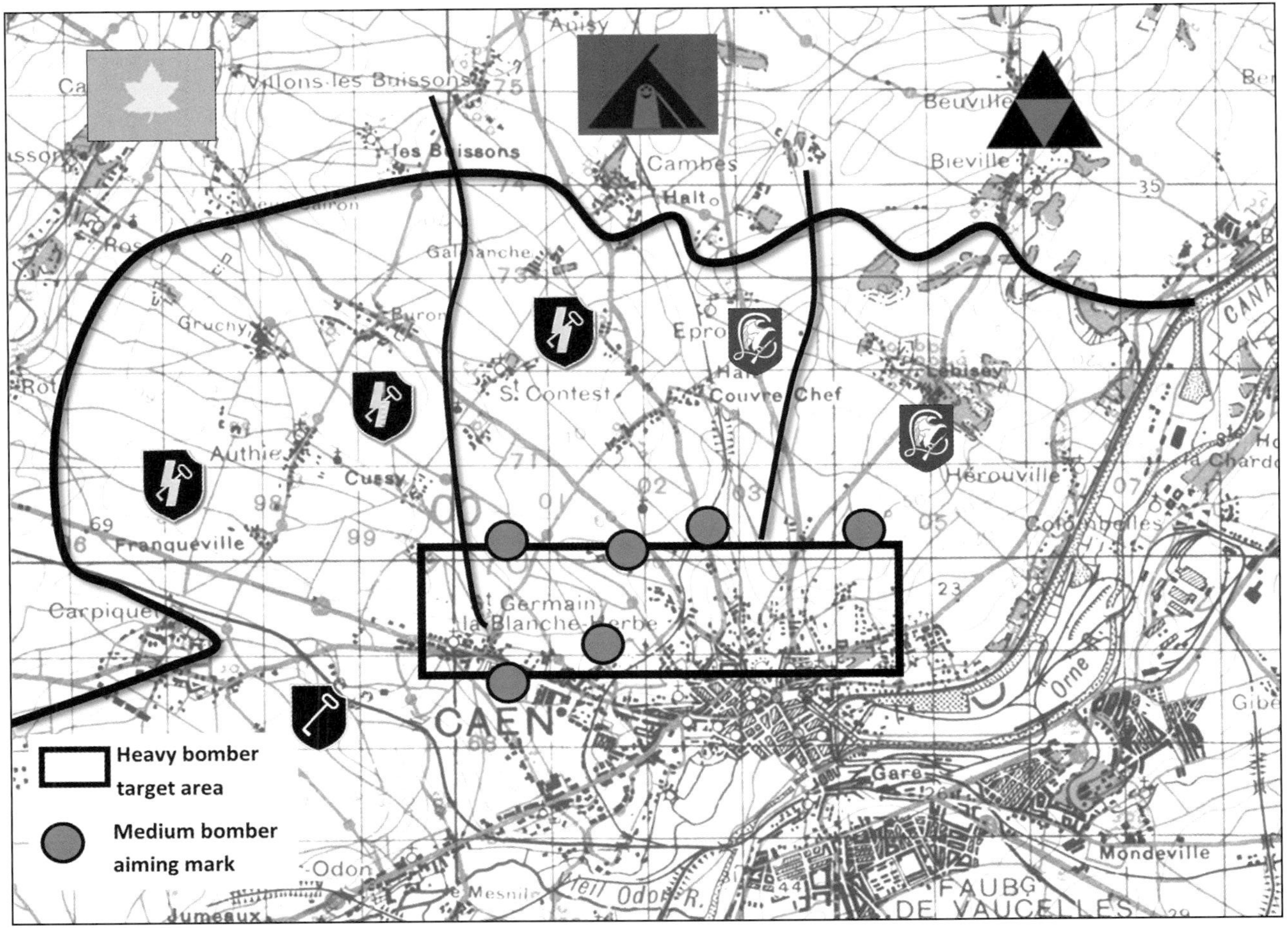

The Situation P.M. 7 July and the intended bomber target area.

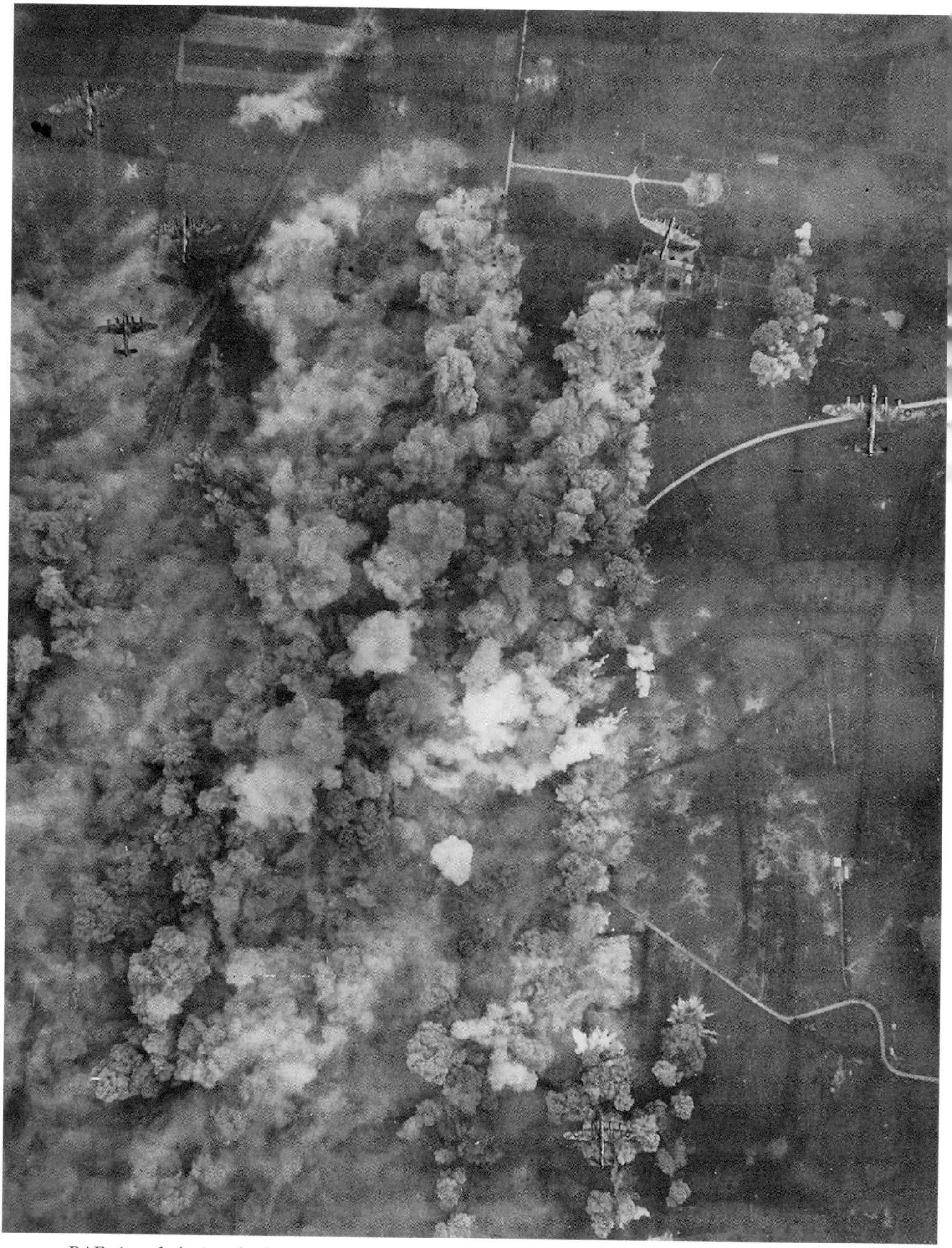

RAF aircraft during the bombing of Caen on the evening of 7 July 1944.

timing was due to the wish of I Corps to assemble and launch their attack under cover of darkness, and for the bombers in such close proximity to their own troops to strike in daylight. It was, however, argued that the forward enemy troops would be isolated from overnight re-supply and reinforcement by the bombing. To help bridge the gap between bombing and H Hour, 15 per cent of the bombs were to have delayed action fuses timed to go off around 0420 hours the following morning.

The target area was nearly 4,000 yards across the front, principally that of 59th Division but overlapping the objectives of the flanking divisions, and 1,000 yards deep. It was placed some 6,000 yards from the Forward Line of Own Troops, meaning that most of the enemy's forward defences were north of the main bombing area; and given their paucity of troops, there were few Germans sited in depth to be hit.

The CHARNWOOD Plan

After a month ashore, Second Army was ready to resume its direct assault on the now well-defended city on the morning of 8 July. The infantry of 3rd and 59th Division were to attack the defended villages to the north of Caen in a phased attack. The Canadian 3rd Division would join the battle in CHARNWOOD's second phase, attacking the defended villages to the west of the city from the north-west.

The 4.5 and 5.5-inch guns were the workhorses of the Army Groups Royal Artillery deployed in support of Operation CHARNWOOD.

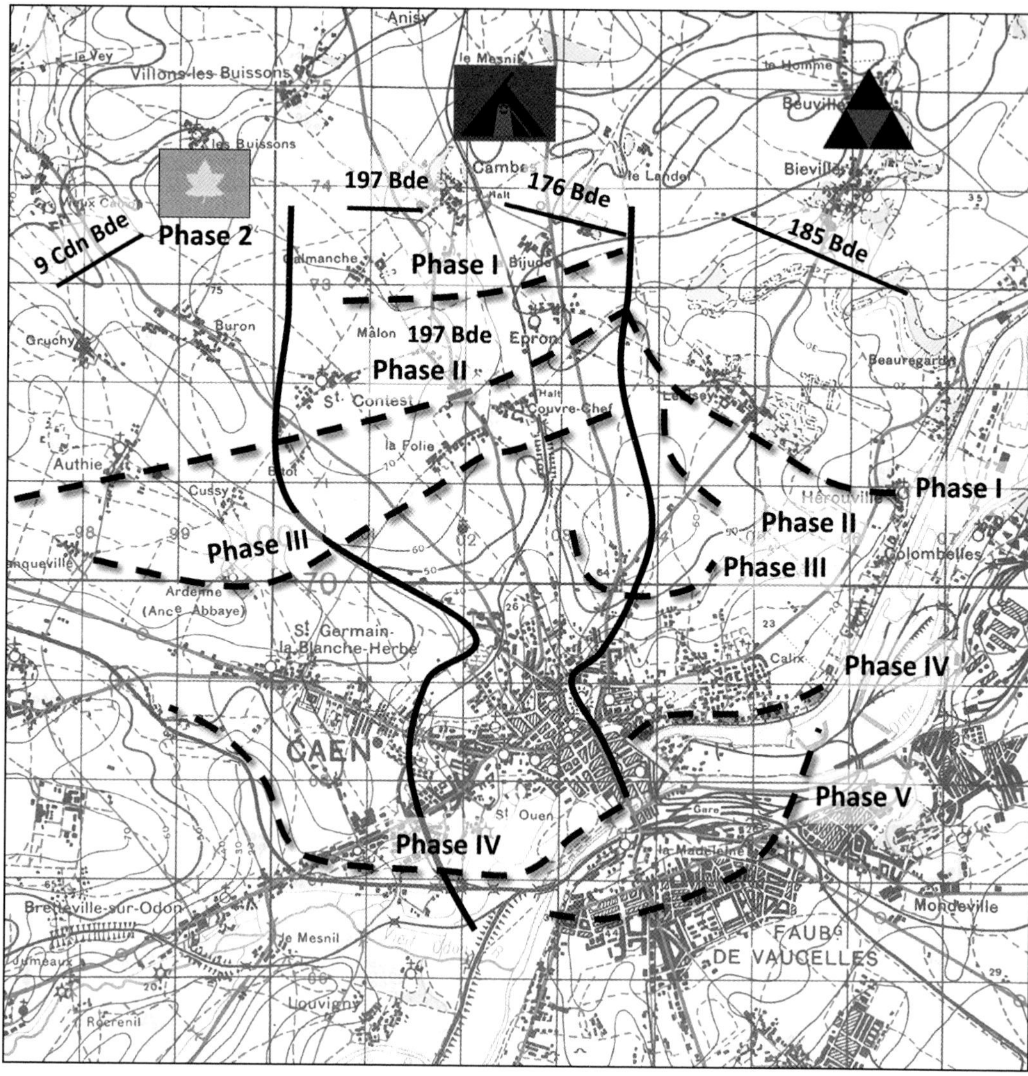

The I Corps CHARNWOOD Plan.

As the British build-up was all but complete, the allocation of support to the infantry assault was lavish.[7] The two British divisions were allocated regiments of Sherman tanks for the first four phases of Operation CHARNWOOD, principally from 27 Armoured Brigade, with the majority of the newly arrived 33 Armoured Brigade, less 1st Northamptonshire Yeomanry, being held in reserve. The 3rd Canadian Division were, as usual, to be supported by the tanks of 2 Canadian Armoured Brigade. The M10-equipped batteries of the anti-tank regiments were to join the attackers on their objectives. As usual in attacks, the armour of 79th Division was parcelled out across the three assault divisions. With regard to artillery:

> The guns to be brought to bear included the resources of five divisions and two Army Groups Royal Artillery, together with the batteries of the

battleship *Rodney*, the monitor *Roberts* and the cruisers *Belfast* and *Emerald*, lying out to sea.

In addition to the naval artillery, this was a total of 632 guns from the AGRAs and the divisional artillery.

The Operation Begins

As dusk fell on 7 July, 467 aircraft of RAF Bomber Command dropped 2,363 tons of bombs on the northern part of Caen. As the Lancaster and Halifax aircraft flew in, soldiers across the Second Army's lodgement paused to look up at the sky above Caen in awe. The Canadian Scots' war diary reads: 'Dense flak went up against the first wave of bombers but then diminished as the enemy gunners ran out of ammunition or the batteries had been overwhelmed by the weight of the attack.' Trooper Farrell of the East Riding Yeomanry was one witness:

> When we saw the bombers come over, it was unbelievable. Can you imagine all these hundreds of bombers coming over? They were not in formation but spread out all over the sky. We watched them dropping their bombs. They all came in left, dropped their bombs and came out on the right. When the first one came in, the anti-aircraft fire was tremendous. However, by the time they'd finished coming in there were practically no anti-aircraft guns left. Because of this, we thought it was great and it would be easy the next day. We went in next morning at first light, and the Germans there were as large as life![8]

Most battalions earmarked for the attack the following morning remarked on a distinct rise in morale at the sight of what I Corps reported to the RAF: 'Everything in front of us is on fire, marvellous.' Fusilier Pollitt of 2/5 Lancashire Fusiliers recalled that he and his comrades 'were beginning to feel that the next day all that would be necessary would be a certain amount of "mopping up" of isolated resistance, before walking into the German positions.' The fall of bombs was not confined to the target area; they tended to detonate further south than intended, many in the central part of the city. It is generally accepted that this was due to the pathfinders erring on the side of caution and dropping their markers too far to the south.

The use of this aerial fire power has been hotly debated ever since. With the majority of the bombs falling further south than intended, there were relatively few casualties amongst the defenders. However, an estimated 300–400 civilians were injured, despite the dropping of warning leaflets.[9] Two tanks of II/12 Panzer Regiment were hit and another two turned over, while further back in reserve, the remaining men of III/26 *Panzergrenadiers* suffered only seven casualties, although the Divisional Escort Company was more seriously hit. More significantly, the headquarters of 31 *Jäger* Regiment was destroyed, undermining the defensive capacity of the 16th *Luftwaffe Feld* Division in front of 3rd Division.[10] Otherwise, only a handful of logistic units passing through the city were caught. Observers,

Panzergrenadiers watch the bombing of Caen from the Abbaye d'Ardenne.

however, claim that after the bombing they saw no evidence of German personnel or vehicle casualties in the city. *Standartenführer* Meyer, whose divisional headquarters was located in a 'barracks' inside the medieval castle just north of the city centre, summed up the impact on the division:

> The front line was so sparsely manned that a bomber attack couldn't cause much damage – 2,500 tons of bombs had merely succeeded in overturning a few SPW [half-tracks].[11]

A Second Army intelligence summary regarded the raid as a success, thanks to *Hitlerjugend* prisoners taken during 8 and 9 July who claimed that no ammunition or food got through to them after the bombing.

Following the heavy bombers, rocket-firing Typhoons, using the last of the daylight, were to attack the villages to the north and west of the main target area, as well as flying interdiction sorties to help seal off the city. The final act by the air forces that evening was an attack by six squadrons of Mosquitoes in the forward area. The RAF account of overnight action to the south of the city reads:

> While the heavy bombers were returning home, the light bombers and intruders of No. 2 Group were on their way to harass and attack enemy movement south of Caen. Road and rail traffic was much in evidence and the

140 aircrews reported very satisfactory results of their night's work. One outstanding feature of these operations was that 26 trains were attacked.

In these attacks, all five railway lines to the area south of Caen were reported as being hit.

At 2300 hours, promptly on the departure of the last RAF aircraft from the skies above Caen, the guns of the Royal Navy and Royal Artillery opened a bombardment across the front that would consume no fewer than 40,000 shells of all calibres. Targets engaged during the night included known enemy defensive positions, the Orne bridges and the identified battery positions of several medium batteries.

As the Allied artillery fire plan got underway, there was nervous expectation by the defenders of an imminent attack. *Standartenführer* Meyer wrote:

> The air raid must have been the prelude to the main enemy assault. Every man was ready, the artillery waited for orders to put a curtain of fire in front of our positions, but we waited. The phones were silent, and we all stared out into the night waiting for the enemy attack. Minutes passed, it was incomprehensible [that] the Allies had not exploited the tremendous bombing.
>
> We were all expecting a big attack and prepared for the inevitable, as we had no illusions as to our hopeless situation. While I anxiously waited for dawn, Hubert Meyer had fallen asleep with his head on the map table. He was an excellent chief of staff.

The Bombardment

An account written by 33 Field Regiment RA states: 'The APPLEPIE [the first heavy blow] was followed by Uncle and Victor targets[12] throughout the night, reaching a crescendo at 0330 hours with a Victor Scale 10 on the celebrated LEBISEY WOOD fired, it is believed, by 20 regiments.' The artillery fire was certainly not all one way. The Germans, in expectation of an attack following immediately after the bombing, shelled Allied positions, but their reply represented only a fraction of the weight of fire they were receiving.

An extract from the I Corps CHARNWOOD Op O, giving the time for concentration of all guns under command of the corps – a VICTOR Target. These shoots were in addition to overnight divisional fire plans.

	Time of engagement	Target area & No.	Map Ref	Ht (metres)	Scale.
(i)	2300 hrs 7 Jul.	LA FOLIE V 108	0213 7161	40	A
(ii)	0245 hrs 8 Jul.	ST CONTEST V 107	0068 7203	65	A
(iii)	0315 hrs 8 Jul.	ST GERMAIN V 6	0020 6900	50	A
(iv)	0330 hrs 8 Jul.	LEBISEY V 104	0474 7200	50	A (twice)
(v)	0400 hrs 8 Jul.	AUTHIE V 298	9840 7150	60	A

(ii) During the op. requests for V

Sturmbannführer Hubert Meyer, the 1a of the 12th *Hitlerjugend* Panzer Division, on a visit to 25 SS *Panzergrenadiers* headquarters in the Abbaye d'Ardenne.

The number of guns that Second Army was able to mass for CHARNWOOD a month into the build-up was impressive:

- Nineteen field regiments with 288 25-pounders and 168 105mm guns, totalling 456 field guns
- Eight medium regiments with 128 5.5/4.5-inch guns
- Two heavy regiments with sixteen 155mm and sixteen 7.2-inch guns
- Warships mounting nine 16-inch, two 15-inch and sixteen 6-inch guns.[13]

Square Wood – Objective SALLY

Under cover of the bombardment, 2 KSLI had preliminary tasks to perform during the night of 7/8 July that would reduce the hitherto broad stretch of no-man's-land in front of 185 Brigade and Lebisey Wood and village to 400 yards. Their war diary recorded:

> As it grew dark the covering parties moved up. 'X' Coy, to protect the right flank, to the cross tracks 038729. The Carrier Pl with one Pl of W Coy under comd were given the task of covering the track crossing just EAST of SQUARE WOOD 038729 and filling in trenches which obstructed the crossing. 'Y' Coy's posn was astride the main rd at 055729. The Carrier Pl and 'Y' Coy carried out their tasks without opposition. 'X' Coy, however, before reaching their objective, met a succession of enemy MG posts. With great determination 'X' Coy assaulted and cleared these posts.[14]

Securing the area around Square Wood, 'holding the important cross-roads on the western end of SQUARE WOOD' and subduing the surrounding positions at night was no easy task, as indicated by Lieutenant Jones' Military Cross citation, earned during preliminary operations with 10 Platoon of X Company:

> On the night of the 7-8 July 1944 Lieutenant Jones displayed courage and leadership much above average. On three separate occasions he led assaults into the face of heavy machine gun fire to silence enemy machine-gun posts, he himself being first into the posts. On the third occasion when leading a party of five men, four became casualties. In spite of this Lieutenant Jones continued the assault firing as he went and put the machine-gun out of action. He displayed throughout a high degree of enthusiasm and unrelenting courage.

Later the following day, 10 Platoon were driven out of the wood by what was reported as airburst shells but were more probably shells detonating in the treetops. Lieutenant Jones recorded that as the platoon withdrew they were lucky to escape a friendly fire incident.

An extract of the CHARNWOOD defences overprint map showing the Square Wood area with known enemy positions marked. What was in the wood was largely unknown due to the obvious limitations of air photography.

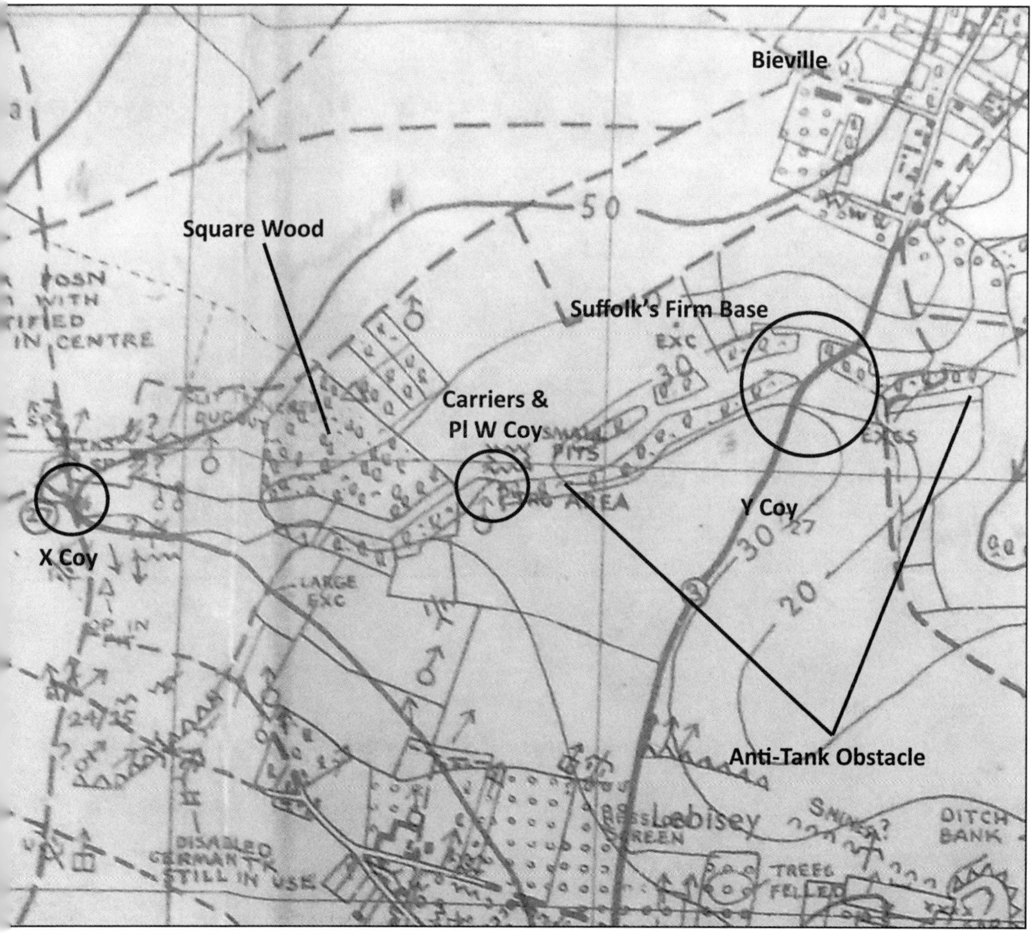

The 7.2-inch Howitzer Mark 6 that equipped some of the heavy Regiments Royal Artillery.

Meanwhile, the remainder of 2 KSLI had assembled immediately to the north of Biéville, ready to go forward to cover the assembly of the rest of the brigade.

At 0420 hours the routine explosion of shells was finally broken by what *Standartenführer* Meyer described as 'artillery fire of unimaginable intensity'. He went on to describe how shells of the bombardment

> from both the land and the sea fell on our front line. The divisional headquarters cellar shook, and plaster and dust fell on the candlelit map table. Our artillery and mortar batteries laid down final protective fires. We had been procuring ammunition for days and [some time later] were trying to give it to our heavily engaged infantry. Fighter-bombers were diving down on our artillery batteries and attacking every vehicle they could see. The Orne bridges were continuously under fire.

The Allied attack on Caen began, ninety minutes before sunrise, with the advance of 3rd and 59th Division. The Canadians would join the advance when General Crocker ordered CHARNWOOD's second phase to begin.

Chapter Six

Attack of the 3rd Division

All day heavy shelling on the bde area, but everyone took it with the thought 'Tomorrow we will put an end to this'. [185 Brigade war diary, 7 July 1944]

Major General Whistler's 3rd Division, with a substantially greater frontage than 59th Division, attacked with the reinforced 185 Brigade under its new commander Brigadier Bols,[1] supported by the Sherman-equipped Staffordshire Yeomanry of 27 Armoured Brigade.

For the attack on Lebisey, 185 Brigade committed two battalions; 1 Norfolks were to capture the wood, and to their right 2 Warwicks, the village, each with the support of a squadron of the Staffordshire Yeomanry. The latter battalion's war diary recorded that '2 KSLI took up a position at SUE, HILDA and HELEN [see map page 134] at 0130 hours in the thickly wooded low ground in front of our position, to cover the Bde Start Line.'[2] On the right flank, the King's Shropshire Light Infantry (KSLI) also had a company deployed for the preliminary task of securing Square Wood (Objective SALLY), with at first light a squadron of tanks of the 1st Northamptonshire Yeomanry (1 NY). On the left flank alongside the canal, 2 Lincolns were attached to 185 Brigade for a battalion advance on the axis of the Caen–Ouistreham road. Once Lebisey had been captured, 2 KSLI's subsequent task (phases 2 and 3) was to facilitate 185 Brigade's advance into Caen by securing Point 64, the crest of Ring Contour 60 (Objective HOCKEY).

Having been relieved by a combination of 8 and 177 Brigade on the division's right flank, 9 Brigade was to move up behind 185 Brigade to the Ring Contour, from where it was to commit the 2nd Royal Ulster Rifles (2 RUR) and the 1st King's Own Scottish Borderers (1 KOSB) to phase four, the capture of Caen and the formation of a bridgehead south of the Orne. The KSLI's attack on the Ring Contour and 9 Brigade's advance into Caen was to be supported by 1 NY. 144 Regiment RAC was in reserve but would come forward to Ring Contour 60 to help hold it against the anticipated counter-attack. Meanwhile, the armoured cars of the corps recce regiment were to attempt to slip through the enemy defences to the Orne bridges.

The Royal Engineers had plenty of work in supporting the attack on Lebisey, starting with 'assault mine clearance and demolitions' for the infantry, followed by the 'construction of two in crossings for each fwd coy' of the anti-tank ditch and a 16ft wide gap through the minefields on each of the four assault company's front, before finally, clearance of main lateral LEBISEY WOOD rd from X rds.' Two troops of flails from 22 Dragoons would work with the Staffs Yeo squadrons to get them through minefields and unmarked patches of mines.

Lieutenant Bunning of A Company, 1 Norfolk provides detail of the overnight artillery 'stonk on Lebisey Wood', which was hit with

> 10-minutes 'normal' each hour from Corps Artillery, cruisers and destroyers, beginning at 0230 hrs. At 0430 hrs until 0520 hrs the guns fire 'rapid', but at 0520 hrs until 0530 they fired as fast as possible, and then lifted to help B Company through the wood and the rest of us to our allotted position.[3]

33 Field Regiment's history describes the barrage:

> The attack proper was opened by a barrage of eight field regiments on this same [Lebisey] wood to support its capture by 185 Infantry Brigade. A simultaneous attack by 59 Division directed at GALMANCHE and ST CONTEST also under a heavy barrage and, with the additional fire of HMS RODNEY, the general effect was of a machine-gun rather than artillery fire. At 0515 hours an intercept on the rear link reported, 'Barrage successful, lifts correct. Sitrep impossible owing to smoke and dust on objective.' At 0546 hours the barrage stopped and immediately [counter] mortar targets were engaged.

Shortly after midnight, 1 Norfolks' Intelligence officer and his I Section set out from the assembly area to mark the battalion's route with white mine tape, forward through Biéville to the FUP. They were followed by A Company, whose task was to form a firm base in the 'Gap' where the road crossed the anti-tank obstacle. Next came the Warwicks at 0230 hours, who noted that their 'Leading Coys reached their Start Line, 400 yds from the North edge of LEBISEY WOOD by 0430 hours, without much def fire coming down, under heavy barrage from the Corps Arty.' The start line (JANET) was in long grass, where the Norfolks, in view of the enemy as dawn broke, were 'instructed to lie very low … until the appointed time for the advance.'

H Hour at 0430 hours saw the Norfolks and Warwicks cross the start line. On this occasion, with German artillery thinly spread across the broad frontage of the British attack, they failed to disrupt the initial advance of 185 Brigade behind the creeping barrage fired by 25-pounders. The KSLI securing the start line and FUP, however, did suffer significant casualties. The leading companies, having begun their move forward on time, were soon joined by the tanks of A Squadron of the Staffs Yeo. They had assembled to the north of the Dan valley anti-tank obstacle so as not to compromise surprise, and passed through the Gap to support the infantry's advance. However, as recorded by the Warwicks' war diarist:

> At about 0440 hours, heavy def fire started coming down on the ground North of LEBISEY WOOD, causing casualties to the Reserve Coys forming up, and the leading Coys moving up behind the barrage. The leading Coys were able to keep well up with our own barrage and did not get very much opposition from the small arms fire, most of the Germans being unable to get out of their positions after our barrage had passed over them

An extract of the CHARNWOOD Defences overprint map covering the 3rd Division's area.

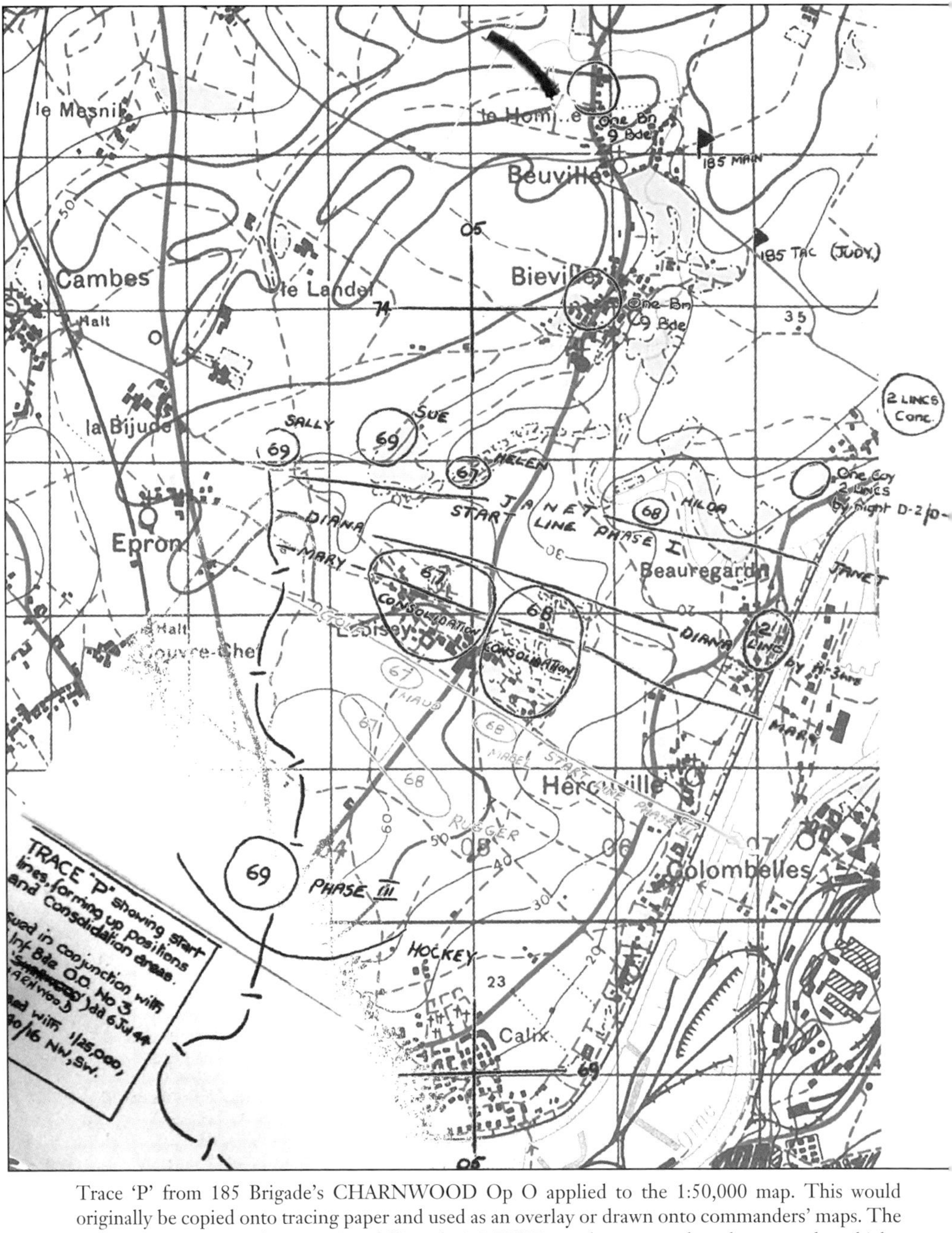

Trace 'P' from 185 Brigade's CHARNWOOD Op O applied to the 1:50,000 map. This would originally be copied onto tracing paper and used as an overlay or drawn onto commanders' maps. The numbers 67 (2 Warwicks), 68 (1 Norfolk) and 69 (2 KSLI) are the same as those borne on the vehicles of the brigade's three battalions. Their use on the trace was for both brevity and low-level security.

> and any positions that did open up were quickly dealt with. 'D' and 'C' Coys reached their objective on the South side of LEBISEY WOOD by about 0600 hours and shortly before this time, the Germans started putting down heavy mortar and arty fire on the wood. The two Tps of tks had a very difficult passage over the tk obstacle on their track, but they came up behind the Reserve Companies and proved of great assistance in dealing with isolated German Positions which were still holding out in the rear of the leading Companies.
>
> Inside the village, A Company had come up against the German Command Post, 'which was an underground rabbit warren' but with the help of 75mm HE fire from an M10, this was 'cleared up.' The Biéville to Lebisey road was mined, but by 0730 hours it had been cleared by the accompanying engineer platoon and the Battalion's support weapons were ordered forward.
>
> The position was quickly consolidated. Enemy mortar and shell fire continued to be very heavy during the morning.

During the fighting, the Staffordshire Yeomanry claimed three Panzer IVs and an 88mm anti-tank gun knocked out, along with a forward ammunition dump destroyed, for the loss of one of the latest diesel-engine Sherman Mk IIIs and two men killed in action.

The ability of the Warwicks to keep up with the barrage was crucial in fighting their way through the Lebisey village defences in just an hour and a half. The fact that 31 *Jäger* Regiment, only recently arrived and not yet inured to heavy artillery fire, had clearly kept their heads down would also have been a factor in the Warwicks' success. On the left flank, Lieutenant Bunning recalled 1 Norfolks' attack on the woods:

> The battle did not last long. All resistance was knocked out of the Germans by the heavy bombardment that preceded the attack. We dug in straight away, and at about 9.30am the order came through to clear the area of all dead. One German did not revive until 10.00am.! 'Bang! Bang! too much!' was his statement as he was escorted away.
>
> The heavy reek of death lingered everywhere, and not only of cattle. I identified several men of C Company . . . and also of the Warwicks who had been killed in the first attack. The bodies had been left in front of the German slit trenches to battle-harden the Germans. In spite of the heavy bombardment by the Navy (*Warspite* and *Arethusa*) cruisers and destroyers and Corps artillery from time to time, I counted less than twenty graves at the eastern end of the wood.

Private Wisewell was an orderly working in 223 Field Ambulance's Main Dressing Station (MDS), supporting 185 Brigade. He described in his diary treating some horrific wounds and how the number of casualties rapidly mounted:

> At 5.00am the first wounded came back, cheerful, optimistic. We splinted fractures, covered wounds with sterile dressings and relieved each other

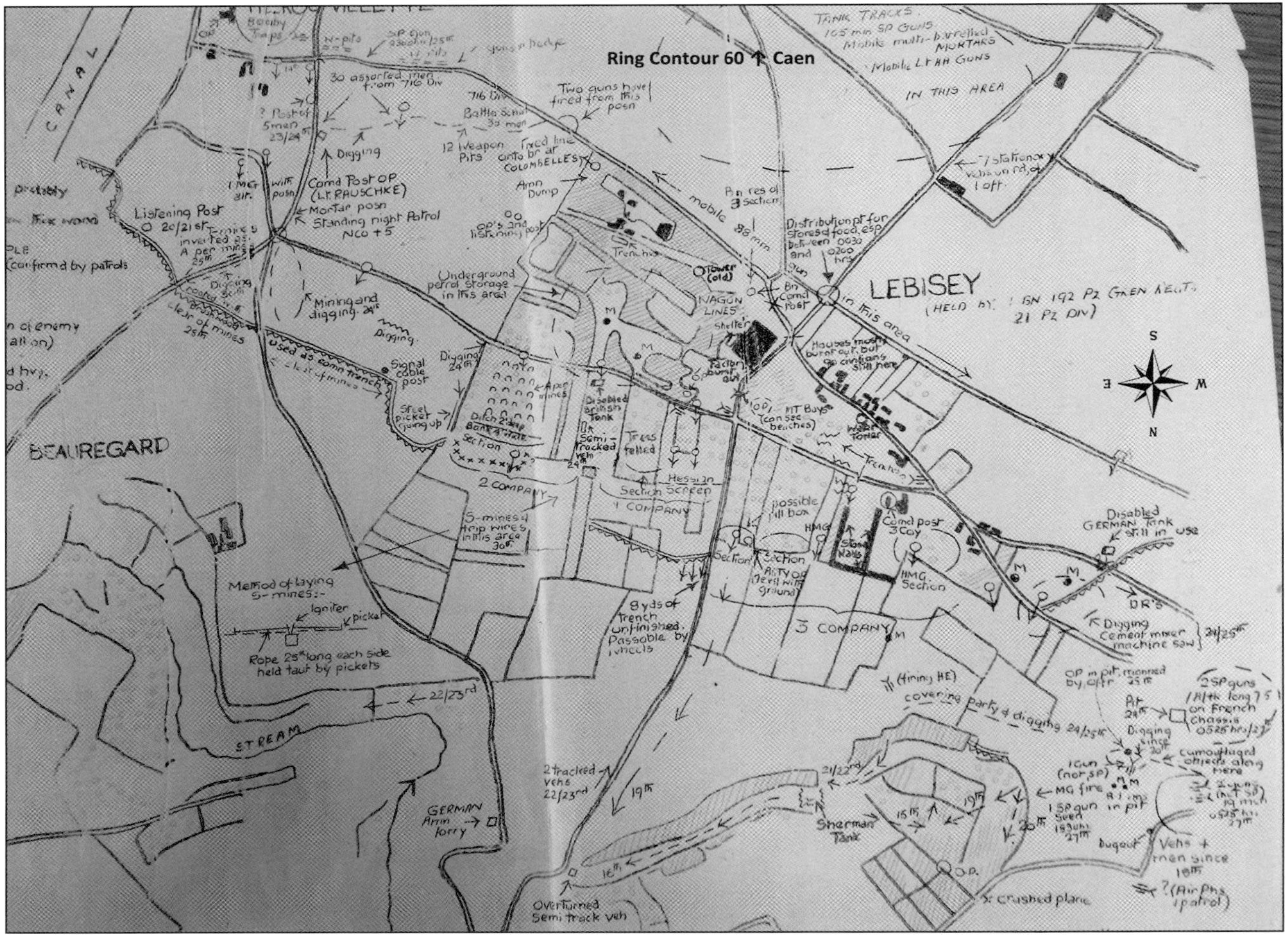

A spirit duplicated intelligence map issued by 185 Brigade's I Section. The detail was largely the product of patrols and observation over the course of a month.

> for breakfast at 6.30am. As the day wore on, sunny and scorching hot, the tide of casualties rose. Dozens and dozens were carried in. Our treatment centre always had three upon the trestles being attended to and soon the approaches were lined with a queue. Hour after hour we worked and evacuated and still the flow continued. Ghastly wounds there were, of every type and state of severity. Heads with skulls so badly smashed that bone and brain and pillow were almost indivisible; faces with horrible lacerations; jaws blown completely away leaving only two sad eyes to plead for relief from pain. Chests pierced through with shrapnel and lungs that spouted blood from gushing holes. Arms were mangled into shapeless masses left hanging by muscle alone and waiting the amputation knife. There were abdomens perforated by shell splinters and displaying coils of intestine, deadly wounds. Buttocks were torn and in some cases spinal injury had followed bringing paralysis. But the leg wounds! Thigh bones splintered; knees without kneecaps; legs without feet; red, mangled flesh and blood flooding the stretcher. And others trembling uncontrollably, sobbing like children, strapped to the stretcher and struggling to be free; screaming and, when a shell landed near the ADS, shouting, 'They're coming again! Oh God, they're coming again.' Not heroes, but sufferers, nonetheless. We ate our lunch of biscuit and corned beef with bloody fingers and when relieved by 9th Field Ambulance at 6.00pm we had treated 466 British soldiers and 40 Germans.

Despite the flow of casualties to the rear, 185 Brigade were pleased with the progress made by the Norfolks and Warwicks. The brigade war diary recorded their progress, with the Warwicks facing a sterner test in Lebisey village that the Norfolks in the woods:

> 0802 1 Norfolk report their sector of LEBISEY clear. Lincs in HEROUVILLE at about same time.
> 1000 2 Warwick after some delay in mopping up report LEBISEY village itself clear.
> 1024 2 KSLI ordered to move forward through the other bns to SOUTH of LEBISEY leaving their one company still engaged near SQUARE WOOD.
> 1203 One coy 1 Norfolk on high ground SOUTH of LEBISEY.
> 1240 One coy 2 Warwick on high ground SOUTH of LEBISEY. Tac HQ moves forward to LEBISEY.[4]

Now they were on the open slopes beyond the village and wood. All of the war diaries comment that they were overlooked from across the canal and River Orne, where despite the best efforts of the artillery and air forces the chimneys of the Colombelles steel works remained standing, almost rivalling the abbey at Monte Cassino as an 'evil eye'. Their towering presence made the laying of an effective smokescreen impractical.

Prisoners of war being assembled to the north of Lebisey Wood by soldiers of 185 Brigade.

A junior staff officer noted in 185 Brigade's war diary with an air of satisfaction and relief:

> 2 KSLI passed under comd 9 Bde and by evening Warwick and Norfolk had withdrawn their forward coys and were consolidated in LEBISEY itself. All very elated at such a complete success and at being at last in possession of a piece of ground that had given us so much trouble. 2 Lincs on left had given us most excellent assistance and were consolidating but undergoing very hy mortar fire as the position was fully overlooked from COLOMBELLES. Tac HQ remained at LEBISEY. Main HQ back at BEUVILLE with the command post established in the recently hewn cavern in the rock where no fresh air ever penetrated nor any shell fragment, and where only the G III [presumably the war diarist] could exist for more than a few minutes.

Photographed east of the Orne, an officer and soldiers of the *Luftwaffe Feld* Division head towards the Colombelles steel works.

The Lincolns at Hérouville

Unlike the battalions of 185 Brigade, some 800 yards east of Lebisey, the 2nd Lincolns, who were to deliver an attack on Hérouville, were not on familiar ground. Their task was to advance from the Beauregard area across half a mile of open country that sloped down to the canal, immediately under the eye of German OPs in the steelworks.

> Lieutenant Colonel Welby-Everard's plan was to hold Château Beauregard with D Company as a firm base where battalion headquarters would be located. B Company was to attack and clear Hérouville, while A and C Companies, right and left respectively, were to exploit from Hérouville to the Colombelles bridge a further 600 yards towards Caen just before the canal basin opens out. There were no tanks in support but a battery of 33 Field Regiment was in direct support [and] guns from the rest of the regiment and 7 Feld Regiment were in support if needed. In addition, the battery's FOOs could call for shoots from division and corps if the situation warranted. There were two platoons of Vickers machine guns and 4.2in mortars of D Company 2 Middlesex and the Lincolns' own 3in mortars were dug-in in the grounds of the château. Other than the indirect fire support this was to be a remarkably self-contained battalion attack.

The Lincolns began to occupy the Beauregard area during 7 July and sent several recce patrols forward to Hérouville; this was all too obvious to the Germans who, once the RAF bombers had departed, shelled and mortared the château area overnight. Major Gilbert of C Company recalled:

> Very early in the morning of the 8th about 0300 hours, we moved from Blainville to Château de Beauregard, which was to be our start line for the attack on Hérouville. I led C Company through the grounds of the château, we came under heavy mortar fire from Colombelles, which killed my CSM, wounded my 2iC and caused a number of other casualties. Not a good start.[5]

The Defences overprint map of the Beauregard–Hérouville battlefield, showing the anti-tank ditch dug prior to the invasion. Note the British cartographer's erroneous use of the name of the nearby hamlet of Hérouvillette on the printing plate.

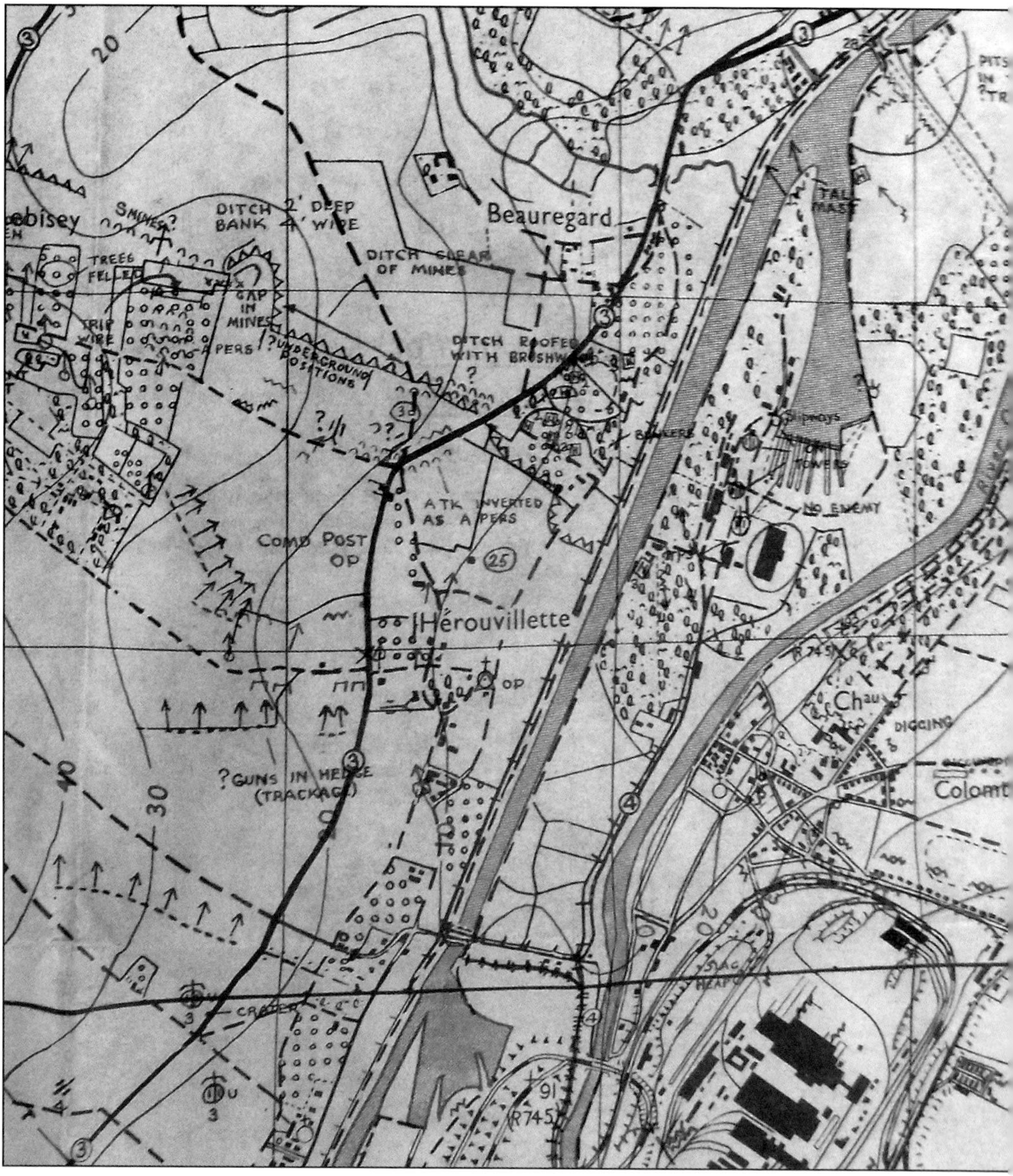

During the night, the Lincolns' assault-pioneers had worked to breach the German pre-invasion minefield adjacent to the anti-tank ditch that ran from the canal, along the southern side of the château's park, to Lebisey Wood. Having crossed their start line at 0430 hours, B Company found the assault-pioneers still clearing a gap in the minefield and marking a safe lane. Consequently, they suffered some casualties from anti-personnel mines but pressed on across the ditch and deployed with two platoons forward. Corporal Elvidge of 12 Platoon described the attack as dawn began to break:

> As we approached a road that ran up into the village a machine gun nest opened up on us. It was located behind a hedge. My section was on one side of the road and 7 Section on the other. The corporal leading 7 Section was shot and dropped to the ground, so I shouted, 'Come on!' and we charged the nest. One of the Germans was shot and killed but the other managed to get away. With 7 Section joining mine we advanced up the hill to the church where we tried to turn right but found a group of Germans in front of us behind a big stone wall. One of my section gave me a hitch-up to look over the wall and I saw Germans all over the place. There was a trench 7 yards inside the gateway full of Germans and another lot in the church doorway. I got down sharpish and started throwing grenades over the wall but the Germans were soon throwing potato-masher grenades back at us. One of my section, Arthur Bellamy, was killed here – it was his 21st birthday. We tried to make our way around the back of the Germans to meet up with 11 Platoon

The church at Hérouville on the northern outskirts of the village and one of the high stone walls that abounded in the village.

> as we had lost all communication with them. As I made my way forward, I was shot in the arm by a sniper from up in the church tower and was simultaneously blown 5 yards by a mortar air-burst, collecting shrapnel in the shoulder and the back. Major Colvin came forward and ordered a stretcher-bearer to help me back. Holding on to his arm, I managed to hobble back to the RAP, where I removed my webbing and was given a shot of morphine.

In the maze of Hérouville's lanes, walls, hedges and buildings, order was inevitably lost, and B Company's battle degenerated into a protracted series of small actions to clear strongpoints amidst the stone-built houses linked with trenches and tunnels into cellars. A reinforced company of I/31 *Jäger* Regiment numbering some 200 men fought hard from advantageous positions but were steadily overcome by the Lincolns. Major Colvin led the fighting by example, as recalled by Lieutenant Curnow:

> I was leading 12 Platoon and [we] were clearing the village. The Germans had turned a 20mm ack-ack gun into an anti-infantry weapon and were firing directly down the centre of the road. While I crouched at the side of a wall Major Colvin stood in the middle of the road firing his .303 rifle from the hip with absolutely no regard for self-preservation.

While B Company was fighting to clear Hérouville, A and C Companies were relieved to be leaving Château Beauregard, which was under continual mortar fire from east of the canal. The Carrier Platoon and the other battalion and attached support weapons were, however, unable to get forward as the anti-tank ditch had yet to be filled in; a single AVRE with a fascine could have improvised a crossing in minutes. By the time the leading section of 6-pounder anti-tank guns were across the obstacle, B Company had cleared a machine gun sited in a hedge that surrounded an orchard in the southern part of the village. In this they had been aided by the Besa machine gun of an armoured car of the Inns of Court Yeomanry, who were attempting to bypass the fighting. However, with the enemy far from defeated, their attempt to slip through the city to the Orne bridges failed, and the squadrons were withdrawn.

By 0800 hours Hérouville was mostly clear, but pockets of resistance remained and it took until midday to fully secure the village, by which time the Lincolns had been ordered not to press ahead with phase two of their attack. This was because the remainder of 185 Brigade was only making slow progress towards Caen from Lebisey. Consequently, the battalion deployed its leading section of anti-tank guns to cover the routes into the village from the south, and the rifle companies sheltered in German defences from vicious mortar and artillery fire.

The Second Bomber Strike

With CHARNWOOD's phase one well underway, at 0700 hours 192 B-25 Marauder medium bombers of the USAAF had struck in a two-hour attack on likely routes and assembly areas for German counter-attacks.The aircrews were under instructions only to bomb positively identified targets. In accordance with these orders, less than half the aircraft released their load, and many bombs fell wide of their targets. Amongst the places hit were the stout medieval buildings of the castle in the centre of Caen where the headquarters of the 12th *Hitlerjugend* Panzer Division was located. *Standartenführer* Kurt Meyer recalled:

> We saw the final wave of bombers heading for us and dropping their bombs. I immediately jumped down into the cellar entrance to our headquarters and ran to the deepest corner. A loud explosion rocked the building and the blast blew the candles out. I could hardly see my hand thanks to the thick clouds of dust, and I could only breathe with difficulty. Hubert Meyer called out to me and more voices could be heard. The blast waves threw a young soldier into the cellar and he cried out: 'We've been buried alive; we've been buried alive', and he was only calmed down with difficulty.
>
> The bombs had hit the garrison church, which was just 50 metres from my headquarters, and had completely destroyed it ... Blocks of stone had been thrown around, some fell on our radio vehicles which were parked up under camouflage nets. Our radios were destroyed, but we soon overcame this [by resorting to telephone (?)].[6]

Following the bombing of Caen the previous evening, in anticipation of an attack on the city, General Eberbach, commander of Panzer Group West, overnight ordered LXXXVI Corps to send II/22 Panzer Regiment west across the Orne and canal to reinforce 16th *Luftwaffe Feld* Division, where tanks of the I Battalion would shortly be in action. With all the bridges damaged or under fire, General

St George's Church, the 'Garrison Church' Meyer referred to in Duke William's castle, central Caen.

The devastated centre of Caen after the battle.

von Obstfelder protested about the time it would take and the losses which would be suffered. He suggested that the *Hitlerjugend* would be best placed to send panzers to support the *Luftwaffe Feld* Division, but *Standartenführer* Meyer, with the backing of his corps commander, Sepp Dietrich, refused, and at 0915 hours, with CHARNWOOD already well under way, Panzer Group West reissued its orders. As predicted, it took 21st Panzer Division until well into the afternoon to execute them.

In the meantime, as far as I Corps was concerned, with good progress being reported by 3rd Division, the operation seemed to be going well; but little information was coming back from 59th Division. Keen to develop momentum and complete the operation in daylight, at 0630 hours General Crocker ordered CHARNWOOD's second phase to begin at 0730 hours with the codeword TALBOT.

Ring Contour 60

Back on 3rd Division's main axis of advance, 185 Brigade reported that Lebisey village and wood had been captured and largely secured at 1000 hours, with 1 Norfolks and 2 Warwicks reorganizing and rounding up prisoners. To complete phase one, both the Norfolks and Warwicks had deployed a company in front of 9 Brigade's assembly area, on the rising ground south of Lebisey (Objective RUGGER), as described in 2 Warwicks' war diary:

> At 1145 hours 'A' Company Gp went forward to take the high ground about 1,000 yards South of the wood. They reached this position without much opposition, but were very heavily shelled and mortared as soon as they got on to the objective, including several salvos from German multi-barrelled mortars. However, they held on to this position until 1500 hours, when 2 KSLI went through them to take up a position on the high ground overlooking Caen. During this very successful attack it was estimated that the German Bn of the GAF Div holding the position was completely destroyed.[7]

The next feature, Ring Contour 60, was to be secured by 2 KSLI, now under command of 9 Brigade. This battalion had been deployed overnight to secure 185 Brigade's start line and firm base and was now accompanied by a squadron of the 1st Northamptonshire Yeomanry (NY) to secure this feature overlooking Caen. This squadron took over the advance from the Staffordshire Yeomanry, who were later released to leaguer in reserve amongst the stumps of what had been Lebisey Wood. There was, however, no immediate move forward by infantry or tanks, as recorded in 2 KSLI's war diary:

> By 1100 hrs LEBISEY was captured and the Bn moved fwd to an assembly area immediately NORTH of LEBISEY. The Bn now received orders to pass through the fwd Bns and occupy Pt 64. Some delay occurred here owing to the difficulty of gathering in the sub-units which had provided the covering parties (X Coy did not rejoin the Bn until 1800 hrs) and due to the

> difficulty of discovering the posn of the fwd Bns and to the shelling of LEBISEY.

The missing X Company on the division's right flank, along with A Squadron of 1 NY, was locked in its own private battle with the 31st *Jäger* Regiment in the area of its overnight deployment near Square Wood and could not be withdrawn. The KSLI's diarist continued:

> However, at 1430 hrs the Bn moved off with Z and W Coys leading, and occupied Pt 64 about 1600 hrs, clearing out a German Pl. The Bn now consolidated. Although the Bn had not seen much Inf fighting during the day it had suffered considerable Cas. Covering parties had received much of the enemy DF fire. The adv over the open ground between LEBISEY and Pt 64 was in full view of the enemy EASTof the River and they shelled the rd continually. The isolated gp of houses on the rd at Pt 64 around which gathered tks and SP guns drew even heavier fire as the Bn dug in.[8]

Well protected from mortar fire, the accompanying Shermans of 1 NY had reported 'advancing in formation over open fields' to Ring Contour 60. 'The advance was not seriously contested by the enemy. The few snipers left in buildings on the hill were soon rounded up and made prisoner. Hill 60 dominated the surrounding country and the roof-tops of Caen lay spread out at our feet.'[9]

Meanwhile, the battalions of 9 Brigade were preparing for action on Ring Contour 60 and beyond. Their war diary noted that 'For the exploitation phases [three and four] 33 Armd Bde (less one regt) and 2 KSLI were put under comd.' Brigadier Orr's plan was to advance into Caen with the 2nd Royal Ulster Rifles (2 RUR) from positions in Biéville, supported by the tanks of the 1st Northamptonshire Yeomanry (1 NY), while the 1st King's Own Scottish Borderers (1 KOSB) were to provide a firm base south of Lebisey. 144 Regiment RAC remained on call in reserve. With a view to the advance into Caen, 2 RUR were only on the move in the late afternoon.

> Meanwhile, the Commanding Officer was making his reconnaissance and evolving a plan with the Commander of the supporting tank unit, the 1st Northants Yeomanry assisted by Major W.D. Tighe-Wood and Captain A.C. Bird, commanding the two forward companies [A left and D right]. At 1430 hours the Battalion moved forward, debouched from Lebisey Wood [to the FUP and advanced] towards Ring Contour 60 at 1730 hours. At this time no news of the progress of the KSLI had reached us, nor had we heard anything of enemy dispositions behind Lebisey Wood.[10]
>
> However, it was obvious from the viewpoint of Lebisey that the Boche was shelling intensively the whole area between the wood and Ring Contour 60, by using as OPs the chimneys of the factories at Colombelles lying on the south side of the Orne to the NE of Caen. These chimneys constituted too small a target for the RAF or for our own gunners, yet they dominated the battlefield, and made the passage of our troops a difficult one.

CHARNWOOD 8 July 1944. Sherman tanks of 33 Armoured Brigade moving up to support 9 Brigade.

The history of 1 NY recorded an unsuccessful attempt to help subdue the enemy artillery fire:

> From this position they overlooked Hill 60 and all the forward slope leading into Caen; and it soon became obvious from the heavy and consistent shelling to which we were subjected, that their OPs were having a busy time. To counteract this, 'B' Squadron (Major the Hon Brassey) and 'C' Squadron (Major D. Bevan) both opened HE fire on the factory, concentrating upon the high towers. It was not long before the factory caught fire and it continued to burn for twenty-four hours.

As with all previous attempts to knock the steel works chimneys down by bombing or shelling, they remained stubbornly upright. Despite the shelling, the

Yeomanry also joined the infantry in sending patrols forward into the city from the Ring Contour.

> An attempt was made to get into Caen on the left flank through the Hamlet of Calix. A patrol of the Recce Troop under the command of Lieut. Vaughan Green advanced through the fields but, as it approached the village, the patrol was put out of action by an anti-tank gun firing from one of the houses. The crews of both tanks were able to escape, thanks to the close support of 'B' Squadron, who engaged the gun with HE at once. Even so, it took the baled-out crews two and a half hours to crawl back 500 yards to safety, being constantly under fire from snipers. By dusk a patrol of the Recce Troop, commanded by Sjt. Jack, with No. 2 Troop of 'B' Squadron (Lieut. R. Morgan) in support, had penetrated to the outskirts of the city by another route.
>
> Owing to the damage done by bombing it proved impossible for tanks to enter the town from the North-East and Sjt. Jack had to go in on foot. By 1900 hours he reached the main crossroads and found that there were only snipers left in Caen. At dusk 'C' Squadron and the Royal Ulster Rifles made a further attempt to enter the city by another route, but again could not get through the cratered streets.

On this 2 RUR added:

> By night a strong patrol of 'B' Company, under Major J.W. HYDE, and two troops of tanks from 1st Northamptonshire Yeomanry attempted to move down into Caen. Progress was soon obstructed by the ruin and havoc wrought in the town and its approaches by RAF bombing. Some mines were encountered, and, at once it was felt that an advance in daylight would save casualties, the march in was postponed until the following day.

The war diary of 185 Brigade summarizes:

> Tk and inf patrols were pushed out to COUVRECHEF, ST JULIEN and CALIX at 2200 one coy 2 RUR with a Sqn E YEO [*sic*, 1 NY] attempted to penetrate into CAEN, but the mass of rubble resulting from our own air and arty preparations rendered the going impossible for tks and very slow for inf as a result it was decided not to push on into CAEN until morning.[11]

Amongst the last to return to the area of the Ring Contour were tanks of 1 NY's Recce Troop.

> Sjt. Bott, who had been sent on a reconnaissance, was seen to be returning, his Stuart tearing up the road at full speed with a German Mk IV hot on his tail. This procession ran right across the 'A' Squadron front. They were only too willing to oblige. No. 1 Troop opened fire, soon followed by a blaze of guns from the Squadron. The Mk IV disintegrated, the turret was blown off and later found 40 yards away from the Tank.

A Shermans of 4 Troop, B Squadron of 144 RAC moving up to Ring Contour 60 on 8 July 1944.

As the 3rd Division's forward troops took up defensive positions for the night, the tanks of 144 RAC were sent forward from Cazelle, where they had been waiting in reserve all day. They drove south to join 9 Brigade on Ring Contour 60 as a part of the defence, reinforcing and relieving 1 NY's squadrons, which took turns to pull back to replenish and service their tanks overnight. For those remaining on the hill it was an uncomfortable night of continual shelling and mortaring, topped with the expectation of hard fighting in the city the following day.

The German Situation

In the face of 3rd Division's attack, the 16th *Luftwaffe Feld* Division had been giving ground and was in growing danger of collapse on the high ground overlooking Caen. However, despite orders from Panzer Group West, they had by mid-afternoon received no reinforcements from either the 21st or the *Hitlerjugend* panzer divisions. With the two corps commanders, Obstfelder and Dietrich, refusing to cooperate and release some of their panzers, General Eberbach crossed the Orne bridges during a lull in the shelling and reached the *Hitlerjugend*'s headquarters in the city, where he spoke to *Standartenführer* Meyer.

> The general thanked me for the division's success in holding the enemy but he did not at that stage know about the collapse of the *Luftwaffe* Division,

> which I briefed him on. He immediately understood how serious the situation was and ordered the deployment of panzers from 21st Panzer Division, which were south [six east] of the Orne.

General Obstfelder, with orders from Eberbach and the situation clearly deteriorating in his corps area, drove to General Feuchtinger's headquarters; tanks of 21st Panzer were soon heading for the crossings of the Orne and canal, but with the Allies expecting such a move, air OPs spotted them. A combination of damage to bridges, rubble in the city and naval gunfire meant they struggled to get through to support the collapsing front. According to Meyer, only 'a reinforced battalion of the 21st Panzer Division crossed the Orne that day' – too late, however, to make a difference.

Luftwaffe Night Bombing

The oft-quoted German soldiers' joke – 'If it's silver it's an American plane, if it's black it's British, if it's invisible it's the Luftwaffe' – might give the impression that the Germans lacked air support during the Normandy campaign. While it is true that with Allied air supremacy very few German aircraft were seen over the beachhead by day, under the cover of night it was a different matter. With Allied combat air patrols having returned to southern England or to their Advanced Landing Grounds in Normandy, the Luftwaffe were able to mount raids in the dark.

Initially, their raids were directed against the shipping off the beaches and the Mulberry harbour, but as the beachhead became more and more crowded, raids were directed at troop or vehicle concentrations further inland. Some of these were mounted by night-capable aircraft of *Slachtgeschwader* 10 flying the Focke-Wulf 190 F or G. This squadron was a dedicated fighter-bomber unit capable of night flying and known to be operational in Normandy. An attack that was sustained, rather than taking the form of a single overflight, indicated that it was delivered by fighter-bombers rather than bomber aircraft.

On the night of 26 July, the Crocodiles of B Squadron 141 Regiment RAC (The Buffs) were located and attacked:

> It was pitch dark as they came in, flying pretty low and dropping flares till the whole area was light as day. They cruised around dropping hefty containers of deadly anti-personnel bombs all round, going for the guns. Ammunition dumps were soon going up, adding colour to the scene. It looked as if they were going to miss this tiny little field, till a lone Bren gun tracer flickered up into the sky. Whoosh! In came the second wave with deadly accuracy.[12]

Every Churchill tank was issued with a Bren gun with a 100-round drum magazine for air defence, and it is possible that the aircraft were able to identify the source of the fire from the tracer rounds. With the crews diving for cover, the squadron bore the brunt of the enemy attack. Ten men were wounded more or less seriously, including the officer commanding, and a considerable damage was done to the Crocodiles, equipment and the logistic echelon's vehicles.

A Bren gun with the 100-round drum magazines in the anti-aircraft role on its tripod mount with an AA sight.

On this occasion the numerous explosions and the effect on men and equipment make it likely that the ordnance used was a sub-munition, the Butterfly Bomb (*Sprengbombe Dickwandig* 2kg (SD-2)) dispersed from the AB 250-3 cluster bomb unit, which could carry up to 108 of the SD-2's sub-munitions.

> When day broke all the trucks were found to have flat tyres, pools of FTF [the Crocodile's flame fuel] were leaking from the punctured drums, and pools of

The AB-250 cluster bomb unit is seen here with one of the other sub-munitions, high explosive or incendiary or a mix of both, that it could carry.

An unexploded Butterfly Bomb caught in a tree before hitting the ground and detonating.

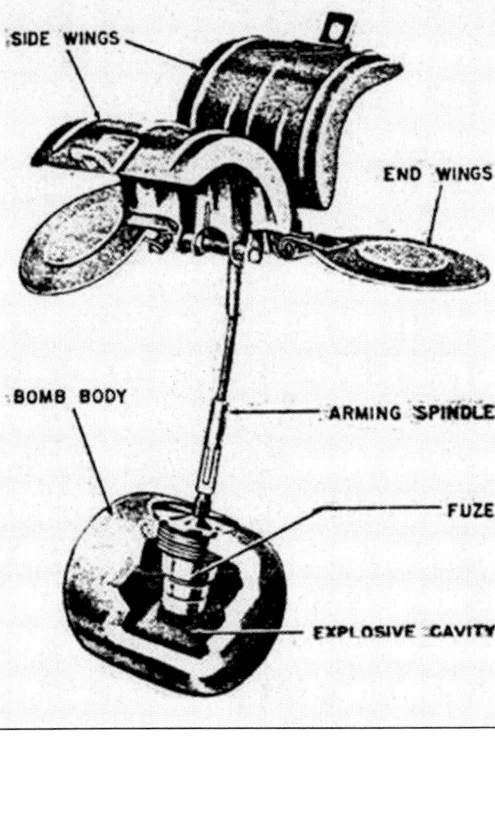

water from the radiators. Whittingham was cursing blue murder about his precious water truck. But by and large the price had been astonishingly light.

Amongst the wounded was Major Spearpoint, who was evacuated to the UK, leaving Captain Ryle to take over the squadron. The following day, the squadron limped back to its base in the fields at Cressons.[13]

On another occasion the *Hitlerjugend* was supported by a squadron of ME-110s; these aircraft, also with a night capability, were to attack the beachhead from airfields in Belgium. This squadron was mainly used at night against RAF bombers, but on this occasion they were tasked with a night bombing raid. *Standartenführer* Meyer was surprised by the arrival of a Luftwaffe general from Holland to witness the strike, which was reported as a 'circus of thirty fighter-bombers'. The first wave of aircraft hit a village, but the second wave 'bombed back' and wounded several of the onlooking Luftwaffe officers.[14]

Generals 'Bolo' Whistler and Crocker.

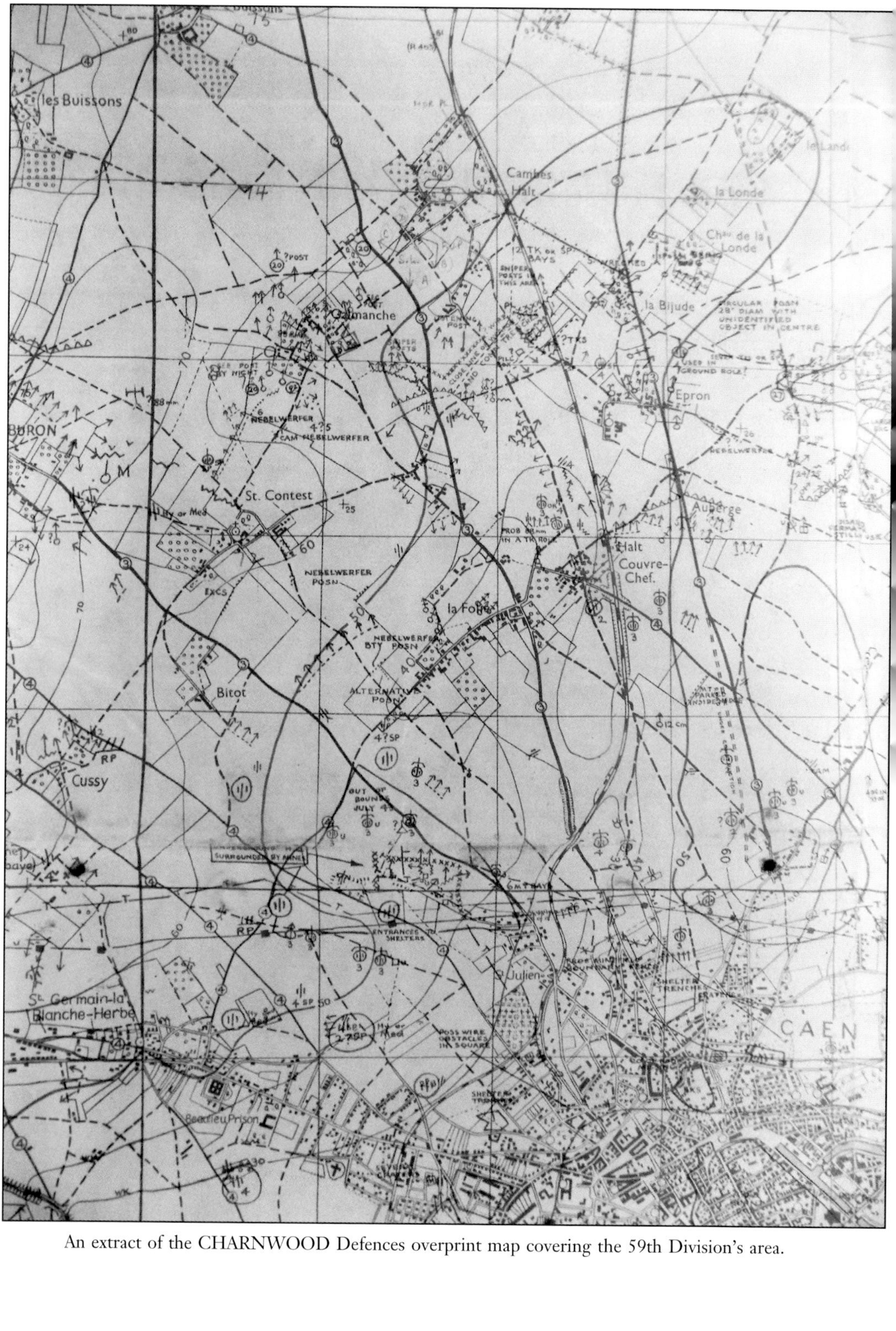

An extract of the CHARNWOOD Defences overprint map covering the 59th Division's area.

Chapter Seven

The Attack by the 59th (Staffordshire) Division

The 59th (Staffordshire) Division had been assembled in Normandy for a week prior to CHARNWOOD; in other words, they were acclimatized to being in an operational theatre and were not rushed into battle the way the 43rd Wessex Division had been during EPSOM. Battle procedure and the orders process for CHARNWOOD was thorough, but as one commanding officer said, 'As a CO I hoped that my unit's first action would be a light one or that we would be put into an area where we would be shelled and mortared for a short while so as to give everyone a little battle inoculation; but this was not so.'[1] In CHARNWOOD the 59th were unfortunate to be up against some of the best German troops in the best-prepared, mutually supporting defensive positions encountered by the Second Army during the campaign in Normandy.

The 59th Division's first battle in Normandy opened with an attack on a frontage of two brigades, 176 and 197. The division's third brigade, 177 Brigade, less 2/6 South Staffs, had relieved 9 Brigade in the defensive positions around Cambes. The divisional history noted:

> The [177] brigade's role in Charnwood was to form a firm base for the division's main attack, and so they were the first to experience the peculiarly grim and menacing atmosphere of this part of the battle area. Enemy activity at this stage was not severe, but the whole place felt evil in a way which no one who went there will forget.[2]

The two assault brigades, 197 on the left and 176 on the right, were to attack on a frontage of just 2,500 yards through a series of villages and mutually supporting enemy positions. The 59th Division's sector was astride the railway line that the Germans used as their divisional boundary between the 16th *Luftwaffe Feld* Division and the *Hitlerjugend*.

On the right, the hamlet of Galmanche, centred on a substantial château/farmhouse, held by II/25 SS *Panzergrenadiers*, was to be captured by 2/6 South Staffords, who were under command of 197 Brigade for CHARNWOOD's phase one. On the left, two companies of 6 North Staffords of 176 Brigade were to capture La Bijude, which was held by a battalion of 31 *Jäger* Regiment. In the open country in the centre was 'the Trench System', a strongly fortified position held by I/25th SS. Though somewhat further back, this position linked up to the west with Galmanche and to the east with the Luftwaffe troops in La Bijude.

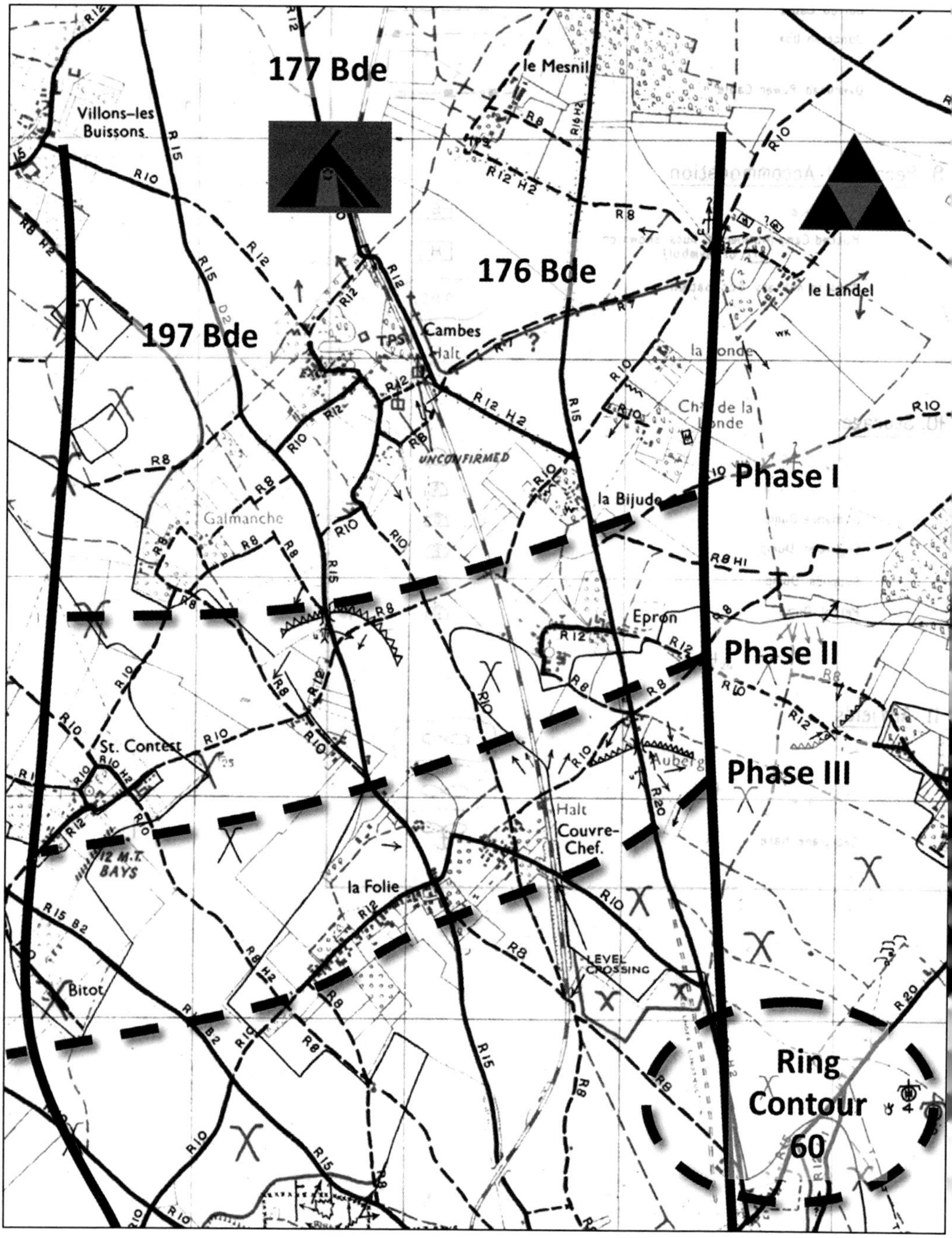

The planned phases of 59th Division's attack on 8 July 1944.

Significantly, its strength having been underestimated, the Trench System was to be attacked by a single company of 6 N Staffs. Once these objectives were secure, in subsequent phases 176 Brigade was to advance south via Epron, and on the right 197 Brigade was to advance towards Caen via St Contest.

Lieutenant Colonel Finlinson commanding the 2/6th S Staffs described the wait for H Hour and the opening barrage:

> It was 4.00am. There was a moon riding high to the sky and away to the east the first pale streaks of a misty dawn were beginning to appear above the horizon. We were waiting in the ruined streets of Cambes [and] all about us on the pavements and in the shelter of the derelict cottages the men of the battalion (the 2/6th) stood or lay waiting for the order that would take us into battle for the first time. Occasionally a German mortar whistled overhead and crumped behind us in the back end of the village. Otherwise, there was complete silence …
>
> The stutter of a few guns that beat the clock and then the mighty roar of massed artillery of all calibres including HM ships riding at anchor in the beachhead. The dark skies to the north became an arc of jagged light over the gun line. The silence all around becoming an inferno of screaming, bursting shells. The ground on which we stood trembled. The time had come. While the guns pounded their shells on the opening line of the barrage, men of the battalion came to life and moved forward in a single line to form up and start for Galmanche …
>
> On the start line visibility was less than 30 yards. The men had been blotted out by the dust and smoke of the barrage and the dawn still came slowly. The leading companies moved quickly across the open stretch of road and in a few seconds were swallowed up in the misty corn that lay between them and their objective.[3]

To the accompaniment for the first time of the 'full roar of the British barrage', the two battalions leading the attack stood up and crossed their start lines at 0429 hours. However, as the bombardment lifted from their objectives, the German defenders rapidly recovered and emerged from dugouts and cellars to man their positions. The divisional historian wrote:

> It soon became evident that our supporting artillery programme was leaving untouched important parts, hitherto unlocated by us, of the enemy defences. These consisted of a large number of light and heavy machine gun positions, linked by an elaborate trench system of pre 'D' Day vintage; the enemy's mortars were well sited and served; and his troops were imbued with a fanatical spirit of resistance.

Attack of 197 Brigade

Before the 2/6 South Staffords had advance much more than 200 yards, A and C Companies came under heavy fire. Colonel Finlinson continued.

> They found themselves heavily engaged by Spandaus from this bewildering system of trenches [surrounding Galmanche and to the east]; there were enemy in front of them and behind them [and] it was a situation for which we were not prepared so soon in the attack. In the half-light the leading

> platoons faltered; those following went to ground in corn and the whole advance came to a temporary standstill while the barrage went on alone.

Brigadier Lingham highlighted a number of mistakes after the battle: 'One was to lose orientation during attacks; another was a failure to use our weapons quickly and effectively when held up by enemy fire.' The suspicion is that, having been thrown into battle without a gentle introduction, when first under fire for real the brigade's soldiers went to ground rather than return fire.[4]

The divisional historian summed up the situation: 'The infantry lost the barrage and remained in the open, suffering heavy casualties from mortar fire as they lay in the standing crops and from MG fire if they tried to move.' The Brigade war diary added more detail in an entry timed 0715 hours:

> 2/6 S Staffords stated that the left hand coy had reached its objective but had been driven off; that the right hand coy was held up and efforts were being

Major General Lyne, one of the senior officers brought back from the Mediterranean 'with sand in his shoes', in his case to command 59th (Staffordshire) Division.

made to get them forward. 2/6 S Staffords stated that the left hand coy had reached its objective but had been driven off; that the right hand coy was held up and efforts were being made to get them forward. During this period Bde comd went forward to 2/6 S Staffords to see the situation for himself. As a result of his visit the unit, which had become considerably disorganised was reorganised into a number of effective bodies of platoon strength.[5]

When 2/6 South Staffs' orders were given during 7 July, B Squadron of the East Riding Yeomanry complained that the infantry had insisted on using a by now somewhat discredited method of tank support. The infantry was to advance in front of the Shermans, which would follow closely and directly behind, deployed in a line of two troops, with the remainder of the squadron similarly arrayed a tactical bound behind them. From the outset of the campaign, the ERY had found themselves extremely vulnerable in a tight formation of this type and had learned to manoeuvre independently during attacks, using cover and folds in the ground to best advantage. This not only reduced the number of tank casualties, but also provided better fire support from crews who were not fighting for their own lives. However, this ignores the morale-boost to the infantry of having tanks in close support. The whole squadron standing off 'to shoot the infantry in' was not popular with the 59th, but the ERY were mounted in Shermans not the more heavily armoured Churchill I tanks. Tactical doctrine for infantry/tank cooperation had been the subject of no fewer than three contradictory directives/ pamphlets issued between November 1943 and March 1944. It is no wonder there were differing ideas. The ERY's historian noted:

'B' Squadron's attack started first, with infantry that had not seen action before. Unfortunately, just as they had assembled to move off to their start line, the Hun put down a devastating fire of shells and mortars onto them, causing not only a lot of casualties but considerable dislocation to their control and command. 'B' Squadron, however, who knew every inch of this ground, rallied what few infantry they could and went on in front alone, in spite of very heavy fire against them of every description.[6]

As recorded above, it took the personal intervention of Brigadier Lingham to rally 2/6 South Staffs and eventually lead them forward towards Galmanche.[7] At 0615 hours they were again moving towards the north-east corner of the objective, with two troops of B Squadron's Shermans taking the lead. In the eastern part of Galmanche the commander of No. 7 Company, *Obersturmführer* Havemeister, whose SS soldiers had sheltered in the cellars and deep dugouts amongst the ruins of the château, recalled the attack closing in on them:

The detonation of shells suddenly lifted off us and moved on to our rear. We could hear the roar of tanks; the attack was about to start. We crawled out of our shelters and into the trenches and we saw innumerable tanks rolling towards us right across our front. Our anti-tank guns had been knocked out

> by the artillery fire, and the few *Panzerfausts* we had did little to give us confidence.
>
> Lieutenant Kinzig of our attached *Nebelwerfer* battery had established radio operators' contact and called for fire on Cambes, and like an express train the rockets howled unexpectedly above us and slammed into the village 1,500 metres away. The strike was supposed to be launched when we were about to be overwhelmed, but it certainly must have helped I Battalion to our right. But the tanks in front of us closed to within 300 metres, and lumps of earth from the exploding shells were flying around us. We could see enemy infantry behind the tanks, but our artillery was still firing at [Villon]-les-Buissons, and didn't we swear?
>
> The tanks attacking us were moving at high speed in the direction of 5th and 6th Companies.[8]

The first tank casualty was the Sherman of A Squadron's Lieutenant Mitchell, who had come up on the right flank to help.

> He was in one of the leading tanks, and a German knocked him out from a hidden slit trench with a *Panzerfaust*; as unfortunately was all too usual with Shermans, his tank caught fire at once. Two of the crew were killed, but Tony Mitchell managed to get out, very badly burnt and [with] one, if not two, legs broken. He was dragged into the trench by the Germans, who treated him very well and bound up his wounds. As it happened, he spoke fluent German, and after some hours it dawned on them he was an officer, so they sent for a German lieutenant to question him. His opening gambit was, 'Why are you so stupid to fight Hitler?' This was considered not worth a reply; and the next question was, 'Why do you attack us here? Anyway, you can never turn us out.' The reply to that was that there were sixty more tanks coming to smarten them up. This made even the German think, especially when he went away to find his company commander killed as well as one other officer and a third of his company. After this they decided discretion was the better part, even of fanatical valour. He took the remainder of his company out of the battle, leaving Mitchell to his fate …

Lieutenant Mitchell, having been abandoned overnight, was found the following day and evacuated to the UK aboard a hospital ship.

Trooper Farrel, a driver aboard one of the B Squadron Shermans heading for Galmanche, commented, 'Yes, the Germans there were as large as life!' and continued:

> This particular day, we were the leading tank [of the troop] and we had to go down a road and we knew at the bottom of the road there were likely to be Germans there … Anyway, we set off down the road and as we went down, we'd to turn a slight bend in the road. We had just got turned round the bend and as I was on the left-hand side of the tank as driver, I could see these Germans going across the road. I automatically got on the mike and said,

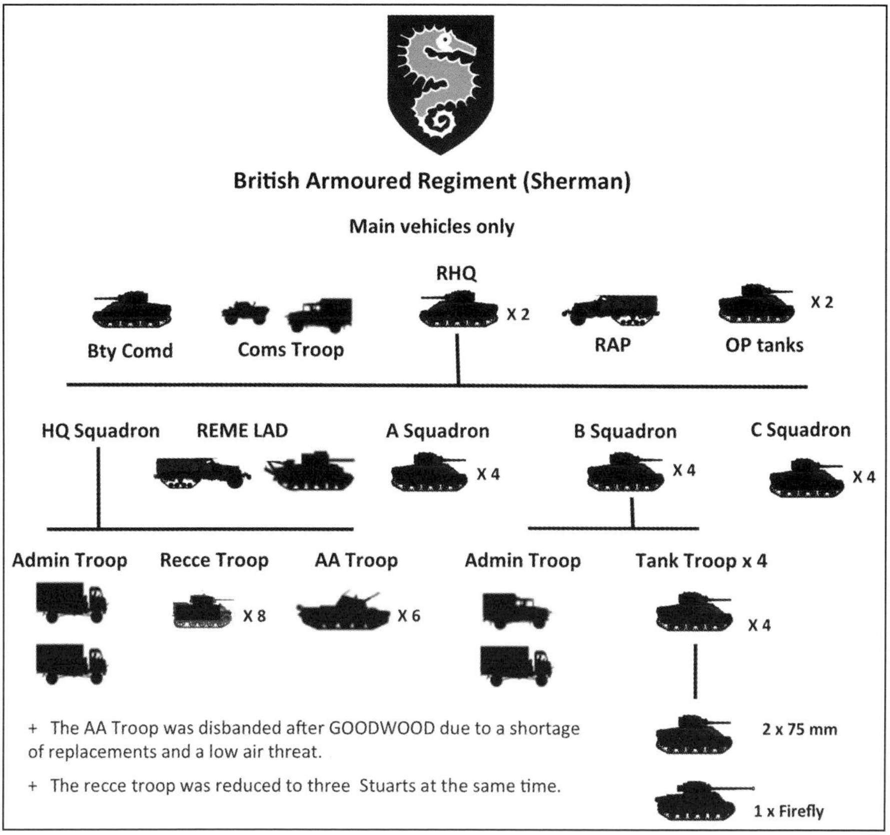

British Sherman Armoured Regiment.

Major Holtby, C Squadron, East Riding Yeomanry, briefing troop commanders in front of his tank.

> 'There are Germans at the bottom of the road, you know!' So, we pulled forward a bit and I helped my co-driver, who had a Browning machine-gun in the front, and together with the other tank with us, we started firing at them.

A revealing entry in 197 Brigade's war diary at 1010 hours reads: 'Personal message from Bde Comd to Adjt 2/6 S Staffordshire: "Our tks are constantly patrolling backwards and forwards between your inf and the objective, you must take advantage of this to get forward."'

> At last, the tide began to turn in favour of the South Staffordshires. Major Garrett, by this time the only company commander left in his battalion, was sent round with what men he could gather in an encircling movement to the right flank, over which the enemy had limited observation. This movement was assisted by the fire from the Gunners and the tanks, and slowly but surely the South Staffordshires were able to gain a foothold in the village of Galmanche itself.

Thirty minutes later, 2/6 S Staffs were reporting 'moving into the nearside of GALMANCHE but opposition on the far side is still strong.' Trooper Farrel's account continues:

> What should have happened was that the infantry were supposed to have knocked out all the anti-tank guns. Well, as we pulled further round the road, next thing a shell hit right about where my head was in the tank! Luckily, we had spare track and spare bogeys on the front of the tank so that protected me a bit. Anyway, it hit the tank, knocked these spare track and bogeys off and took about the width of a finger and thumb out of the front of the tank. Incredible really, that all that happened but nobody was hurt. However, all the white paint that was on the inside of the tank came over my face.
>
> For the moment I didn't know what had happened. Straight away, the crew commander said, 'Reverse! Right?' So, I reversed but I forgot about the bend and as I reversed, the tank went up a mound and we were almost lying over. So I thought, 'What do I do here? If we pull forward, they're going to have another go at us.' Anyway, the engine was 'revving up' and we couldn't stop it. So I knocked the engine off and we all baled out, into this ditch and then up the road to get away. The Squadron Leader in charge of us saw what was happening and he asked what had happened. We told him and then he said, 'Get down that road again.'
>
> So, we had to go back and retrieve the tank. We waited until it had quietened down a bit. I ran over the road, jumped in to see if it would start up again and luckily it did! Then we pulled it down and got it on the level. All the other four lads jumped in and then we had to pull back, because it needed repairing. That was the first time we were hit.

> Because the tank had been hit and the controls were a bit haywire, we had to pull back and to take it to the maintenance area they had established by then. We got it sorted out in a couple of days.

Other Shermans further to the west pressed home the attack, and 'So well did they go that, in fact, on their own they overwhelmed the defences and killed a large number of the enemy by bouncing delayed action 75mm shells on to their slit trenches'.[9] This is somewhat exaggerated as far as Galmanche is concerned. What had happened is described in the 59th's divisional history:

> Our leading companies came under heavy fire within 200 yards of the start line, and though elements of one company entered the outskirts of Galmanche and a few tanks got round the village to the south-east, our attack on this flank round the village to the south-east, our attack on this flank came to a full stop.

Infantry of the 59th Division and a carrier belonging to the anti-tank regiment moving forward.

Ensconced in what remained of the château, *Obersturmführer* Havemeister witnessed what happened to No. 5 Company as the weight of the British attack fell on the II/25th's left flank:

> The enemy tanks drove over the Company's trenches and bunkers and started to rotate their tracks in an attempt to bury our men. Soon the enemy infantry arrived and examined our forward positions under fire from us but did not take cover in them. Eventually the infantry followed the tanks, and we were not attacked in our rubble fortress. It was now quiet, but we could still hear the noise of fighting further to our left.

During the battle, *Hauptsturmführer* Thierey, commander of No. 6 Company, personally knocked out three ERY Shermans with *Panzerfausts*, before he was killed hunting down a fourth.

As the Shermans rolled on around Galmanche, mortarman Karl-Heinze Decker of No. 8 (Heavy) Company, II/25 SS *Panzergrenadiers*, who had been in position south-east of the farm for a month, saw them coming towards him:

> The Allies began their big push inland during July 1944. We were often active with the mortar, firing at the enemy, but all the while being pushed back due to overwhelming numbers. I remember one particular occasion, in truth I'll never forget it, the mortar was set up, and I was in a hole in a hedge nearby . . . I'd been there for a while when I began to hear this distant rattling sound. The noise got louder and seemed to be coming closer. A few minutes later an Allied tank rattled past my hole in the hedge. All the hatches on the beast were closed as it went by, and there I was in a hole in the hedge with my pistol in my hand. If I'd had a *Panzerfaust* I might have been able to disable the thing, but as it was, I could do nothing but watch it go by.
>
> I came out of my hiding place and watched the brute rumble off into the distance. I suddenly realized that my comrades who had previously been nearby were no longer around. Next moment I was being fired at by enemy infantry who were coming along at some distance behind the now almost disappeared tank. As luck would have it there was a cornfield on the other side of the hedge. I dived through the hedge and into the cornfield. I crawled across the field as fast as I could on my belly. The enemy soldiers kept firing across the top of the corn. Every so often they would fire into the field itself when they saw the corn move as I made my way further across the field. Eventually I reached a stone wall at the opposite side of the field. I chose my moment then sprang across the wall. On landing on the other side, I found a couple of equally bewildered German soldiers. I was safe. I considered myself lucky that the enemy did not have any phosphorus ammunition, as the corn was ripe and dry, and it would have burned easily!

The 2/6 S Staffs reported that Galmanche was taken at 1327 hours, but the reality was that the château was still held by remnants of II/25 *Panzergrenadiers* until the following morning. *Obersturmführer* Havemeister and a handful of

Only a few of the *Hitlerjugend*'s 75mm anti-tank guns were by this stage of the battle still in action with the *Panzergrenadiers*.

No. 7 Company held on tenaciously in the ruins, surrounded by Shermans of B Squadron. As noted by the ERY's historian, they 'sat there for five hours machine-gunning any movement.' During that time, 'they lost five crew including [Major Platts] the squadron leader from snipers.' Two tanks were knocked out and two damaged. For 2/6 S Staffs, however, pinned down with scant cover and unable to advance, being halted short of Galmanche was a thoroughly unpleasant culmination of their introduction to battle.

Panzerfaust ('Panzer Fist')

The Germans led the way in exploiting the Munro Effect of focusing explosive force and produced the first hollow-charge weapons, which they used to blast their way into the Belgian fortress of Eben Emael at the start of their 1940 campaign.

How the *Panzerfaust* worked

On detonation, the warhead's explosive charge compressed a shaped metal liner and focused it into a high-velocity superplastic jet or self-forging fragment, which burnt its way through armour, penetrating to a theoretical depth of up to six times the diameter of the charge. The hollow charge was, however, less effective if the warhead failed to hit its target square-on at 90°.

The warhead was propelled by a rocket, with exhaust exiting the rear of the launch tube to produce a balance that was 'recoil-less' as far as the user was concerned. The launcher tube was discarded.

A sketch of aiming and firing the weapon. Note the *Panzerfaust*'s back-blast that limited its use in confined spaces.

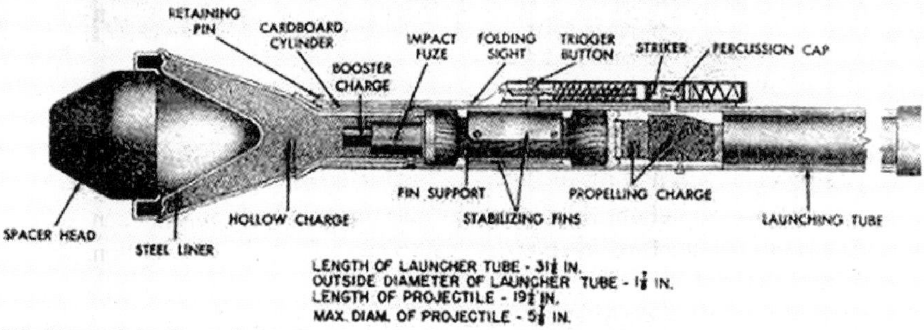

Workings of the *Panzerfaust*.

Deployment

The first prototypes of the *Klein Gretchen* version began to appear in 1942, but by 1944 the weapon was available in four variants suitable for ranges from 30 to 150 metres. The *Panzerfaust* was an infantry section weapon, which when available in numbers was successful in keeping Allied armour from motoring onto defensive positions, particularly in villages and close country. Because of its back-blast the weapon could not normally be fired from within the cover of a building, for example.

Panzerfaust 100.

In response to the *Panzerfaust*, Allied tanks lacking 'bazooka plates' would typically use sandbags and logs to up-armour, but the most successful counter-measure was the application of tank track links which produced a spaced armour that helped to defeat the shaped charge.

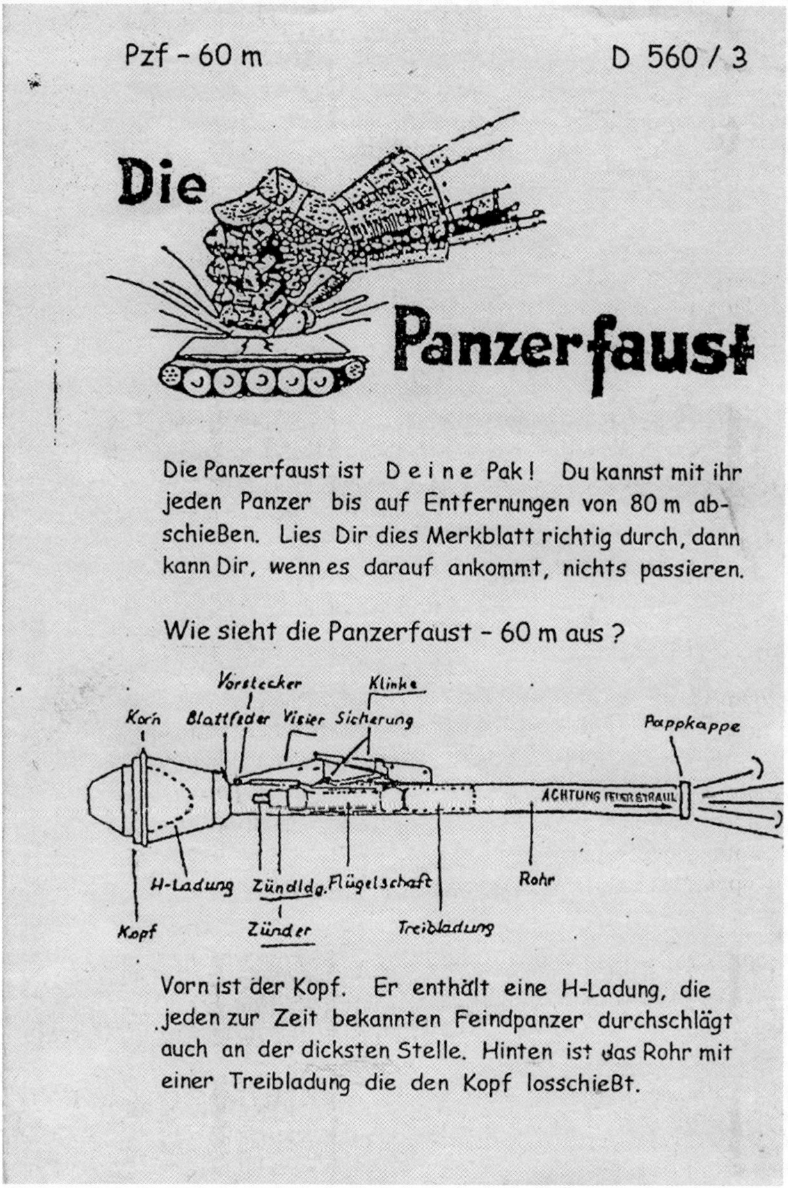

Pzf - 60 m D 560 / 3

Die Panzerfaust

Die Panzerfaust ist D e i n e Pak! Du kannst mit ihr jeden Panzer bis auf Entfernungen von 80 m abschießen. Lies Dir dies Merkblatt richtig durch, dann kann Dir, wenn es darauf ankommt, nichts passieren.

Wie sieht die Panzerfaust - 60 m aus?

Vorn ist der Kopf. Er enthält eine H-Ladung, die jeden zur Zeit bekannten Feindpanzer durchschlägt auch an der dicksten Stelle. Hinten ist das Rohr mit einer Treibladung die den Kopf losschießt.

The front page of a very simple instruction manual for the *Panzerfaust*.

A grenadier and *Panzerfaust* in action.

Only 6 per cent of British and Canadian tanks were knocked out in Normandy by hand-held anti-tank warpons, but later in the North-West European Campaign, with the *Panzerfaust* filling the vacuum created by the loss of anti-tank guns, this rose to 34 per cent.

176 Brigade – La Bijude

On the 59th's left flank, 176 Brigade were to fight their way through the German defences astride the railway line, including the hamlet of La Bijude and a part of the trench system to the west and the village of Épron. The brigade's three battalions were to attack sequentially, each supported in turn by a squadron of the 13/18 Hussars (13/18 H).

> The Regiment was to support 176 Infantry Brigade. B Squadron was to support 6th Battalion of the N Staffordshire Regiment in the capture of LA BIJUDE. [In subsequent phases] C Squadron was to support 7th Battalion of the Norfolk Regiment in the capture of EPRON and A Squadron, with 7th Battalion of the S Staffordshire Regiment in Brigade Reserve with the probable task of capturing COUVRE CHEF, after the successful outcome of the other two attacks.[10]

The 6 North Staffs advanced with two companies forward, astride the railway, with B Squadron's Shermans in close support and C Squadron 'shooting them in' from near Château de la Londe. Their first objectives were La Bijude, held by Luftwaffe troops, and immediately west of the railway well prepared positions held by I/25 SS *Panzergrenadiers*. The latter were largely spared, thanks to the intervention of the *Nebelwerfer* strike on Cambes mentioned earlier that disrupted the attack by the leading companies of 6 North Staffs. As recorded in the divisional history, on the other side of the railway line '6 N Staffs gained an initial success, capturing La Bijude by 0730 hours, but both forward company commanders became casualties and a subaltern found himself the senior officer present.' Captain Neave, Adjutant of the 13/18 H, wrote:

> They appeared to be having not much trouble and our supposition was pretty correct, they had moved out to the west and were now getting in some deep-dug trenches west of the village in very strong [German] positions. Then 'B' Squadron troops went into the village and then the infantry turned their attention to the trenches where they immediately became stuck. The result was nil and eventually the [tank] troops in Bijude began to get a bit anxious as the infantry had left them and they were surrounded by about fifty Boches. One of their tanks was knocked out and, after killing quite a number with Browning fire they withdrew further into the village.

Having fought their way into La Bijude, with both 6 N Staffs company commanders becoming casualties, an inexperienced subaltern officer, optimistically believing that being on the enemy position equated to taking it, had fired the success signal flares. This was unfortunate, as with both No. 18 wireless sets having been knocked out he was later unable to report that the Luftwaffe *Jäger* were far from beaten. They launched a counter-attack almost at once and drove the remnants of the two N Staffs companies back to the area just north of the cross-roads between La Bijude and Château de la Londe. According to the 13/18 H, C Squadron commander's Sherman was hit and B Squadron's Shermans were left alone in the centre of the village for some time. In the confusion of battle, at the end of CHARNWOOD's first phase it is clear that the 59th Division's two battalions did not fully hold their objective.

During the fighting on 8 July CSM Lawley won a well-deserved Military Medal:

> By 06.30 hrs, his Company Commander and all Platoon Commanders were wounded or missing and took no further part in the action. CSM Lawley showed great coolness and courage and moving about under heavy machine gun and mortar fire reorganised the Company. At approximately 08.00 hrs, he was severely wounded in the shoulder and continued in command of the Company for at least half an hour and organised forward fire positions for PIATs to deal with enemy Machine Gun and sniper posts situated in derelict tanks. He then collapsed. His coolness and leadership under heavy fire and power if endurance when severely wounded setting magnificent example which was particularly needed at this juncture of the battle.[11]

As already noted, General Montgomery aimed to give newly arrived divisions a gentle introduction to battle, but in its first operation 59th Division was making a

Lieutenant General Crocker, his ADC Captain Cross and driver Lance Corporal Marsden view the battle on 8 July 1944.

slow and costly start against determined opposition from both SS *Panzer-grenadiers* and the Luftwaffe *Jäger* troops. The latter, defending La Bijude, clearly benefited from being adjacent to the *Hitlerjugend*, as further east in 3rd Division's area their resistance was less effective. *Standartenführer* Meyer added:

> I/SS-*Panzer-Grenadier-Regiment* 25 was covering the right flank, and its fire was disrupting the relatively easy advance of the 3rd Infantry Division into the area of *Luftwaffe Feld* Division, which was almost destroyed.

Most of this fire, thanks to the Germans' well-coordinated overlapping and interlocking arcs of fire, fell on 6 N Staffs, but the KSLI company around Square Wood on the divisional boundary also reported fire from the west. Meyer was, however, still concerned that if La Bijude and Épron were lost, the British would turn his right flank. He commented:

> Our neighbour to the right, the 16th *Luftwaffe Feld* Division, was not up to the job. It was shattered by the renewed bombing and this ad hoc division's

> will to resist collapsed under the weight of the enemy's firepower. The British 3rd Infantry Division advanced into the Luftwaffe division's defensive positions and soon threatened our division's right flank.

In accordance with the *Führerbefehl* that Caen was to be held, *Obergruppenführer* Dietrich refused the first of Meyer's requests to withdraw. With I/25 *Panzergrenadiers* holding the trench system, Meyer deployed a handful of the available panzers and the Divisional Escort Company to his right flank south of La Bijude. This was to prevent an outflanking move, contain the enemy and provide support to the *Luftwaffe Feld* Division.

59th Division – Phase Two

With little more than the success signal from La Bijude, Major General Lyne lacked either accurate or detailed information on the progress of the attacks, largely thanks to a failure of radio communication between the two Stafford battalions and their respective brigade headquarters. Other factors were the pressure of CHARNWOOD's timings, which were proving to be over-ambitious across the board, and the need to conform to the advances of the flanking divisions. Consequently, with corps headquarters ordering the Canadians to begin the second phase, General Lyne faced a dilemma. The divisional history explains his decision:

> About 0600 hrs, some 1½ hours after H Hour, the Divisional Commander was faced with the problem of deciding upon H Hour for Phase II. The information available at divisional HQ on the results of Phase I was over-optimistic; and though the divisions on our right and left flank were making some progress, they could not get much further unless we played the part

Unlike the 3rd and 3rd Canadian divisions, the artillery regiments of the 59th Division were equipped with towed 25-pounder guns rather than the 105mm Priest.

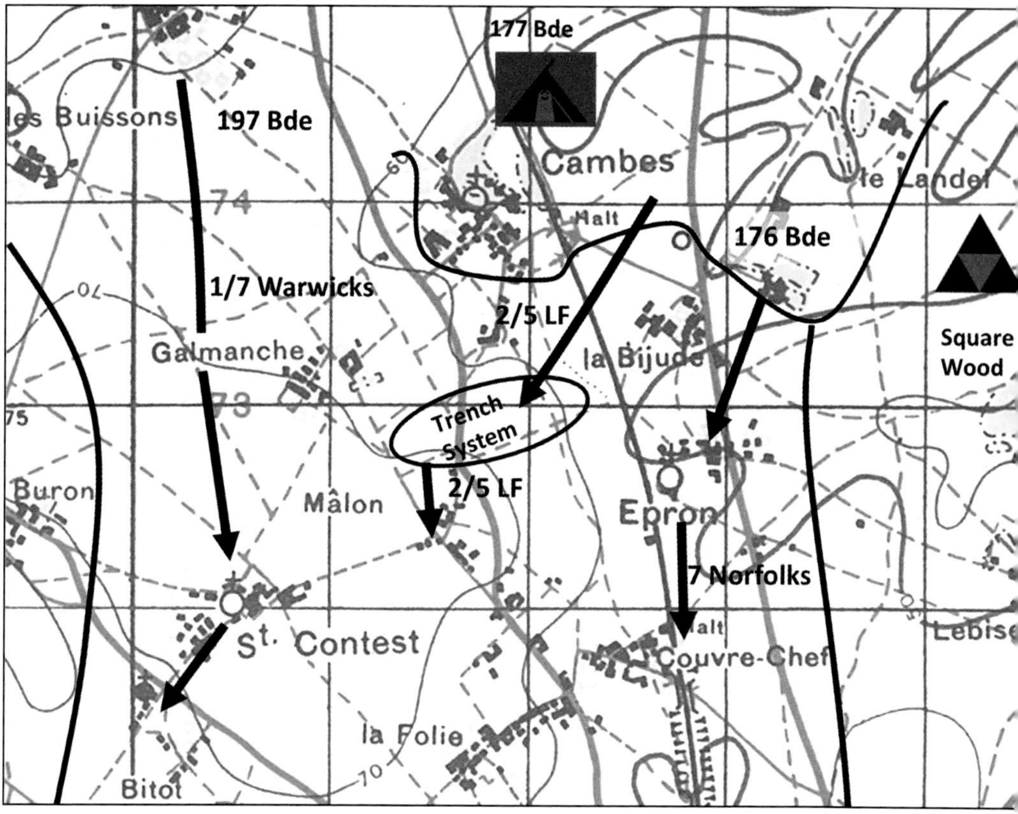

Plan for phase two of the 59th Division's attack.

> expected of us. At 0620 hrs the order reached the battalions concerned that Phase II would start at 0730 hrs.[12]

In this phase the second wave of battalions was to advance around Galmanche and La Bijude, which were still far from secure at this time. 176 Brigade's 7th Royal Norfolks on left were to advance past La Bijude and take Épron and Couvre Chef. On the right, 197 Brigade's objectives were: for 2/5 Lancashire Fusiliers, Mâlon, and for 1/7 Warwicks, St Contest and, 600 yards further south, the hamlet of Bitot.

The problems facing the 59th in the second phase were twofold. In the centre astride the divisional axis the substantial trench system held by I/25 SS *Panzergrenadiers* was still intact; and, on the division's right flank the Canadians were yet to break into Buron, where *Untersturmführer* Kandler's platoon of Panzer IVs was in action firing across the divisional boundary.

The Battle for Épron and St Contest

Assembling in the fields to the east of Château de la Londe, 7 R Norfolks crossed their start line on time, but the leading companies, A and C, were soon under fire. The most significant casualty early in the battle was Lieutenant Colonel Freeland's tactical headquarters radio set. Its loss simply exacerbated the shortage of information that he and other commanders had when making decisions, and it added to the confusion of a battle with multiple events and different interpretations of them. However, all the CO knew was that the leading companies had gone around La Bijude, which as far as he knew had been taken by 6 N Staffs. 'After a lapse of approximately 25 minutes it was obvious that a heavy battle was being fought by the main effort companies.' Little did Colonel Freeland know, but most of the firing was coming from La Bijude. Knowing, however, that a stiff fight was underway, he decided to launch B Company to assist via the left flank, but they were already under fire from enemy positions to the east across the divisional boundary. An attempt by a platoon to attack the Germans was stalled by heavy fire. The situation was resolved by the accompanying tanks of the 13/18 H firing smoke to that flank, which enabled B Company to move on south. Eventually, a message was received from Captain Pettifer via a B Company runner at 1030 hours:

> I am establishing temporary firm base astride road SOUTH of LA BIJUDE 028732. Have 7 tks and 4 [M10] A/TK guns, ammo of all types urgently required. Have met remnants of C Coy and amalgamated with Major Smith in comd. No N STAFFS here. Consider EPRON can be taken as soon as org and control are established. A Coy believed not in EPRON, at present am mopping up to BIJUDE. 1030 hrs.

This was the only message received by Colonel Freeland during the action on a barely operable replacement radio. In his report Colonel Freeland noted that 'Coys must send runners back to Tac HQ if wireless is not working.'

> This message confirmed that things were not going too well with the main effort and that an attack round the right flank with tks had more chance of success especially as 6 N STAFFS. were reported to be in possession of LA BIJUDE, D Coy was then sent by the CO to RV WEST of the Chateau [de la Londe] and to wait for the CO and tks to join them. While the CO was waiting for the tk sqn to come the Bde Comd arrived but did not know anything about how the attack was going or how the N STAFFS were faring. The CO reported the situation to the Brig as he knew it and told him of his intention to attack round the right. The Brig agreed with this action.
>
> On arriving at the FUP for D Coy and tk attack the Brig informed CO that remnants of the main effort and mopping up coys had been coming back in front of the Chateau and that control was required to get them together again.

The solution to La Bijude proposed by Brigadier Fryer was to call forward the single troop of Crocodiles allocated to the brigade. This was the first time the 59th had flame-throwers grouped with them, and Captain Dean, B Squadron's 2iC, objected to the plan:

> It was now seriously suggested that the position be flamed by 8 Troop alone supported by a mere sixteen infantrymen already well and truly pinned-

> down. John's wiser counsels fortunately prevailed. He pointed out that the position demanded a full-scale attack . . . and that to put the Crocs in without adequate infantry to kill the enemy and occupy the ground was merely to lose the Crocs on the strong anti-tank gun defences to no purpose whatsoever. A sound axiom rarely disputed later, after bitter experience: 'No infantry, no show'.

It took the intervention of the commanding officer of 141 RAC (The Buffs) to stop the proposed solo attack by the Crocodiles.

While the other companies were being re-formed behind the château by the Second in Command of 7 R Norfolks, and discussions were being held over the use of Crocodiles, Major Crocker's D Company group advanced but soon discovered that not only were there no N Staffs in La Bijude, but the enemy had almost fully reoccupied it. Major Crocker on his own initiative attacked La Bijude with a troop of 13/18 H in support, some time after midday.

> One [platoon] on the right of the rd working through the ruined buildings [Lt Bartlett], and one pl on the left on the open ground and hedgerows [Lt Bushell]. One pl in res. Considerable machine gun and mortar fire was encountered from the hedgerows surrounding the village and the buildings on the southern outskirts. The whole time heavy mortaring continued and one complete sec of Lt Bushell's pl was hit by a bomb bursting in the trees above them. A/tk (suspected Tiger) was firing from that SE.
>
> Major Cotter, the tk sqn comd, who was in direct comd of the tp of tks, himself was assisting Bartlett's pl from the area of the rd in the SE corner of LA BIJUDE: his tk was almost immediately knocked out by a bazooka and set on fire. The crew bailed out successfully and Major Cotter continued to direct the fire of his tks on foot. Bartlett's pl cleared the buildings and then started on the hedgerows SOUTH of the buildings where there was considerable enemy opposition and it was while silencing a machine gun position with a few men that Bartlett was killed carrying out a very gallant act.
>
> On the left Bushell's pl was under heavy fire from all directions and the pl sgt, Sgt Flowers, was killed by mortar bomb. The tks in this area gave first class support.

By 1400 hours the village of La Bijude, or rather its ruins, were in the hands of the depleted ranks of 7 R Norfolks; but having secured it they still had to take their own objective, Épron. While Colonel Freeland was reorganizing the remnants of his battalion, orders were received from brigade headquarters instructing him to clear Épron, the outskirts of which had apparently been reached by the 13/18 H. The information on which Brigadier Fryer made this decision came from receipt of an incorrect code word, and it took the man on the ground, Colonel Freeland, some time to convince him that the tanks were not in Épron but on Ring Contour 80. He also stated that attacking with a single company where three had already failed would not deliver success.

On the right flank of the division, having crossed their start line on time, the leading troops of 1/7 Warwicks were advancing.

> 0730 zero hour. The battalion began its advance on St Contest with B and C coys forward, A Coy acting as mopping up Coy and D Coy in reserve. Heavy SA fire was now encountered from the direction of GALMANCHE and C Coy was held up. B and D Coys also pinned down by mortar fire. A Coy pushed on and eventually reached the objective at 0900 hours.

Forty minutes later, however, a message was received in Headquarters 197 Brigade from the commanding officer 'describing the whole situation as uncertain'. His three much reduced companies of Warwicks were struggling to hold their positions in St Contest against determined enemy resistance in the buildings, and 'consolidation on the objective did not take place.' Once again, a battalion was on its objective but cannot be said to have held it. As will be explained later, 2nd 5th Lancashire Fusiliers (2/5 LF) were in even greater trouble at Malon.

It was clear to General Lyne that the enemy in the SS trench system south of Cambes was standing firm, and that 7 Norfolks were not strong enough to take Épron without reinforcement. He therefore ordered 177 Brigade to take over responsibility for Galmanche. In the centre, 176 Brigade brought up three of 7 S Staffs companies to take on the SS trench system, while their fourth rifle company was to reinforce the Norfolks at Épron. Having relinquished responsibility for Galmanche, 197 Brigade on the right flank were to now to renew attempts to secure St Contest. This regrouping and replanning took time, further denying the 59th Division the possibility of developing momentum and maintaining pressure on the enemy.

Infantry of 197 Brigade moving forward. The rear man is carrying his platoon's 2-inch mortar.

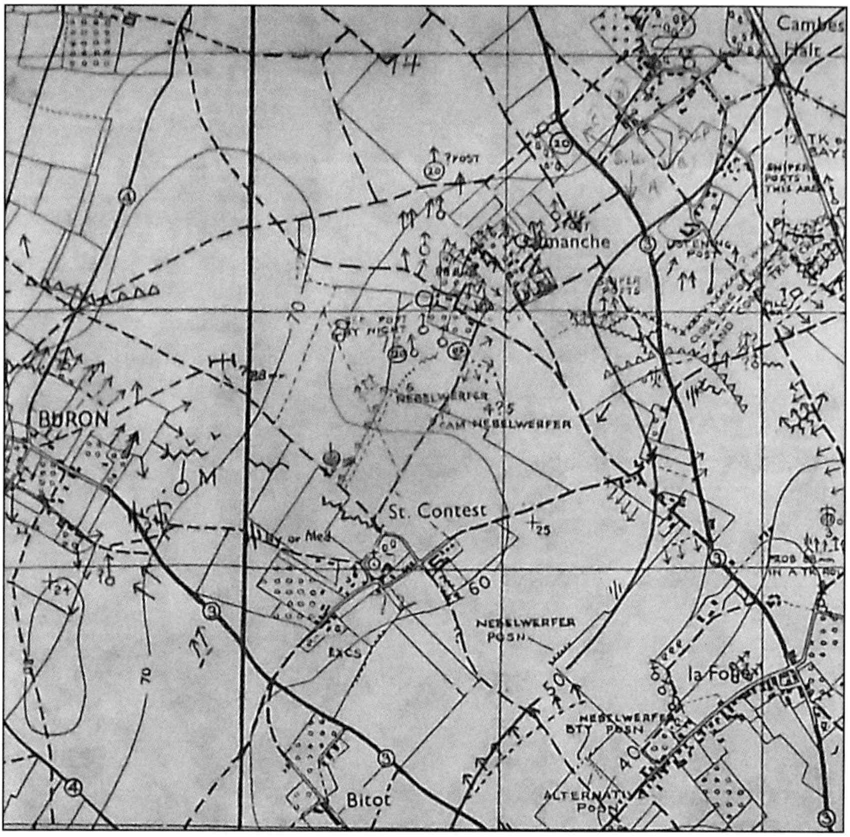

The area of operations of (above) 197 Brigade and (below) 176 Brigade in phase two

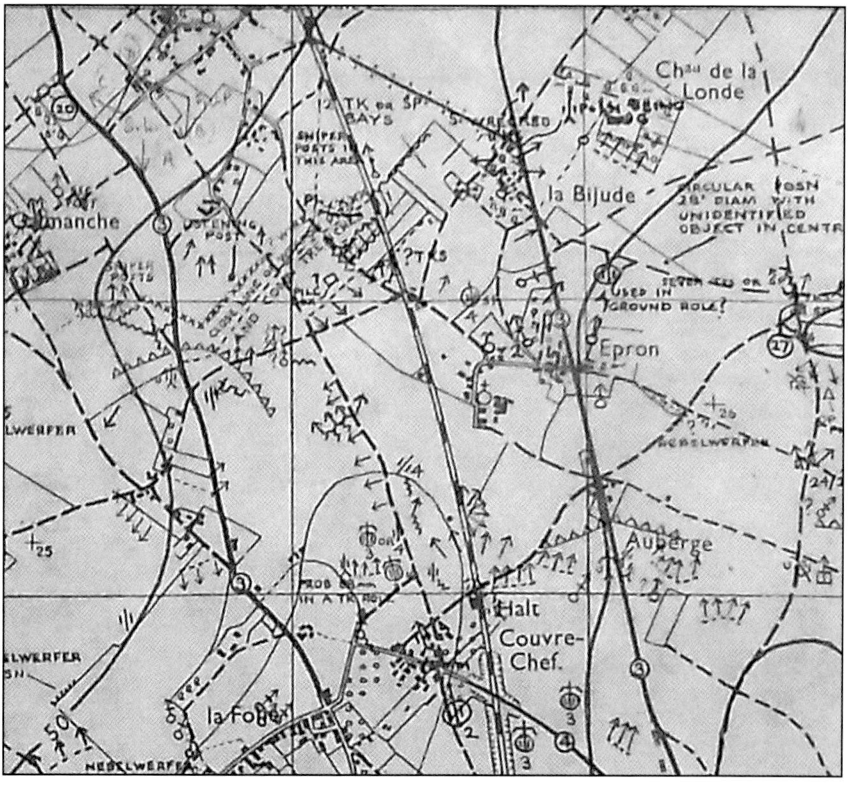

Chapter Eight

Enter the 3rd Canadian Division

Operation CHARNWOOD would see the Canadian 3rd Division and tanks of 2 Canadian Armoured Brigade return to the villages of Buron and Authie, where they had had a bloody engagement with *Standartenführer* Meyer's 25 SS *Panzergrenadiers* on D+1. A month later, they faced the well developed defences of the same SS regiment, and the fighting at Carpiquet had shown all too clearly that attacking the *Hitlerjugend* and closing in on Caen from the north-west would be difficult and costly. Consequently, it was planned that the attacks by the 3rd and 59th Division against arguably softer defences north of the city in the opening moves of CHARNWOOD would outflank the *Hitlerjugend*, compromise their defences and prompt their withdrawal. As we have seen, *Standartenführer* Meyer had requested to withdraw his division south of the Orne early on 8 July but had been refused, and now the *Hitlerjugend* was to fight for its life in a brutal battle against the equally committed Canadians.

Meyer had, however, wondered why Major General Keller's 3rd Canadian Division had not attacked the thinly spread ranks of 26 SS *Panzergrenadiers* and a handful of panzers to the west of Caen in the first phase of CHARNWOOD. The Canadians' blow in the operation's second phase fell further north, while the western approaches to the city were only subject to demonstrations by 7 Canadian Recce Regiment and a squadron of the Inns of Court Yeomanry. The 43rd Wessex Division was to occupy the village of Verson south of Carpiquet, firstly as a diversion and then as flank protection. However, the planned attack on Carpiquet barracks by 8 Cdn Brigade (Operation TROUSERS) was delayed.

The Canadian part of CHARNWOOD would begin at 0730 hours and was of course preceded by a bombardment that included naval gunfire from ships including *Rodney*, *Belfast*, *Emerald* and *Roberts*. The latter was a monitor mounting a pair of 15-inch guns.

> *Roberts* was in support of the Canadians and one of their objectives was the fortified village of Buron, to the north-west of Caen. Having registered the target on the evening preceding the attack, the monitor opened fire at H–60. Her allotment of ammunition was forty rounds, and a Canadian captain watching the shoot at the O.P. offered a prize of twenty 'Sweet Caporals' for each round seen to fall in Buron. All the rounds fell in the village. The Canadian was 'set back' a matter of eight hundred cigarettes, but he paid up without a murmur.[1]

Major General Keller, Commander 3rd Canadian Infantry Division in Normandy.

The attack was to be led by Brigadier Cunningham's 9 Cdn Brigade from the north on a narrow frontage. A pair of battalions were to attack the village of Buron, 1,000 yards west of Galmanche, and the smaller hamlet of Gruchy, which were held by the well dug-in III/25 *Panzergrenadiers* and the regiment's support companies. The Highland Light Infantry of Canada (HLI of C) attacked the substantial village of Buron on the brigade's left, while the Stormont, Dundas and Glengarry Highlanders' (SDG) objective was Gruchy, 500 yards further west. The Sherbrooke Fusiliers provided armoured support and the North Nova Scotia Highlanders (NNS) were initially in reserve, but with orders to exploit from Buron to Authie once the HLI of C had captured the village. In the third phase, 7 Cdn Brigade were to attack Cussy and the Abbaye d'Ardenne; the latter had been the headquarters of 25 SS *Panzergrenadiers* since D+1.

The attack was preceded by another heavy bombardment, this time by 188 assorted guns.

> Beginning at H Hour, four field regiments would shell the enemy's positions forward of the villages for ten to twenty minutes to allow our troops to close in across the open ground in front, while the mediums and heavies pounded strongpoint sites among the houses and beyond. The concentrations would then move forward to cover the further stages of the advance.

An officer of the SDG wrote: 'The artillery fire is unbelievable. Nothing like it has ever been heard. The dust is now so great as to obscure the sun.' The bombardment kept the Germans' heads down as the HLI of C and the SDG

The phase two attack by 9 Canadian Infantry Brigade and the phase three attack by 7 Canadian Infantry Brigade.

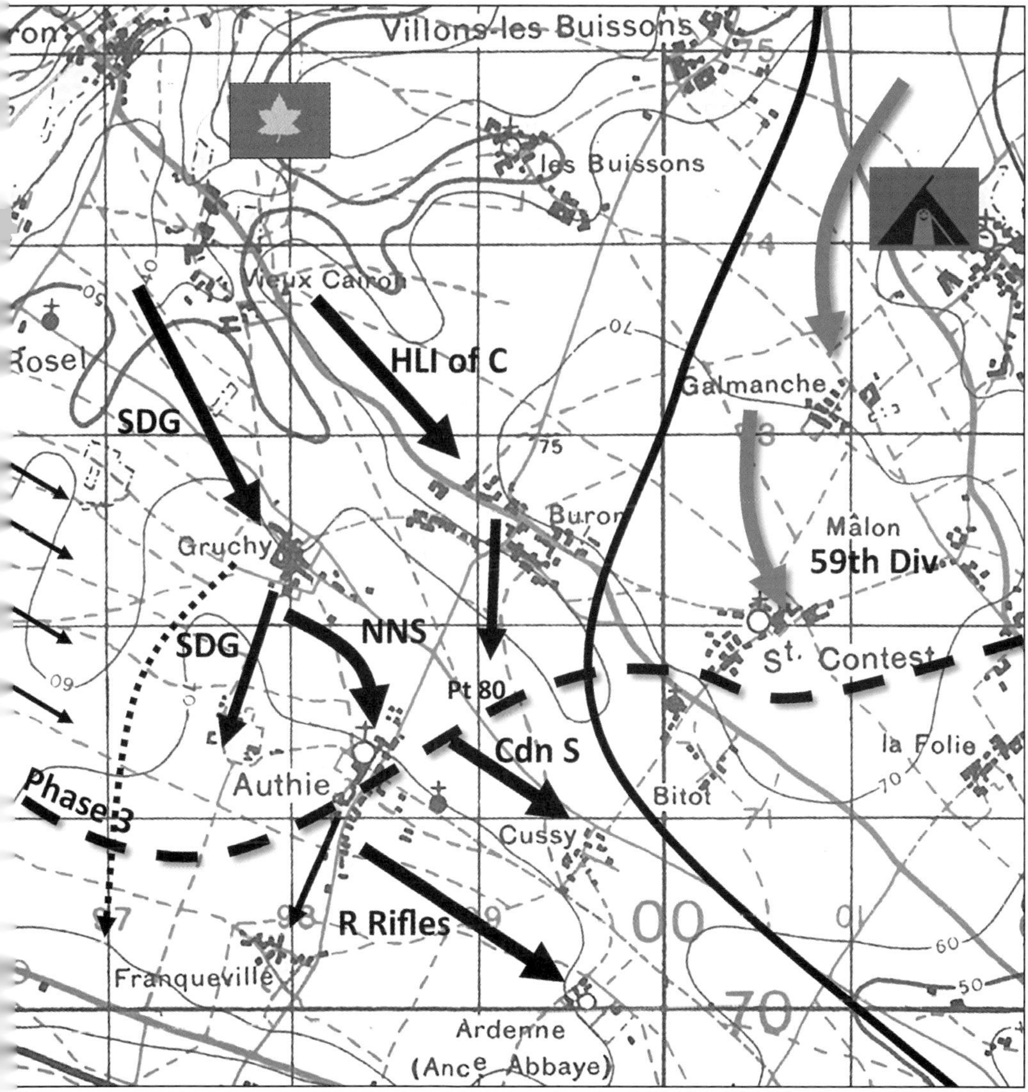

advanced across 1,000 yards of open ground. Nonetheless, as noted in an entry in 9 Cdn Brigade's war diary,

> there were still those [Germans] who the shelling had left intact in slit-trenches and weapon-pits hidden amongst the grain, where they would wait with their automatic weapons, until our men stumbled blindly upon then.

Buron

The HLI of C advanced from their start line near Vieux Cairon, attacking with two companies, "B' Coy going on the left flank from LE BOISSON along the east side of the LES BUISSONS–BURON road, and 'D' Coy going on the right along the VIEUX CAIRON–BURON road.' On the flanks of the infantry were the Shermans of the Sherbrooke Fusiliers, two troops of A Squadron leading, two following in support, squadron headquarters next and finally No. 4 Troop in reserve. The first obstacle to be overcome was the anti-tank ditch. The HLI's war diary states:

> Little opposition was met on the ground until the A/Tk ditch was struck and both coys came under MG fire from the ditch. The ditch and auxiliary defensive positions behind it were cleared after some heavy close-in fighting and many enemy were killed and about 20 PWs were taken.[2]

In the area of the obstacle, the infantry advancing in the open suffered casualties, as did A Squadron, which struck mines and was engaged by the 88mm guns in depth to the south-west. On the right, No. 1 Troop with D Company lost three of its four tanks, while No. 2 troop also lost Shermans to anti-tank fire from II/25 *Panzergrenadiers*' 75mm guns to the east. Unlike the ERY and the 59th Division, the Sherbrookes were operating to the flanks of the infantry companies, but this made little difference. Finding themselves in the enemy's arcs of overlapping fire, there were too few tanks to give the attack any punch. No. 4 Troop was brought up from reserve to replace those Shermans that had been knocked out.

The HLI's diarist noted that 'the battalion command group suffered, for having followed in hard upon the heels of the riflemen, they now lay in the open field, insistently calling for support.' In front of them covering Buron 'the A/tk ditch, which cut both the LES BUISSONS–BURON and VIEUX CAIRON–BURON roads was substantial at around 12ft wide and 15ft deep.' The obstacle in turn was covered by fire from 'a ring of defensive positions most of which contained MGs'.

> These brought down continuous and devastating fire on our tps and it was almost impossible to advance through. Many times our tps were pinned to the ground by it, only to get up and go on as soon as it let up. The tks had to be called fwd on several occasions to aid the inf fwd.

The mines that so concerned B Squadron on the right flank proved not to be a great problem, and eventually the HLI's commanding officer had to order the

An extract of the CHARNWOOD Defences overprint man covering the 3rd Canadian Division's area.

Sherbrooke squadron forward to help break through the Buron defences, with main armament firing HE and Browning machine-gun fire.

To help the infantry break through the SS defences and into Buron, the Canadians had been allocated AVREs and flail tanks, but moving slowly and at close quarters, the funnies needed enemy anti-tank guns to be suppressed. However, with the Sherbrookes suffering tank casualties, this had clearly not been achieved and the Shermans contributed little to the break-in battle. The war diary recorded:

> 'D' Coy under Major J. H. Anderson was the first coy into the village. The tks were not able to follow them in as they struck a minefield on the rt flank. 'D' Coy had to smash its way through alone and clean out all the trenches that comprised the defensive system. They suffered hy cas doing this and progressed on to the orchard on the right fwd side of the village with only half a coy. In the orchard Sgt. Herehenratter reorganized the remnants of two platoons and led the attack to clear out the orchard. Cpl Weitzel already wounded here distinguished himself by leading two men left of his section into an attack on two well sited MG posts. When both of them were hit he carried on and knocked out both posts before he himself was killed.
>
> Meanwhile, 'B' Coy was encountering heavy opposition on the left flank. They charged again and again but were faced with a strong reinforced coy equipped with at least double the usual number of automatic weapons. Tks were called for but were out of communication. Then contact was finally made the tks feared to move fwd because of the minefields. It was sometime before they could be told that the left flank was free.

Out in the fields, the SS *Panzergrenadiers* of 9 Company were the first to be overwhelmed in hand-to-hand fighting, and before long the rest of III/25 *Panzergrenadiers* were also fighting at close quarters. *Untersturmführer* Kandler's five Panzer IVs were also driven back into Buron from the northern edge of the village by artillery fire, but they were still able to cover the flanks. Once the panzers had been driven back, a Canadian officer recorded that the Shermans then 'browsed about the slit trenches immediately in front of Buron, shooting up anything and everything.' However, supporting the infantry in Buron at close quarters was of course an uncomfortable role for the lightly armoured Shermans, and No. 2 troop lost its remaining tanks to *Panzerfausts*. The number of men of C Company HLI still on their feet was dwindling rapidly, and by mid-morning no company was at more than 50 per cent strength.

The HLI were reported as having reached Buron at 0825 hours and at 1010 were in the centre of the village, where they had the remnants of the defenders cornered. 'Here the SS sprang to life and some valiant fighting with rifle and grenade was required to deprive them of it.'

> With the support of the tks 'B' Coy was able to break their way through the defensive ring and proceed to clean up the enemy MG posts one by one. These posts were very well dug in and it was necessary to approach the pit to

Walking wounded. SS prisoners of war being escorted back from Buron.

> the very edge before the enemy guns in them could be silenced. It was very sticky for a long time. In fact several isolated pockets offered up resistance until next morning.

Securing the village was not a speedy process, and the SDG war diarist, clearly taking note of conversation on the brigade radio net, noted, 'The Brig in a very nice way … prods the HLI who are taking a long time in going through BURON.' Despite being under continual fire from St Contest and Bitot, the process of consolidation was underway. As elsewhere, however, 'amongst the rubble individuals and small parties of the enemy clung on desperately fighting throughout the day.'

By late morning the Germans were ready to launch the inevitable counter-attack.

Counter-Attack

Appeals from *Obersturmführer* Millus that his III Battalion was surrounded in Buron resulted in the Panthers of *Hauptsturmführer* von Ribbentrop's 3 Company being ordered by 25 *Panzergrenadiers* to counter-attack the village. Von Ribbentrop recalled that his two platoons were supported by the SPWs (Hanomag half-tracks) of the III/25 which had significant firepower of their own.[3,4]

> Unfortunately, radio communication with the SPWs did not work, I could not speak to the commander of the SPWs, an army *Hauptman* [Steger], by

> radio, who could not in turn speak to his battalion headquarters in Buron, and I stressed strongly from the turret of my panzer the absolute necessity of advancing together.[5,6]

Thus, the attack began without proper coordination between panzers, SPWs and dismounted infantry. Von Ribbentrop continued:

> My company started the attack with one panzer platoon advancing to the left of Buron and two on the right. We advanced in two quick bounds, with a platoon taking turn to give covering fire just as we had practised on exercise.

Unterscharführer Freiberg was commanding the third Panther platoon on the right and recalled:

> Our first attack from the Abbey [Ardenne] went in the wrong direction. When we tried to engage an enemy target our main gun failed. Since my crew could not repair it, I made the appropriate call on the radio. The answer was to continue on and use the panzers' machine guns. Driving fast, we crossed the open terrain to the village of Buron.
>
> As were passing an opening in a wall there were two explosions and two Panthers burst into flames. We immediately fired the machine guns into the opening, where I spotted movement followed by a flash, and we were hit on

Hauptmann Fritz Steger (left), commander of the III Battalion's Hanomags. *Unterscharfuhrer* Heinz Freiberg (right).

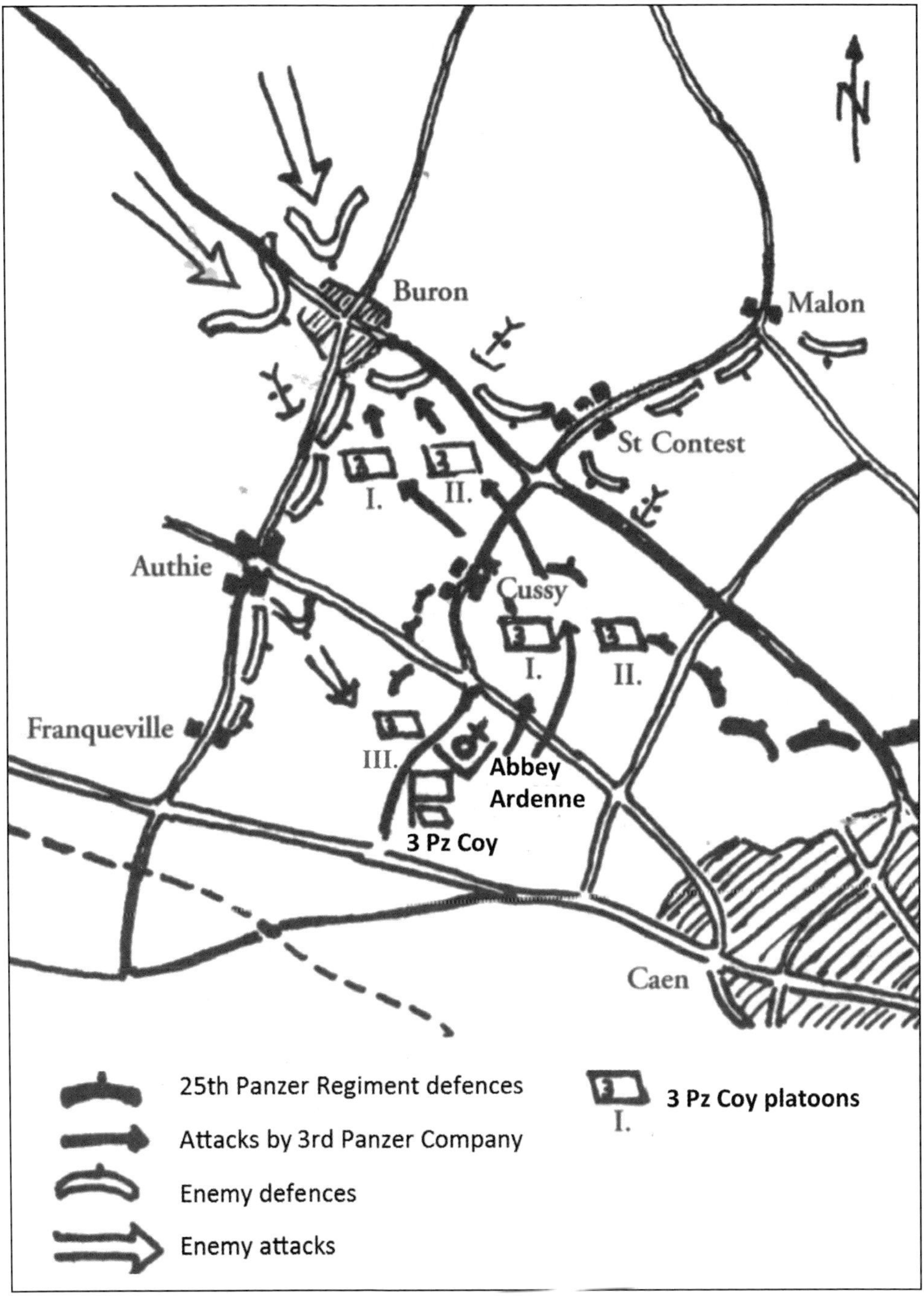

A sketch of the action of 3rd Panzer Company at Buron on 8 July.

> the gun mantlet [the thickest armour on the Panther] and the armour-piercing shell fell into the tank and the gunner was wounded in the face. I also had a small splinter wound to my left arm. We, the turret crew, bailed out and because of the heavy fire took cover behind the panzer. The driver and radio operator in the hull had not noticed what had happened and sat there with the engine idling. I remounted the panzer [onto the engine deck] and shouted, 'Reverse march!' through a throat mike which was hanging out of the turret.
>
> After reversing a few metres, the aerial mount which I was using as a foothold was shot off along with the heel of my boot! After pulling back 500 metres we reached our grenadiers, where my gunner and loader had arrived on foot.[7]

Von Ribbentrop and the rest of his Panthers were still fighting south of Buron.

> We reached the outskirts of the village and engaged some tanks but were now faced with a new problem around the village: the hedges and ditches, which were confusing. At that moment a Canadian Pak [anti-tank gun] must have opened fire; two or three vehicles went up in flames to my right and we had no other option but to withdraw to the start line.
>
> From here the platoon on the left engaged a column of enemy tanks and supported the hard-pressed infantry in Buron. The rest of the company's panzers were positioned around the Abbey all day, enduring heavy artillery fire, but preventing the Canadians from advancing.[8]

The HLI's war diary noted that 'B Coy was in for a shaky time when it was attacked by eight Tigers [*sic*].' The HLI's commanding officer, Lieutenant Colonel Griffiths, brought two troops of M10s of 62 Anti-Tank Regiment into the village and reported that 'such a formidable defence, together with that of the supporting squadron of 27 Cdn Armd Regt [Sherbrooke Fusiliers], proved too much for the German armour ... The counter-attack was repulsed and the tanks [and M10s] in support of that coy did noble work in knocking out six of the eight and driving the other two away at the cost of three SPs.'[9] German records show that this attack had cost von Ribbentrop seven Panthers knocked out or damaged, but the Canadian infantry was also paying a heavy price in the battle for Buron. The fighting was 'bitter', and the battalion's war diary noted:

> Mortaring, and shelling by the enemy from ST CONTEST and BITOT on the left flank were exacting a heavy toll by the minute. So continuous and severe was the shelling that even slit trenches were not safe. The enemy followed his old habits of bringing to bear all the fire he possessed on his own position once it was overrun.
>
> During the afternoon the enemy continued to shell every corner of the village systematically and inflicted many cas on our tps. There were too many cas for our S.Bs. to handle and not enough Jeeps or stretchers available to handle all the cas.

Gruchy

Meanwhile, an hour and five minutes after receiving the codeword TALBOT to initiate CHARNWOOD's phase two, the Stormont, Dundas and Glengarry Highlanders (SDG) began their 1,000-yard advance across open fields to Gruchy at 0735 hours.Two companies were leading, with B on the right noted as holding the main effort, and A on the left. This smaller objective, with fewer buildings for the enemy to shelter in, was almost certainly more effectively neutralized by the Allied artillery bombardment than Buron. The war diary recorded at 0745 hours after a speedy advance that 'Fwd tps have reached fwd enemy [outpost] posns and have not yet drawn fire', but at 0749 'they now come under mortar and medium arty fire.' The German defenders, the Pioneer Company of 25 SS *Panzergrenadiers*, recovered from the bombardment and as observers watched B Company disappear into the smoke and dust surrounding the village, the sound of small-arms fire increased. In addition, 'A Coy was held up on the LEFT by MMG fire.' The Sherbrooke Fusiliers' diarist observed that 'The Arty can shake the Hitler Youth but it can not stop them killing until they are dead.' Meanwhile, mortar rounds fell amongst the SDG's reserve companies following up in the open.

The SDG's uncommonly full war diary is worth quoting at length for a flavour of the battle:

> 0816 Bde ask us if the Arty program in going too fast and we reply 'yes'. It is therefore slowed down as it is evidently a long slogging match to get anywhere today.
>
> 0825 The NNS are told to be ready to move at short notice. The HLI are having a difficult time at BURON and are pinned down. We ask Bde to put down Arty fire on AUTHIE as the enemy is lively in that direction.
>
> 0830 The tanks [B Squadron] are mopping up between BURON and GRUCHY. C.O. asks Bde to give some counter mortar fire as fwd coys are now under continuous mortar and arty fire. Bde replies that they will try if we can spot the direction. From 0815 to 0900 hrs VIEUX CAIRON and the rear parts of the Bn again under heavy mortar and rocket fire.
>
> 0900 The enemy A/Tk gun[s] between GRUCHY are now reported as knocked out. Our tanks being shelled.
>
> 0920 [Code Word] 'FLOUR ABLE' Fwd troops in GRUCHY.
>
> 0925 No movement or fire from the Chateau [de St Louet, west of Authie].

At 0945 hours the battalion reported that 'after some close and severe fighting' Grunchy was in their hands and that 'the CO is regrouping for Step II in the operation.' The SDG's diarist continued:

> The NNS are ordered to go in from the RIGHT. The HLI are having a difficult time at BURON and their communication with the tanks is not that it could be. NNS are told to move on fast as possible.

A Vickers machine gun of the Cameron Highlanders of Ottawa joins the fire plan with the .303Z enhanced range bombardment round.

> 0950 The Unit [SDG] is now ready to take the CHATEAU ST LOUET.
> 1005 HQ again mortared and shelled . . . Our 3″ pl is doing a good job; each mortar having fired over 200 round so far today.

One of the jobs allotted 7 Cdn Recce Regiment was the task of 'mopping-up' once the Infantry overran their objectives. Lieutenant Ayer was supporting the SDG with the sixteen carriers from B Squadron's scout troop blazing away. The regimental historian wrote:

> Unfortunately, the infantry were having a hell of a time. At Buron the Highland Light Infantry had already received 400 casualties [*sic*], while at Gruchy, the S.D.G. had been stopped by very heavy machine gun fire just outside the town. Lt. Ayer, who, with his 15 or 16 carriers, was waiting for the S.D.G.'s to push on, saw this. So, without hesitation, he charged right

> through them, in real old cavalry style, right into the middle of an enemy company position. With grenades and Bren guns firing at point-blank range, they drove the enemy from his dug-outs, killing dozens, wounding others, and capturing 25 or 30 prisoners. This act of extreme gallantry on the part of all ranks allowed a complete battalion of infantry to advance into Gruchy. This fact was confirmed later that evening when Lt Pavey was talking to ... commanding officer of the S.D.G.'s. He said, 'I'd like to thank that Officer. Without his aid along with his crazy carrier crews, I doubt very much if we would have got into Gruchy.'

The SDG and the recce carriers had fought well in Gruchy and, in the process, the young *Hitlerjugend* soldiers of the 25 SS *Panzergrenadiers*' Pioneer Company were reported by regimental headquarters as being 'annihilated in the fighting' and 'dying in their positions'. The Canadians, however, reported a number of Germans withdrawing in the direction of Buron who were shot up by the Shermans of the Sherbrookes' B Squadron, which had followed the infantry through and around Gruchy. Those Germans who escaped would have strengthened the defences of Buron.[10]

Ring Contour 80

Just south of Buron (see map page 179) is a piece of high ground that dominated the subsequent objectives of Authie, Cussy and Abbaye d'Ardenne, all of which were important CHARNWOOD objectives. The significance of this unspectacular piece of ground was explained by General Crerar to fellow Canadian General Simmonds:

> The possibilities in that direction depended on our ability to secure control of Buron and the push out into the open over the face of the very gentle rise leading to our objectives on the farther side. As long as this deadlock persisted, we were condemned to immobility, an embarrassment of which the enemy was quick to take advantage with his artillery and mortars.[11]

According to the Sherbrooke Fusiliers, the problem was that 'In the early afternoon the enemy held the high ground SOUTH of BURON, and it was A Sqn, with Sp of medium arty alone that was responsible for regaining the initiative upon which the success of the div plan depended.' Having secured the exits to Buron some time previously, 'Five tks under Comd of Maj S.V. RADLEY-WALTERS reached the high ground SOUTH of BURON.'[12] They were eventually joined over the course of several hours on this key piece of terrain by the M10 tank destroyers of the British 62 Anti-Tank Regiment RA, attached from Corps Troops, two machine-gun platoons and a company of HLI of C to hold the ground. According to the HLI's war diary at 1600 hours, the depleted '"C" Coy was ordered up to high ground to the south of BURON', and the Canadian CMHQ report concluded: 'Thus precariously established, the position held firm. An uneasy situation had been set right. The advance could be resumed.'[13]

Authie and Château de St Louet

To complete the next phase of the divisional plan, 9 Cdn Brigade was to capture the ground to the south. The village of Authie was to be attacked by the North Nova Scotia Highlanders (NNS), while the Château de St Louet farm complex was to be secured by a company of the SDG. This latter objective was 1,000 yards south of Gruchy and 500 yards west of Authie.

During the late morning, with fighting in the villages and fields still going on, the *Hitlerjugend* observed fresh Canadian troops assembling in orchards south of Buron and Gruchy. Consequently, every German gun, mortar and *Nebelwerfer* that could be spared engaged the Canadians as they formed up for their attack. Heavy casualties, particularly amongst the NNS's officers, resulting from this strike were confirmed in the war diary. This German fire, combined with delays in Buron and in securing Ring Contour 80, meant that the advance on Authie and the château did not begin until 1430 hours.

Preceded by the now familiar heavy bombardment, which crept south towards the objectives, the NNS and a company of the SDG set off. Shermans of the Sherbrookes provided fire from Ring Contour 80 to the east while others were in close support. The regiment recorded at 1515 hours 'With the tide turning in

Soldiers of the SDG waiting in their assembly area to be called forward to battle.

our favour, all three sqns gave sp to the Nth NS Highrs into AUTHIE and the SD & G Highrs into CH DE ST LOUET.'

However, the *Nebelwerfer* regiment supporting the *Hitlerjugend*, and every mortar within range, continued to engage the Canadian infantry and tanks that were following closely behind their protective barrage. By 1530 the Canadians were reported as having broken into both objectives, and they had been secured within the hour. The open fields of fire surrounding the objectives, which had been of considerable advantage to the Germans, now became a disadvantage as they withdrew. Though the SS offered some resistance, the opinion was that 'their enthusiasm had waned, and parties of them were observed … to be withdrawing southwards in disorder.' Then, 'The fugitives were shot down by our

A Canadian 3-inch mortar team. The limestone spoil from the mortar pit has been camouflaged.

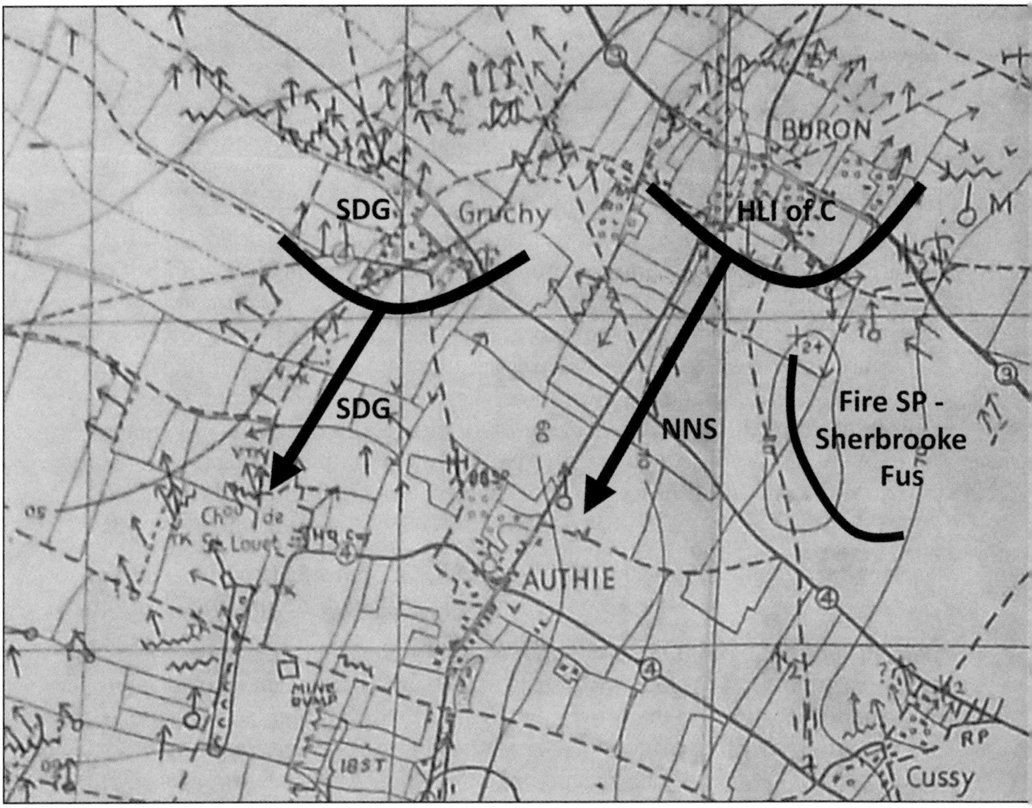

The Canadian attacks on Authie and Château de St Louet.

artillery and some of the armoured cars of 7 Canadian Recce Regiment approaching from the west.' The SDG, however, took twenty-five prisoners in the château area and had this to say of them:

> They are all boys of 17 to 18 years of age and are supposed to be some of Hitler's best troops. They are certainly fanatics. They are sick and tired of the war and that they have had no mail, papers or news for the 4 weeks they have been opposed to us.

The capture of Buron, Gruchy, Authie and Château St Louet effectively completed CHARNWOOD's phase two in the 3rd Canadian Division's area. Phase three, which was to be undertaken by 7 Cdn Brigade, would see a change of direction of the axis to the south-east, with the objectives being Cussy and the Abbaye d'Ardenne.

Chapter Nine

The Afternoon Attack of the 59th Division

Starting at H Hour and advancing on a narrow frontage of just 2,500 yards in the centre of I Corps' CHARNWOOD assault, the inexperienced 59th Division was facing a severe test. Pitted against enemy troops in very well-prepared defensive positions, the leading battalions of 176 and 197 Brigades had made slow progress during the morning. With the SS trench system south-west of Cambes still firmly in the hands of the *Hitlerjugend*, Galmanche only tenuously held and 7 Norfolks lacking the combat power to take Épron without reinforcement, Major General Lyne recast his plan – 'The divisional commander brought HQ 177 Inf Bde into the battle, 2/6 S Staffs reverting to their command.' With all three brigades committed to battle, Brigadier Elrington (177 Brigade) was now responsible for Galmanche and deployed a company of 5 S Staffs to come under command of 2/6 S Staffs to assist in breaking the resistance around the château and farm complex. It was only later that the parlous state of the 2/6th was realized, whereupon the battalion was withdrawn to Anisy and the 5th Battalion took over the taking of Galmanche. Meanwhile, 176 Brigade brought up three companies of 7 S Staffs to take on the SS trench system, while the battalion's A Company was to reinforce 7 Norfolks in their fight for Épron. Having relinquished responsibility for Galmanche, 197 Brigade were to now concentrate on advancing south to take St Contest. The regrouping involved in General Lyne's revised plan put the 59th Division well behind the 3rd Division and meant that the latter had an open flank to protect. It was hoped that this rejuvenated attack would deliver momentum to the division's advance on Caen.

St Contest and Mâlon

The small village of Mâlon was the site headquarters of II/25 SS *Panzergrenadiers*. By this stage in the operation it was probably defended by a mixture of members of the regiment driven back from the area of Galmanche, while St Contest was held by 11 Company of the III Battalion.

Since before dawn the battalions of 197 Brigade that were to launch CHARNWOOD's second phase had been moving forward behind the assault battalions and had been halted in their FUP since 0400 hours, waiting while 2/6 S Staffs attacked Galmanche. As normal, the Germans engaged areas where follow-up troops were likely to be forming up. Fusilier Pollitt of 2/5 Lancashire Fusiliers

(2/5 LF) recalled marching before dawn to Cambes, where they were to wait in an adjacent field and

> were directed with instructions to dig slit trenches. We needed no second bidding and at once set to work on the soft ground. In no time at all my trench was 18in deep but at this point I struck a flinty subsoil with my spade and it became impossible to dig deeper.
>
> How much time had passed since the flare had given the enemy warning of our imminent arrival it is difficult to say, but now at last they began to react. First indication of enemy action was of several indistinct sounds followed by what seemed like a substantial flight of geese immediately overhead and then an urgent 'swishing' sound followed by seven sharp explosions very close at hand. Some sixth sense alerted me to danger and I jumped into my shallow slit trench and lay face down. The trench was just deep enough to allow my body to be below ground level but it was a close thing and being face down I couldn't be absolutely sure no part of me was exposed.

The SS mortars were soon followed by the *Nebelwerfer* bombs of 93 *Werfer* Regiment.

Pollitt continued:

> The Germans had opened fire with their seven-barrelled mortars known to us as 'sobbing sisters' or 'moaning minnies'. Their distinctive screaming noise as bombs fell to earth was designed to put us in a state of panic. Fear they quite often generated, but I never saw British troops in a state of panic throughout any actions that I took part in. As I lay in my entirely inadequate shelter I at first counted the bombs in the knowledge that after the seventh there would be some respite, but the barrage achieved such a level of intensity that the bombs were falling continuously. The noise was incredible, soil was being thrown into the air and pieces of equipment left at the side of the trench were being damaged or destroyed. This was our first experience of coming under shell fire.

With the shells of the artillery barrage passing overhead as phase two of the Corps' plan began, 2/5 LF advanced on Mâlon and the 1/7 Warwicks on St Contest. The latter were supported by A Squadron of the ERY. Lieutenant Colonel Jerram described 1/7 Warwicks wading through the standing crops to St Contest:

> The roar . . . was terrific. It was quite impossible to hear any one gun or shell or another man speak; there was just a surging roar and the whole landscape was blotted out in smoke and dust. Simultaneously the same sort of thing was going on at Buron with the Canadians. German mortar bombs were coming back, bullets from all directions with an occasional 88-mm shell passing like an express train.
>
> During this advance C Coy were to be mauled in a vicious German flanking attack and held up by minefields and stubborn defence by 12th SS.[1]

The multi-barrelled 150mm *Nebelwerfer* 41.

Major White was awarded the MC for 'his determination and coolness' in keeping his company moving despite half his men becoming casualties, and leading the rest to take St Contest. This was a baptism of fire that Captain Phillips recalled:

> On the right Lieut. Jack Pritchard's platoon had had to assault a thick hedge planted on the earth rampart typical of the Norman countryside. At least twenty weapon slits were cut in this hedge. Beside them were cover trenches enabling the ... 12th SS to live through our barrage ...
>
> On the left a great swathe had been cut in the standing corn, clearing a field of fire for a machine-gun position which appeared as no more than a slight mound among the stubble. Between the machine gun and the corn, the open field ... was strewn with trip-wire grenades. Barbed wire lined the edge of the crops where our riflemen emerged into the open.

The catalogue description of an Army Film and Photographic Unit (AFPU) team's film of the attack provides a succinct description of the action:

> Two universal carriers, one carrying an OP detachment from 116th Field Regiment RA and the other ('Dog Star' [see photograph, page 266]) carrying Tactical Headquarters of the 1/7th Battalion Royal Warwickshire Regiment's 'D' company and tanks from the East Riding Yeomanry's 'A'

The Warwicks photographed at the beginning of their advance.

> Squadron [advanced] towards the village of St Contest. Shermans belonging to the tank squadron's HQ troop in particular a Firefly armed with a 17-pounder gun manoeuvre behind the crest of a low ridge in front of St Contest to take up hull-down firing positions and to avoid mortar bombardment while one or two infantrymen dig-in in the foreground; smoke from bursting mortar bombs flares up in the waist-high wheat. An RAF Typhoon fighter-bomber supporting the attack flies low overhead. One of the HQ troop Shermans opens fire with its co-axial Browning .30 calibre machine-gun on positions impeding the Warwickshires' assault.[2]

Untersturmführer Kandler was in action with his five Panzer IVs from positions alongside III/25 *Panzergrenadiers* south of Buron across the divisional boundary. From here he was able to engage the British tanks advancing around Galmanche and south towards Mâlon and St Contest. He later recalled:

> From this location we could engage the Englanders in their flank at almost 90 degrees. Although the range was between 800 and 1,000 metres, the flank of a Sherman made a larger target; it was also the thinnest armour and was more vulnerable than the frontal armour. My gunner Willy Schnittfinke had quick reactions, which was vital for our survival, and responding to my orders and target indications over the intercom or by the pressure of my legs on his shoulder, he calmly identified the target with accuracy. We could easily see our hits and we alone knocked out five enemy tanks. We also engaged enemy infantry with our *Spandaus*; watching the tracer through the gun sight we could see that we inflicted heavy casualties and were forcing them to take cover. During this time, we fired 10,000 rounds of machine-gun ammunition.
>
> The area we fired from [near Buron] had plenty of hedges which provided us with cover and after firing we moved a short distance to new positions to

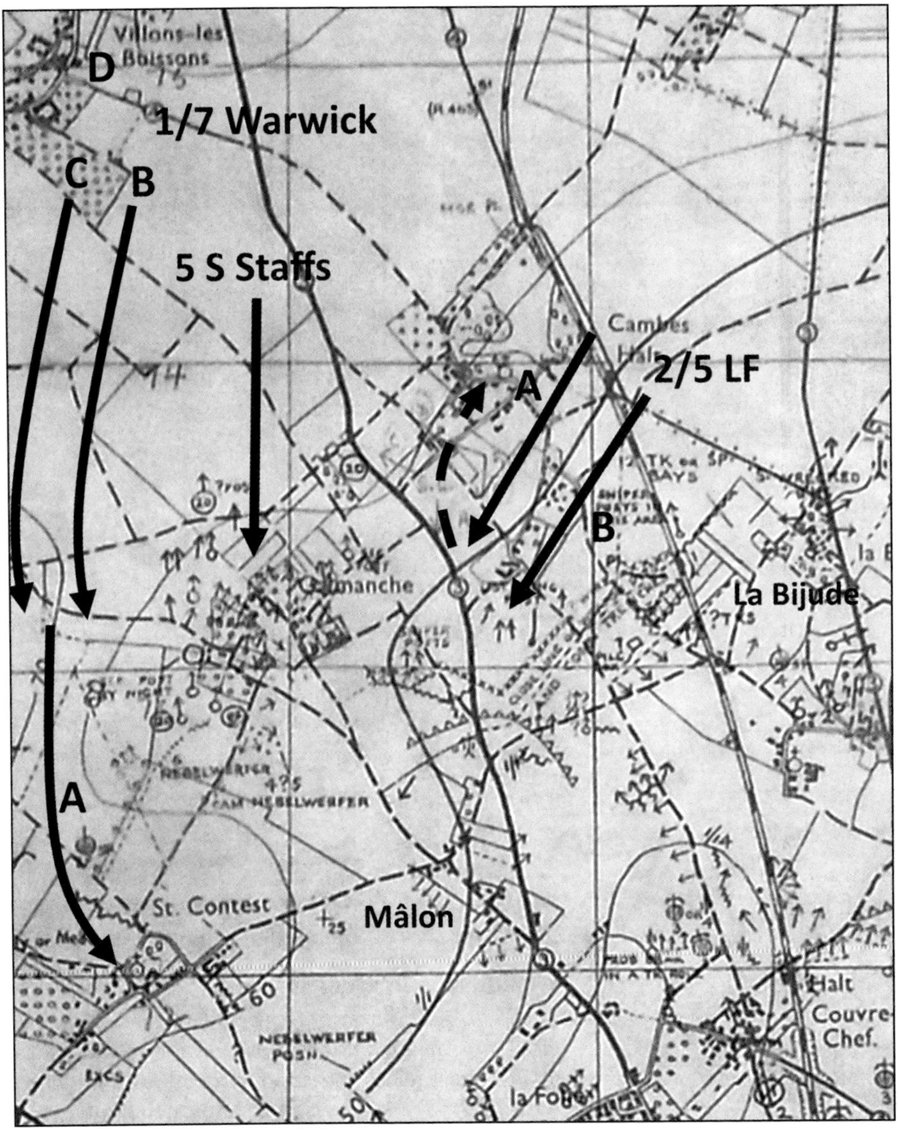

The advance of 1/7 Warwicks and 2/5 Lancashire Fusiliers in CHARNWOOD's second phase.

> stop the enemy targeting our muzzle flashes; consequently we did not lose a single panzer.[3]

The Warwicks' C and D Company were pinned down by machine-gun and mortar fire, but suppressive artillery, tank and small-arms fire permitted the mopping-up company, A Company, to come up and deliver the battalion's assault on St Contest. They entered the village at 0900 hours, and 'a patrol sent forward to Bitot established that the main enemy forces had withdrawn.' As usual, however, this was not the end of the fighting.

> Snipers who had been overrun continued their fire throughout the day until captured. Consolidation on the objective did not take place at once owing to a temporary breakdown in communication and owing to the fact that isolated M.G. positions continued to hold out.[4]

Major Knight recorded that '1/7 R Warwicks had a long day of confused, hard, plugging fighting with very heavy casualties; but by nightfall they were firmly established on their objective [less Bitot], to the great benefit of the Canadians on their right.' The soldiers of 9 Cdn Brigade would dispute the timeliness of this, but the fact is that the wide interlocking and overlapping fields of fire between villages in this generally open area were ideal for the Germans' defence based on fire. Such was the *Hitlerjugend*'s deployment that both the 3rd Canadian and the 59th Division received heavy flanking fire from across their neighbour's boundary.

The divisional history also provides a glimpse of 2/5 Lancashire Fusiliers' attack on Mâlon in the centre of the 59th's attack:

> 2/5 LF had the misfortune to come under very heavy and accurate fire as soon as they appeared in the open among the standing crops, through which the enemy had cut lanes of fire. This fire came not only from the low ridge directly to their front, but, more serious still, from those evil trenches south-west of La Bijude. The leading companies lay down in the corn, control was consequently lost and they remained there, suffering heavy casualties from mortar fire.

The Fusiliers had advanced into an enemy fire pocket and were pinned down in the open despite several attempts to get forward. The battalion's war diary records:

> By noon after several rallies only a small advance had been made. 'A' Coy were in the southern part of CAMBES at pt 018733 and 'B' Coy were on the rly at sq 0275. Casualties had been heavy. 3 Coy Comds and the IO were amongst them. 'D' Coy was brought in to reinforce 'A' Coy, who at that time was only approx. 1½ pls in strength. 'C' Coy were covering 'B' who had also suffered heavy casualties. All this time Bosche mortar fire was still falling and our own mortars were out of action.[5]

The German account of the battle is more complete. *Sturmbannführer* Waldmuller's I/25 *Panzergrenadiers* stood in the way of 2/5 LF's advance on Mâlon. In those 'evil trenches' out in the fields, they had survived the heaviest of the Allied bombardment and, as described by Kurt Meyer, the battalion 'Stood like a bulwark on the battlefield, unshaken despite the enemy's enormous superiority in men and equipment. They defeated every attack and the Tommies failed to

A marked air photograph from 2/5 LF's war diary of the enemy defences around Mâlon. Note the forward edge of the Germans' trench system.

overwhelm the battalion.' This was largely due to the intervention of *Sturmbannführer* Prinz's Mk IVs of II/Battalion 12 SS Panzer Regiment. One of the panzer company's war diaries recorded:

> Because a new breakthrough was reported, the recce platoon of the regiment, with the Flak Platoon of the II Battalion and the command tank, led by the Commander [Prinz], were detached forward to La Folie. The breakthrough by armoured fighting vehicles reported by the regiment did not prove to be real, and the panzers reached Mâlon without engaging the enemy; there they supported the *Panzergrenadiers* [I/Battalion] and elements deployed east of La Folie, covering out towards Hill 64 [east of the divisional boundary].

When General Lyne came forward in the early afternoon to review the situation personally, and with 2/5 LF having suffered 111 casualties, he ordered the battalion to withdraw into Cambes at 1630 hours under cover of a barrage. For Fusilier Pollitt and his platoon, the GOC's decision came just in time:

> Exactly when this decision was made, and how long it took to filter through to our company, I know not, but at the precise moment when our little group was about to move more clearly into the sights of the German machine gunners, a runner came from company with instructions for us to return to where the rest of our men were waiting on the road in front of the village. Much later, we took shelter in a nearby stand of trees, where I lay down and, without even digging a trench for protection, I slept.
>
> This day, without a shadow of doubt, proved to be the worst day of the whole war. We had failed to gain our objective and A, B and C companies

Soldiers of 2/5 Lancashire Fusiliers advancing to battle.

had suffered appalling casualties. Rumours circulated that more than half the battalion had perished, but later this figure proved to be greatly exaggerated. We had not however taken a yard of ground that we had been able to hold.

The 2/5 LF subsequently became the reserve for attacks later that day. The fire from the *Hitlerjugend* defenders in Mâlon and the surrounding area, from well-prepared defensive positions, along with the supporting panzers, was simply too much for the Lancashire Fusiliers to face.

St Contest was eventually secured by 1/7 R Warwicks with A Squadron ERY, but they were pinned down in the ruins by the *Hitlerjugend*'s artillery and mortar fire and were unable to dig in until that evening. The 59th Division had penetrated the *Hitlerjugend*'s positions but they had certainly not broken through. As during EPSOM, German positions held out, and small groups and individuals fought on, successfully slowing the tempo of the division's operations throughout the day.

The Capture of Épron

Meanwhile, the Adjutant of the 13/18 H, Captain Airey Neave, was uncomplimentary about the mounting delays, in this case, in launching the attack on Épron:

> Why the operation was so slow up to this point I cannot say except that there is little doubt that this Brigade is far behind what it ought to be in fitness for battle; they seemed to lack a proper grasp of things and this in addition to their other shortcomings had caused them an enormous quantity of unnecessary casualties. But the opposition as far as we could make out at this stage was not more than two companies in the trenches and a bunch of well-trained snipers in Épron.
>
> However, the result was as usual, and we were left sitting on objectives without support and our tank casualties were about 8 – Delaval's tank was knocked out by a bazooka and Toto had his arm broken.
>
> At about 2030 the big attack went in on the trenches and at the same time Delaval pushed into Épron. The barrage was terrific, and flame-throwers and flails performed with some success as well.

With the attack to be delivered by his own D Company 7 R Norfolk and the fresh A Company 7 S Staffs, plus the depleted C Squadron 13/18 H and its RHQ tanks, Colonel Freeland continued his report:

> At 2030 hrs the tks moved into the hedgerows and opened a devastating fire against all buildings and hedges in EPRON using 17 pdr, 75mm (HE and Browning). After 5 mins of this the inf went in and D Coy attacked magnificently.

The Crocodiles of Lieutenant Beechy's 8 Troop 141 RAC have a slightly different story. They joined the attack at H Hour and set off, only to realize that the

Captain Airey Neave photographed later in the campaign as a prisoner of war.

infantry had not followed. Corporal Hischier commanding one of the Crocodiles recalled:

> There were strong anti-tank positions there, as we had feared. Later we crossed the start line behind a troop of Sherman flails. My troop leader noticed our infantry had not joined in behind so we were ordered back. Unfortunately, this had primed Jerry that an attack was imminent and the shelling was extremely heavy. Once again we set out and saw our flail was well on the way to the railway embankment. As the flail turned to one side I went up over the embankment, heart in mouth as my thin underbelly showed briefly. Then we were among the trenches. I gave a long squirt of flame up the left-hand one, saw my troop leader close to me just the other side of the right-hand trench. The turret gunner was using the Besa to good effect when

he had a double feed. I told him to use the 75mm on HE and gave him gun control. He scored a hit some 100 yards ahead in a low bush in which something blew up.

Jerry helmets showed in the trench in front and the flame thrower swept along it. Then my face hit the periscope and a sheet of flame flung me into the bottom of the turret. I couldn't breathe as the flames roared out of the driving compartment. Struggling upwards I somehow pushed the hatches open, lifted myself up. The gunner and wireless operator were following me so I rolled over the side of my tank and flattened myself to the ground, looking for the driver to appear. But we had been hit by a 75mm through the flame-thrower mounting and both driver and flame-thrower gunner had been killed instantly. As my other two crewmen joined me grenades came sailing over us. We promptly rolled into the right-hand trench. I then realised how badly we were burned, unable to use our pistols.

Following their false start, Crocodile commander Lieutenant Beechy wrote:

> We must have had every anti-tank gun ranged on us, after withdrawing the first time we had given our position away. We had hardly started out again when a Flail tank went up on our right and our troop corporal's tank [Hischier's] on out left also got it.

A note in the squadron war diary exemplifies the technical problems with the Crocodile at this stage in the campaign, having been rushed into service:

> Right from the start Lt. Beechey could only get unignited shots from his gun and shortly afterwards had his gearbox compartment penetrated by a 75mm which almost completely dislocated his steering. Nevertheless, moving in wide circles, he continued to give fire support and direct his Tp Sgt. Shortly afterwards the Sgt's [fame] pressure failed, and he came out of action.

Captain Harry Bailey added details of the dramatic arrival of 7 and 9 Troops on the scene:

> Then into this twilight arena Sydney and Peter roared and clattered to the rescue. Released from 197 Brigade only minutes before and without any knowledge of the plan or ground they came belting up and over the railway, charging in with a furious onslaught of steel and flame. The flaming was magnificent. Peter just 'went to town.' Never before or since did such a 'rod' of flame spew forth from any Croc as that which [Trooper] Staples now sent seething and roaring over cowering Germans in their trenches. Serve you right, you bastards! Into the trenches, over the trenches, into dugouts and round corners the stuff boiled and licked. Old Staples was down there in his seat muttering Cockney imprecations as he sweated with the gun, heaving it this way and that against the heavy stiffness of the pipes. And into this blazing wrath Partridge the gunner was slamming out the 75s as fast as he could go. Sgt Norrington was doubling up, making up for what he'd missed

> at Carpiquet. Sgt. Decent's pressure gone – these were the early days when Crocs were just about as constant as fickle womankind – but making up for it with Besa [which] he liberally applied. Rowland Beechey, halted now, was using up his last few rounds. And now in this weird setting of dusk and burning flame the infantry came on.[6]

Alongside the demolition rounds of the AVREs, the Crocodiles of B Squadron successfully flamed the defences and buildings of Épron, significantly helping the Norfolks and A Company 7 S Staffs to break into the village. However, Captain Neave, who had come forward to watch the attack, commented, 'Again the tanks reached the objectives first and it was dark shortly afterwards.' D Company was, however, soon in the village,

> clearing the houses and Orchard EAST of the X rds and going through to AUBERGE on their own accord. A Coy 7 S STAFFORDS having a larger area to capture took longer but by 2200 hrs the village of EPRON and buildings of AUBERGE were firmly in our hands and only a few snipers remained to be 'winkled out'. Tho A Tk guns and MMGs were moved fwd quickly and they were all in post by dark (22 A Tk guns in all). The tks then withdrew to rear rally. Fwd coys then sent out patrols but only negative info was gained.

The Crocodile's armoured trailer contained 400 gallons of flame fuel and the cylinders of gas that threw the flame up to 100 yards.

Galmanche and the SS Trench System

Galmanche and the trench system in the centre, between the château and the railway line, were to be attacked by 177 Brigade at the same time as 176 Brigade's assault on Épron at 2030 hrs. Galmanche was the objective of 5 S Staffs, and the trench system was attacked by 7 S Staffs, less A Company. The latter enemy position had been a persistent thorn in the flanks of the attacking battalions and, as the 59th advanced south on either side, the SS defenders had stubbornly held on. Both attacks were supported by armour, with 5 S Staffs having AVREs to help reduce the Galmanche Château, alongside a renewed bombardment of the objectives. In the case of the 7th Battalion's attack on the trench system,

> the tanks suffered severely, in the open country, from the fire of well-sited 'eighty-eights' and had to withdraw; and there was insufficient weight of artillery to have much effect on the well-entrenched enemy. So, 7 S Staffords had to fight their way through the maze of trenches with their own weapons. They did this to some purpose and advanced well westwards of the railway. But night found them too disorganised to hold on in the foremost positions gained and they had to withdraw once more behind it.

Overnight, the trench system remained in SS hands, but a short distance to the west, with AVREs and Shermans of the East Riding Yeomanry in support,

By the evening of 8 July the Galmanche Château and its garrison were virtually surrounded, and the building had been reduced to ruins.

5 S Staffs put in a company attack on the château. The divisional history attributes the surrender of some of the *Hitlerjugend* defenders to the 'flying dustbin' demolition rounds fired into the farm and château complex by the AVREs. Not all the SS defenders surrendered, and neither Galmanche Château nor the trench system were fully secured until the following morning.

Panzerabwehrkanone 40 (PaK 40)

The main anti-tank gun of 12th *Hitlerjugend* Panzer Division was the 75mm PaK 40. It had been under development during the late 1930s, but only when pre-war intelligence reports were received in 1939 of new, heavier Soviet tanks was the project spurred into final development and production. It proved to be a wise decision, confirmed by encounters with the heavy KV1 and sloped armour of the T34 during Operation BARBAROSSA in 1941.

Due to the urgent need to deploy a new anti-tank gun, the 75mm barrel was to be fitted to the PaK 38 carriage, designed to take a 50mm barrel which had been rendered obsolescent by developments in Soviet armour before it could be deployed. However, due to the diversion of aluminium to aircraft production, a similar steel version was quickly produced. The first PaK 40s were fielded on the Eastern Front during November 1941, and with a range of nearly 2,000 yards were an immediate success, resulting in wholesale production by Krupp and Rheinmetall. Thanks to the success of the PaK 40, the large and vulnerable 88mm Flak 36/37, which had temporarily filled the gap in anti-tank capability, could be substantially withdrawn from the front into its anti-aircraft and artillery role.

This photograph of German soldiers training with the PaK 40 shows the low profile of the gun.

The PaK 40 was based on the L/46 gun barrel, with a muzzle velocity of 990m/s, and could take on the armour of all Allied tanks in Normandy. In trials against armoured plate, at 60 degrees the ballistic-capped Pzgr 40 anti-tank munition could penetrate 126mm+ at 100 metres, 108mm at 500 and 87mm at 1,000 metres. By 1944 the tungsten shell had been replaced by a 40-1 steel version with reduced penetration. Amongst other munitions, the gun also had a high-explosive shell which had a useful maximum indirect firing range of over 8,000 yards. By late 1944 the L/46 gun, on a variety of mounts, was perforce becoming a dual-purpose anti-tank and artillery weapon.

As a towed weapon, the PaK 40 was the standard equipment in most infantry and *Panzergrenadier* regiments' heavy companies and in the *Panzerjäger* battalions of infantry divisions. The L/46 gun was also taken into use on a variety of mounts, including Panzer IVs, Marders and on the Lorraine Schlepper conversion in the unmodified and later modified format L/48. These were largely for use in panzer and *Panzergrenadier* divisions.

When fully dug-in the gun presented a target area of less than 18 inches to the front, but in a large open gun pit both gun and crew were very vulnerable to airburst munitions. During MARTLET and EPSOM, 26 SS *Panzergrenadiers* lost most of their guns, necessitating the deployment of panzers forward in the anti-tank role. In the case of Operation MITTEN, the inadequate PaK 36 and 38 anti-tank guns held by 16th *Luftwaffe Feld* Division and the importance of holding Caen dictated that Panzer IVs and Marders had to be deployed in defence around Château de la Londe.[7]

A PaK 40 being towed by an Sd.kfz.10 half-track.

After firing, the breech automatically ejected the cartridge case and re-cocked the firing mechanism. Following loading of the shell, the breech also closed automatically, allowing a theoretical rate of fire of fourteen rounds per minute.

A 75-mm PaK 40 positioned to fire through a loop-holed Norman stone wall.

Summary of 59th Division's Attacks

The 59th Division was considered to be well trained, but in its first battle it was up against a determined and skilled enemy. When measured against their more experienced flanking formations' advances south, the 59th was not successful. One suspects that 'well trained' equated to 'well drilled', and that the experienced General Lyne had had little time since taking command to make a difference. Battalions had yet to grasp the realities of war and understand the wiliness, commitment and flexibility required to defeat the Germans. In common with most infantry divisions, they had had little training with armour. In addition, most of the divisions that had been in the UK for the duration of the war so far and had been committed early in the campaign had benefited from extensive cross-posting of veteran officers and SNCOs from the Mediterranean. Far fewer, however, had been made available to the 59th, which was to be the last British infantry division to deploy to Normandy. Finally, as already mentioned, despite lavish artillery support, the battalions of the 59th were committed immediately to a very difficult battle, rather than being eased into combat as Montgomery would have preferred.

Even though much of the *Hitlerjugend*'s towed anti-tank artillery had been destroyed by artillery bombardment, there were still sufficient guns, plus those of panzers, to keep the ERY at a respectable distance, breaking the necessary intimate cooperation between tanks and infantry. The loss of tanks to *Panzerfausts* at close quarters in the villages and surrounding orchards strongly indicates

The limit of the 59th Division's advance.

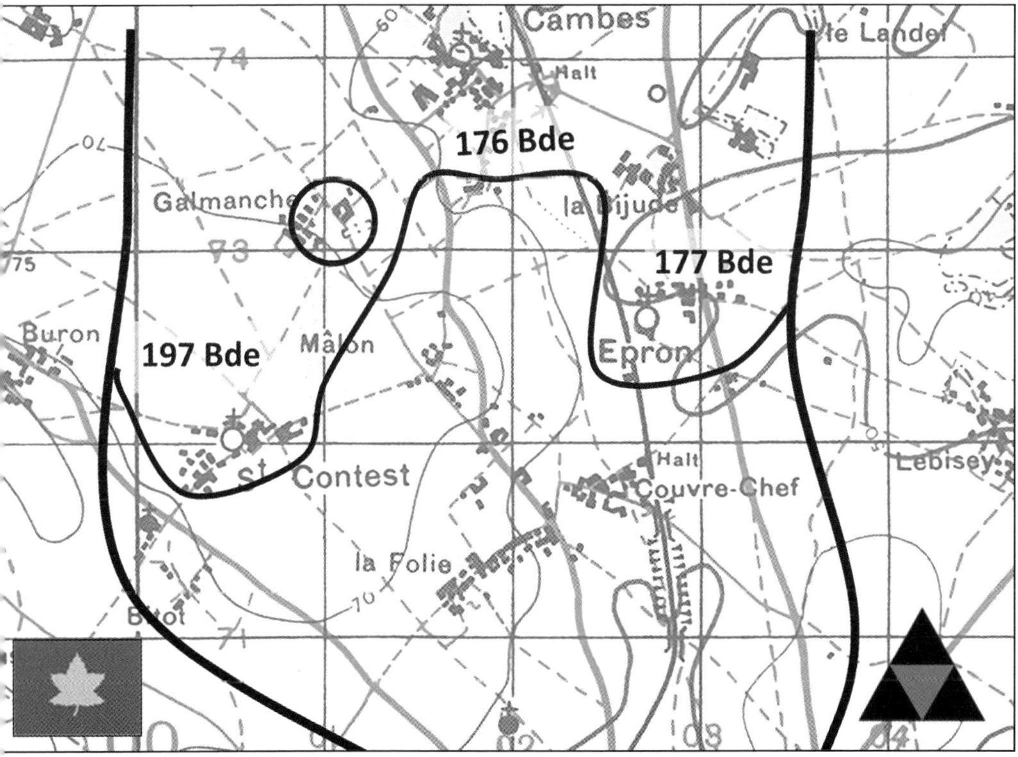

that tanks and infantry were not working together but fighting for their lives in their own separate battles.

The level of casualties suffered by the division has been held up as evidence of failure, but while they were undoubtedly heavy, they are comparable with those suffered by other divisions in their first battles, for example, 15th Scottish during EPSOM and 43rd Wessex in JUPITER.

A post-raid photograph of the bombing of the northern outskirts of Caen.

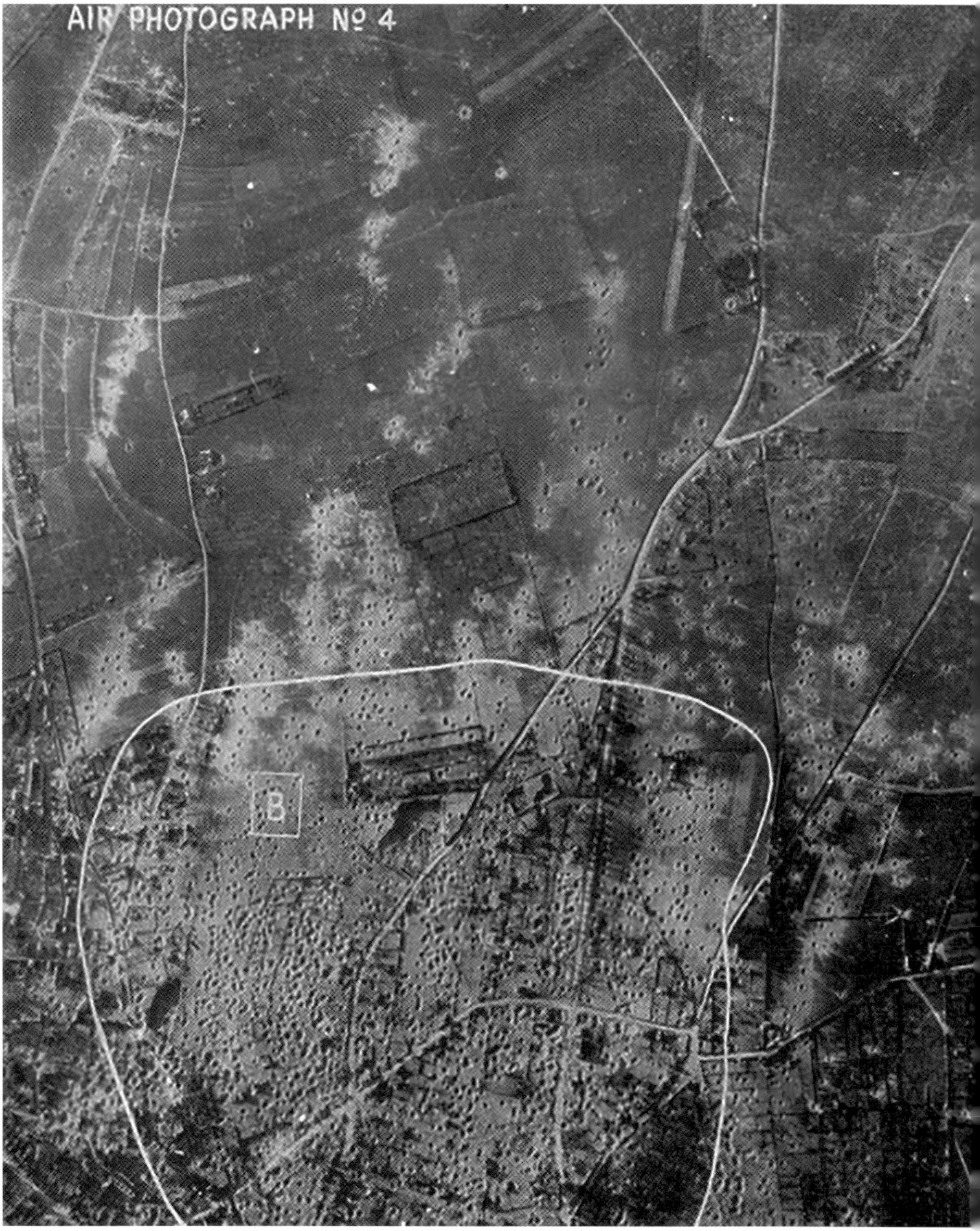

Chapter Ten

Abbaye d'Ardenne and Cussy

In Phase II of Operation CHARNWOOD, in the villages of Buron, Gruchy and Authie, Brigadier Cumming's 9 Cdn Brigade faced opposition every bit as severe as had been anticipated. While 7 Cdn Brigade moved up to take on phase three, 9 Cdn Brigade's final objectives were still being secured, the cutting the N13 Bayeux road and the taking of the hamlet of Franqueville (see map page 179). The former was achieved by a company of the NNS by 1700 hours. The brigade's war diarist recorded that 'The enemy had evidently decided that the mile of country over towards Carpiquet was no longer tenable: following up the withdrawal, Nth N.S. Highrs had comparatively little difficulty in taking possession of Franqueville.' The NNS war diary goes on to explain that 'As soon as AUTHIE was adequately cleared "Charlie" Company put a patrol forward to Franqueville and although thin on the ground were able to hold it.' The Sherbrooke Fusiliers make it plain that this was not a solo endeavour on the part of the infantry: '1600. The remnants of A and C sqns put the Nth NS Highrs into FRANQUEVILLE.' Despite being 'thin on the ground', C Company and the Shermans were able to hold Franqueville against a counter-attack launched by the *Leibstandarte*'s III/1 SS *Panzergrenadiers*. The village was, however, not considered to be secure until 2100 hours. However, from the high ground around Franqueville the NNS and tanks were able to control the N13 road.

Off to the west on the Bayeux–Caen road, General Keller ordered the Inns of Court Yeomanry with squadrons of 7th Cdn Recce Regiment forward towards Saint-Germain-la-Blanche-Herbe, with a view to getting into the city and seizing the bridges.

The Defenders

The abbey was the headquarters of 25 SS *Panzergrenadiers*, while Cussy was held by a battery of the 12th SS Anti-Aircraft Battalion, commanded by *Hauptsturmm-führer* Ritzel. The SS gunners found themselves fighting as infantrymen as well as serving their three surviving 88mm guns against both ground and air targets. They occupied positions 200 yards north of Cussy and in the village itself. So thinly spread had the *Hitlerjugend* become after a month in battle that it had become the practice of support weapon companies, artillery batteries and even the division's logisticians to hold ground, in order to provide depth to the division's defences. The abbey itself, held by the headquarters staff of 25 SS *Panzer-grenadiers* and men who had withdrawn from the villages, proved an altogether sterner test that lasted into the night.

An Allied soldier is ready to take on the enemy from a badly damaged building.

During the afternoon while General Eberbach was still at the *Hitlerjugend*'s headquarters in Caen, as *Standartenführer* Meyer recalled, 'Alarming reports arrived'.

> The enemy had broken through between the II and III/25th SS Panzer Grenadier Regiment, that is to say, between Galmanche and Buron. He had taken St Contest and was able to bring the approaches to the Abbey Ardenne under fire.[1]

Himself under fire for much of the latter part of his journey, Meyer drove out to the Abbaye d'Ardenne and later wrote:

> I wanted to see the situation for myself and make the necessary decisions in the middle of the fighting. The Führer's order not to give up Caen could no longer be executed. We could hold out for perhaps a couple of hours longer, but there wouldn't be any survivors from the division. I struggled against allowing the division to be destroyed.

Returning to his headquarters, he was again on the telephone to Headquarters I SS Panzer Corps making the first of several fruitless appeals for a withdrawal as the situation continued to deteriorate. He reported details of the Canadians' advance to Sepp Dietrich's staff as each successive defensive position fell.

For the Germans, the battle for the Abbey began early in the afternoon when the Canadians were seen assembling south-east of Authie. In this case the

Panthers of I/12th SS Panzer Regiment were brought forward. Their war diary reads:

> At 1300 hours [1400 Allied time] the 1st Company, commanded by *Hauptsturmführer* Berlin, and the Recce Platoon, commanded by *Untersturmführer* Fiala, with six and four panzers respectively, as well as two of the 3rd Company, were deployed in defending the Abbey Ardenne. During the artillery bombardment that lasted hours, two of the tanks of the 1st Company became total losses due to direct hits, and three more tanks were seriously damaged. One of the panzers of the Recce Platoon was hit in the fuel tank, and the track of another was hit. The Platoon Commander's panzer was hit by an anti-tank gun, though without any particular effect: the optics were damaged, and the turret machine gun was out of action because of the hit.

General Eberbach, the replacement commander of Panzer Group West, before being promoted and having the tip of his nose shot off.

Young *Hitlerjugend* recipients of the Iron Cross Second Class.

Lieutenant Brown, commanding the Regina Rifles' D Company, had gone forward to carry out his recce and recalled that the tank casualties in this preliminary engagement were not all suffered by the *Hitlerjugend*'s panzers:

> We found the village of Authie but the Novas had not secured the whole town and were, in fact, hanging on for dear life. Our tank support arrived; about twelve Shermans surrounded me in a field right behind the village where I lay waiting for my company to arrive. Why the tanks chose to remain exposed, I don't know, but one by one they were destroyed by 88mm guns located near the Abbey. It was the most devastating display of German anti-tank power that I had seen to that date. Our tank crews bailed out of their burning Shermans and were machine gunned from the mounds beyond Authie. I could do nothing until our companies arrived.[2]

The 1st Hussars' war diary confirms that they were in action before they reached their designated start line but claims they lost 'only two tanks'. The following extract from the diary confirms that other tanks were hit but not necessarily knocked out and a total loss:

> MAJOR W.D. BROCK'S tank was hit but was saved by extra tracks welded on the front. Sgt LUMLY's tank was set on fire, but the crew stuck with it, extinguishing the fire and bringing it back from the action.[3]

Cussy

It was as early as 0955 hours on 8 July that General Keller had ordered 7 Cdn Brigade to move forward in readiness for CHARNWOOD's third phase. The 1st Canadian Scots' war diarist noted that 'From early in the morning from when the barrage started until late in the evening the scream of artillery and the thud of mortars thundered in our ears.' He and the 1st Canadian Hussars also recorded that while moving forward to their FUP they cleared up pockets of resistance that had been missed during 9 Cdn Brigade's advance. Such were the cumulative delays caused by overcoming resistance in Buron, flanking fire from St Contest, and so on, that time slipped away into the afternoon.

The war diary of 7 Cdn Brigade records:

> At approx. 1300 hrs 7 Cdn Inf Bde was in posn in the assembly area – the two fwd bns – the Regina Rif and 1 C Scot – were being heavily mortared including moaning minnies by the cartload, 88mm HE, armour piercing and larger shells, 150 mm.
>
> By 1700 hrs the situation cleared up – the 9 Cdn Inf Bde were now in possession of GRUCHY, BURON, CHATEAU DE LOUET, AUTHIE and FRANQUEVILLE. The Brig then advised 7 Cdn Inf Bde that our H-Hour was 1730 hrs. All three units – the Regina Rif and 1 C Scot R first and the R Wpeg Rif in reserve – crossed the SL on time under heavy shell fire.[4]

However, following the sundry delays further north, it was only shortly after 1800 hours that the Abbaye d'Ardenne and the nearby village of Cussy were attacked by 7 Cdn Brigade. The Canadian Scottish advanced on the small village of Cussy and the Regina Rifles on the Abbey. They were supported by the Sherman-equipped squadrons of 1 Hussars, while the Royal Winnipeg Rifles were the brigade's reserve located near Buron. When 7 Cdn Brigade's much delayed attack began, even though the overall situation 'looked more and more promising', the fact that the orchards south-west of St Contest and the hamlet of Bitot had not yet been secured by the 59th Division was an added difficulty.

Lieutenant Colonel Cabeldu's plan for the Canadian Scots' attack on Cussy was for A and C Company to lead across the start line. A Company, however, had a gun and infantry position north-west of the village to clear. Once this position was taken, B Company would pass through and attack the village on the right, alongside C Company on the left. D Company was the battalion's reserve. The battalion's war diarist recorded:

> The leading coys 'C' and 'A' in extended line formation began their 'WALK' to Cussy and beyond ... It was a sight to see – with these seasoned battle-hardened troops from CANADA overcoming enemy resistance and carrying through to the defeat of the defenders.

Captain Ramsey, the 2iC of B Company at the time of the battle, penned a far more realistic account of the fight in the right half of Cussy:

> The road leading through Cussy on the right was the logical approach for our Coy, and 11 PL (left forward), commanded by Lt Ross, was ordered to move up this road clearing that side of Cussy and reorganise forward right of the village. 10 Pl was to move up on the right side of the road. As 10 Pl

started on their way, they were met by an enemy Tiger tank [*sic*] which came down the road on A Coy's right flank. Maj Lendrum fired a red Very light in the direction of this tank to attract the attention of our supporting armour. CSM Fill and Sgt Frost quickly went back about 200 yards to the carrier and brought up a PIAT. By the time we had primed the bombs and Sergeant FROST had placed the PIAT in the hedge to fire, one of our supporting tanks and A Coy PIAT both got direct hits on it and it went up in flames with cheers from A, B and C coys. By this time B Coy with 11 Pl forward was moving along the hedge. 10 Pl on the right engaged an enemy 2.5cm AA and A/Tk gun near the road and several Germans ran from the gun to the Abbey. At this point we came under intense fire from the right flank – still no sign of the Regina Rifles. Coy HQ at the junction of the road and hedge was in a very precarious position exposed to enemy fire, therefore I directed them all in to vacated enemy AA and A/Tk gun positions in getting there we suffered 3 casualties from MG fire and had to pull the two least injured in on top of us cutting their webbing off to enable them to get down the narrow German slit trenches. To now no report had come from 11 Pl, so 10 Pl commanded by Lt Park, was ordered forward on the right of the road to come up on 11 Pl's right as originally intended. 12 Pl was furiously digging in to get protection from the intense MG and mortar fire directly directed mainly from the Abbey.

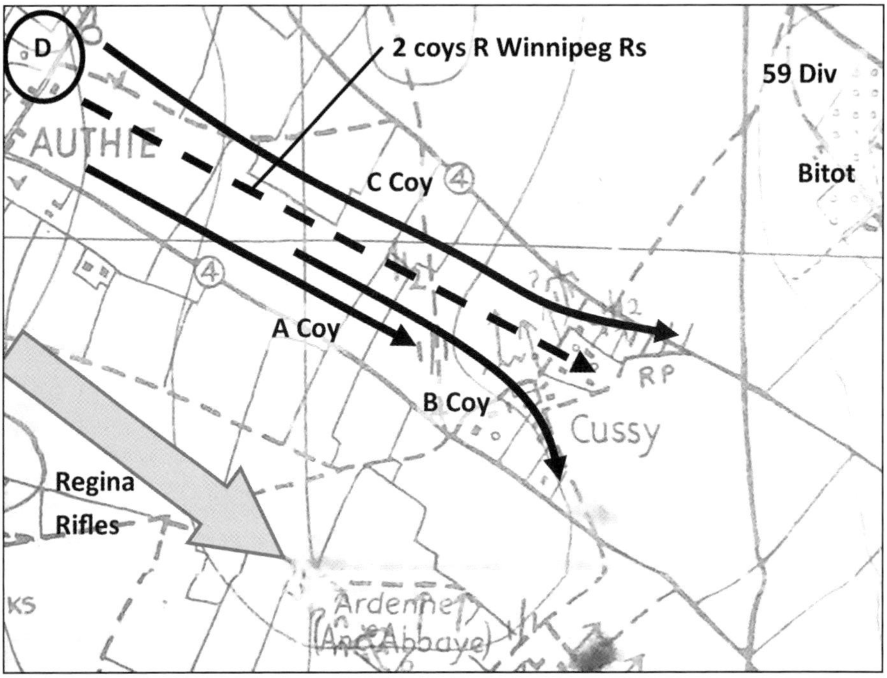

The 1st Canadian Scottish attack on Cussy.

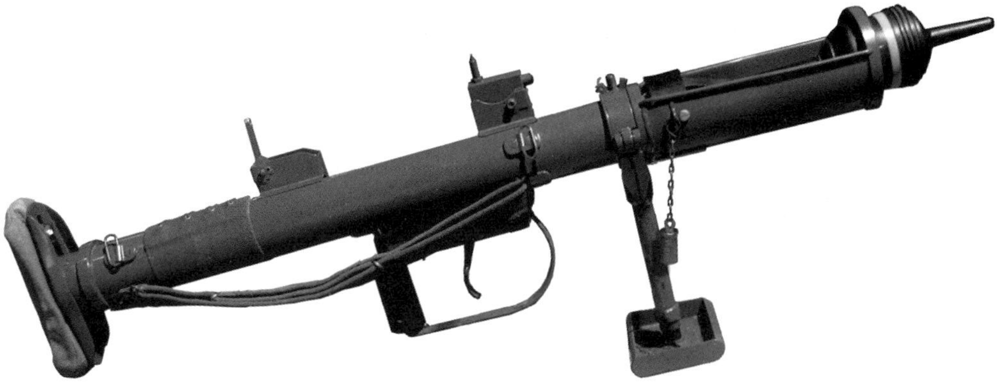

The Projector Infantry Anti-Tank (PIAT). The shaped-charge warhead was fired from a spigot by a powerful spring, which unlike the *Panzerfaust* had neither a back-blast nor an obvious firing signature.

The Canadian Scottish regimental historian's account of C Company's attack on the left of Cussy is similarly robust:

> Halfway to its objective the company came under terrific crossfire from Bitot on the left and the abbey on its right front. Machine gun fire from Cussy was thickened by enemy tank fire, one on the company right flank and another from an old burnt-out tank the enemy was using as a machine gun post near Bitot. This caused about 20 casualties even before the company hit its objective.[5]

The brigade war diary noted that 'This nuisance on our flanks was not sufficient to save the enemy in Cussy despite a strenuous defence.' The historian continued:

> 'On arrival on our objective,' wrote Major D.G. Crofton, 'Our men went in with the bayonet and let out blood-curdling yells which put to flight at least seventy-five Germans who were manning two 88-mm, two Howitzer guns, an anti-aircraft gun and other defensive positions.'

As was so often the case, holding gains was not at all easy, with the brigade war diary recording that 'By 1900 hrs 1 C Scot R reported … that they were being vigorously counter-attacked. Due to this counter-attack by tanks and infantry they requested immediate help.' Captain Ramsey explained the situation in B Company's area:

> Our #46 set would not work but from the sounds on the left and in the village, we deduce that hot fighting was going on left. Lt Ross of 11 Pl arrived with this runner to report the arrival of his platoon forward of the village. He also reported the presence of twelve enemy tanks commanding the right flank plus three MMG positions mutually supporting and fire from the Abbey, which was still German held. He had roughly one section left under Sergeant Proverbs and had left them reorganised on the right of the village

> when he came back to report. Lt Ross was lying on the edge of the trench and talking when he was hit so we pulled him in. The coy comd at this juncture was struggling along the trench searching for a wider spot for the [radio] set when he found three Germans cowering in the corner. We had now three groaning wounded, three Germans and the remains of our Coy HQ, plus two remaining sigs trying vainly to get connection on the set that would not work.

The Scots' 6-pounders were rushed forward to the village, where they deployed three guns, with the remaining crews acting as infantry. According to the war diarist, they 'spent the hottest time of their lives during this action.' Six enemy tanks were also claimed by the Scots from 6-pounders and PIATs. Also in action in Cussy were the brigade's reserve, the Winnipegs, whom 7 Brigade

> ordered to send two rifle coys [B and D] with two A Tk guns and plenty of SAA to the 1 C Scot R. This having been done, one coy of the R Wpg Rif plugged the gap between the two coys of the 1 C Scot R – the other coy remained in reserve. Things began to quieten down in CUSSY apart from the occasional shot by enemy snipers not yet ferreted out. At approximately 2300 hrs CUSSY was firmly in our hands.

Colonel Cabeldu praised 'the close spirit of co-operation' with the 1st Hussars and the supporting machine-gunners of the Cameron Highlanders of Ottawa, adding that 'Only one unforeseen eventuality arose. Both flanks were open.' The CO and his FOO decided that Bitot, the hamlet between St Contest and Cussy in the 59th Division's area, had clearly not been captured and could be engaged, as there was no sign of British troops. Bitot was duly shelled and enemy fire from that quarter suppressed.

The last of the defenders of Cussy, with *Hauptsturmmführer* Ritzel acting as gun layer, claimed to have knocked out three Shermans, but the remaining SS anti-aircraft gunners were overwhelmed, with Ritzel and six men mounting a last stand amidst the rubble. Nearly every SS soldier who had stayed at his post in the village was either killed or captured, but the Canadian Scottish had to beat off a counter-attack. Ritzel's action is recorded as buying time for the growing number of casualties to be evacuated from Abbaye d'Ardenne.

The Abbaye d'Ardenne

The Regina Rifles' companies only started to move forward between 1700 and 1725 hours and, with the Canadian Scots' attack underway, they were badly delayed from, reaching their FUP by shelling. There were further delays while casualties were evacuated and the assault troops were reorganized. According to Lieutenant Brown of D Company,

> it was almost 1800 hours when Baker, Charlie and Dog Companies reached us [in the FUP]. The artillery programme had already been fired on the

> mounds and the Abbey with the result that we were now to make an infantry assault without immediate artillery preparation and without any tank support.

Lieutenant Colonel Matheon's plan for the Regina Rifles' attack was to use three of his rifle companies. B on the left were to attack an abandoned enemy anti-aircraft position referred to by the Reginas as the 'Mounds', while a squadron of the 1st Hussars neutralized the enemy still in the Franqueville area. Then, D Company in the centre and C on the right were to assault the Abbey, while the already badly under-strength A Company was in reserve.

The attack did not get underway until after 1830 hours. The officer commanding D Company described the company moving forward on an axis passing

The Regimental Medical Officer of the Cameron Highlanders of Ottawa treats a casualty prior to evacuation.

through B Coy and with fire and movement to within 500 yards of the Abbey. Lieutenant Brown added more detail:

> Baker [B Company] lost more than half their hundred men in reaching the 'mounds', and were under constant machine gun and mortar fire. We had a devil of a time getting beyond Baker as we were so exposed, running and crawling through the grass and weeds. Charlie Company was on our right and being driven onto our line of advance by machine gun fire from the direction of Franqueville to the west.
>
> When we finally got going, the advance was awfully slow because of the relentless machine gun and rifle fire. The two forward platoons began to use fire and movement effectively, but it was heavy going. We had already lost

The Regina Rifles' attack on the Abbaye d'Ardenne.

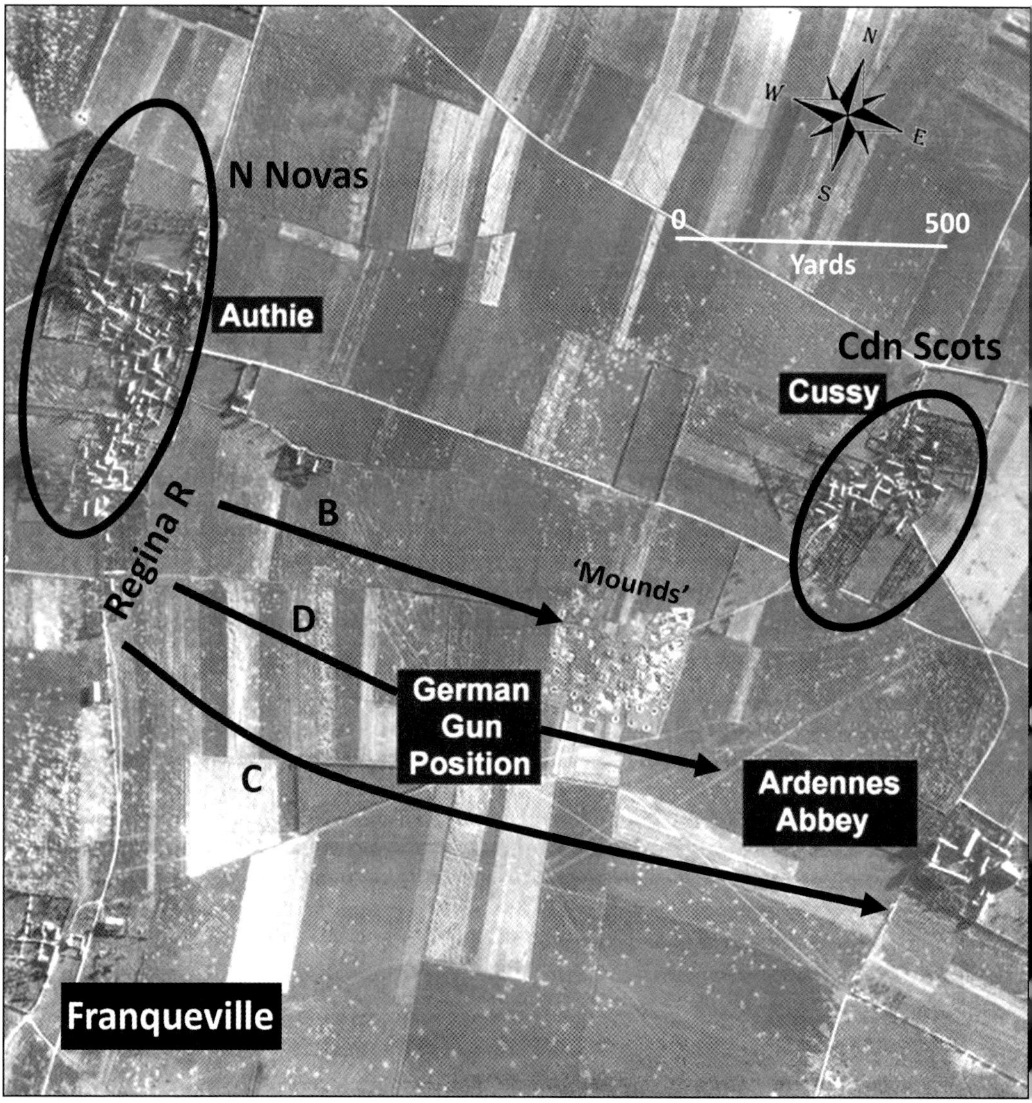

several men and were forced to crawl and run in short bursts to avoid heavier losses. We had to limit our losses if we were to have anyone left for the final assault.

Without working radio communication, Brown 'was in a quandary':

> We needed another artillery programme to be fired at the Abbey. Machine gun fire from the tower of the church and from other locations around it was holding us at bay. I sent my runner back to find Hec Jones and ask him to contact the artillery and have them fire a stonk on the Abbey and surrounding buildings. This turned out well as the shells hammered the buildings thoroughly and we were able to move more quickly. But it was already near 2100 hours, and we were just over halfway between the mounds and the Abbey.

C Company had advanced, but with further to go in the open suffered cruelly, and the wounded Major Tubbs gave the order for the survivors to withdraw. D Company advancing from the area of the Mounds pressed home its attack as described by its commander:

> We were then pinned down with heavy MG fire from 2 tanks at the corner of Abbey, dug-in pill boxes and an MG on top of Abbey. 16 Pl went left flanking but were forced to withdraw under heavy MG fire. We then moved 17 and 18 pls in an assault on the Abbey undercover of 2″ mortar and tank smoke at about 2230 hours and gained our objective this was consolidated and dug in the side of the buildings.

The *Hitlerjugend* had the support of two panzers at the Abbey and had well protected positions built into the surrounding wall. The Reginas' war diarist also reports a 'sniper, in the abbey church's tower, armed with an LMG'. In the two and a half hours of the fight the SS defenders beat back several advances that closed in on the Abbey.

> During these engagements the 1st Company knocked out four Shermans, the Recce Platoon five Shermans, an anti-tank gun and one or two companies of enemy infantry, partly in close combat.
>
> The crisis had been averted with the advance of the Canadian tanks being finally halted within 100 yards of the Abbey buildings and driven back. The *Panzergrenadiers* then had to force enemy infantry out of the surrounding hedgerows and orchards but the aid station in the Abbey was now overflowing with casualties.

With his division in peril, *Standartenführer* Meyer was driven back to the Abbaye d'Ardenne:

> The monastery's orchard looked like an inferno. Round after round exploded outside the regimental command post. Taking advantage of a pause in the shelling, we rushed toward the building. Dead soldiers were

Canadian infantry and Sherman in the tight confines between high stone walls and stoutly built stone houses.

scattered around the vicinity of the headquarters. While leaping out of the car, I recognized the body of the commander of the headquarters company. Shrapnel had killed him.

We stumbled into the old building to find the commander of SS *Panzer-grenadier* Regiment 25 [*Sturmbannführer* Milnius] in the cellar. He was wounded ... The ceiling seemed to be moving above us, even though it was deeply embedded in the earth and supported by enormous arches. We heard continuous booming ...

Flame-thrower tanks [Crocodiles of 10 Troop, B Squadron 141 RAC] were raging around the positions of the *III./SS-Panzer-Grenadier-Regiment 25*. Burning *Panzergrenadiers* jumped into the air and then collapsed. Flame-thrower tanks were the most feared weapons.[6]

The Reginas continued the fight. Out on the edge of the orchard, now just over 100 yards from the Abbey's perimeter wall, Lieutenant Brown struggled to keep control of his company as they attempted to get forward under cover of fire from 13 Field Regiment RCA:

I found myself ... prepared for the final dash. The mortar smoke was fired and created a perfect screen. The two platoons rose from the wheat and

> firing on the run, we all made the dash towards the walls. There were many slit trenches and dugouts into which we threw grenades. Some of our men fell but we overwhelmed the remaining dazed enemy troops. Dick Roberts and I patrolled down the wall to a place where a huge hole had been torn in it. There luck was with us again. We stood in the opening looking into a courtyard where a German tank was slowly turning its turret towards us. I said, 'There's a tank' and Dick responded, 'Yeah, and it's a German tank.' Machine gun fire missed us by very little as we jumped clear of the hole and lay there, puffing and fuming. The tank seemed immobile for otherwise it wouldn't be sitting in an open yard like that.

Lieutenant Brown's own platoons and those of both C and D Company, had fought through the SS defences but, having reached the walls surrounding the Abbey complex, found it impossible to break in against a resolute defence by HQ 25 SS *Panzergrenadiers* and the remnants of III Battalion. Overnight, the survivors of the Canadian companies scraped the earth to gain what cover they could, mostly around the northern and eastern sides of the Abbey.

As full darkness fell on 8 July, the 3rd Canadian Division had battled their way through very well-prepared defences, in country favourable to the German defenders, whose tenacity, in accordance with Hitler's instructions, had thwarted I Corps' aim of capturing the Orne bridges during 8 July. In fighting against unbeatable odds, in what most of the *Hitlerjugend*'s commanders considered to be

A wounded Panzer IV crewman of 6th Panzer Company being treated by *Panzergrenadiers*.

a trap, they suffered irreplaceable losses of manpower and equipment. The British and Canadian, however, with casualties averaging 175 men per battalion in a single day of battle, were also burning through the available infantry battle casualty replacements.

Overnight

The Regina Rifles had reached the Abbey walls and gained a foothold in the buildings, but in darkness it would have been impossible to clear the Abbey complex in detail. They spent an unpleasant night at close quarters with the enemy, being machine-gunned and mortared. It was only shortly after dawn on 9 July 1944 that they began clearance of the Abbey.

Elsewhere in the divisional area, as the battle moved on or otherwise died down as night set in, the experience of the HLI of Canada was typical. Not only had they to put the village of Buron into a state of defence but also to return the battalion to operational effectiveness.

> The LOBs [left out of battle] were sent for and the Bn was reorganized. They dug in completely to hold what they had taken and endeavored to get the rest of their cas out. Towards eight o'clock the enemy shell fire slackened as ST. CONTEST, BITOT, etc., on the flanks were taken and with the 7 C.I.B. attacking all along the south the Bn gained a respite. It remained for the Coys to clear up the snipers still in their orchards. In several attempts aided by tks they were unable to flush them out and they remained until next morning when 'C' Coy sent a party to clear them away.
>
> Night fell on the quiet, smoking village of Buron, which had witnessed one of the fiercest battles ever fought in the history of war. It was the HLI's first big fight, and 8 July will go down in its annals as a day to remember. The ranks were sadly depleted, and reorganization showed them to be thin on the ground – too thin to stave off a counter-attack in the night. Yet they doggedly dug in, determined that their day's work would not be in vain and, though dead tired, ready to go on to CAEN the next day if the opportunity presented itself. One hundred per cent stand-to was maintained during the night, but the enemy had expended all his energy during the day, and with the exception of a few snipers trapped behind the lines all was quiet and the night passed without incident.[7]

CHARNWOOD's Right Flank

South of the hills separating Carpiquet airfield and the River Odon, the 43rd Wessex Division had the task of capturing Verson as an adjunct to CHARNWOOD. They had already taken it once from the *Leibstandarte* during Operation WINDSOR, but with the Canadians' failure to secure the barracks they were in an uncomfortable salient and had been withdrawn. On 8 July, the 7th Somerset LI of 214 Brigade renewed the occupation of Verson, which had remained as no-man's-land, despite the Canadian attack (Operation TROUSERS) on the

The Abbaye d'Ardenne after the battle. In the foreground is a knocked-out Fiat 626N ambulance.

Carpiquet barracks being delayed until the following day. The Somersets' historian wrote:

> On July eighth the whole battalion moved up and dug in around Verson, entering the desolate rubble strewn street during the night, and making 'an awful clatter over the piles of broken slates'. It was not a popular move since it placed them in the narrow salient between Carpiquet and the high ground South of the river Odon, which was under fire from both sides, but it was necessary in that it rendered the enemy positions on the aerodrome untenable, secured the right flank for the famous Canadian attack on Caen, and opened the way for 43rd Division to drive across the Odon towards Hill 112 [in Operation JUPITER].[8]

The Germans were clearly alarmed by the threat to the west of Caen and the possibility of an advance north of the Odon in the Verson area and ordered assembly of another *Kampfgruppe* of 21st Panzer Division, which two days earlier had been relieved in the line. *Leutnant* Ratzinger joined the division as a replacement at the beginning of July, but during the following week, due to officer casualties, he had been elevated to command of No. 1 Company I/192 *Panzergrenadier* Regiment. His diary for 8/9 July, taken from him when he was captured several days later, provides a glimpse of the difficulties both sides faced amidst the hedgerows when in battle:

> I took over command of the coy at 1100 hrs and set out to march to ETERVILLE, where a tank *Kampgruppe* is to be formed. Immediately after leaving cover we are subjected to low-level air attack. Fortunately, without casualties. At 1320 hrs we move into the assembly area WEST of CAEN. Recce by a tank officer and myself. During afternoon slightly injured in right buttock by shell fragment. We attack at 2130 hrs with arty, but skilful sniping by enemy operating from the hedges during the hours of darkness forces us to dig in. Three of our tanks were knocked out. The infantry has to be sent ahead. Murderous arty and mortar fire over our position the whole day. Heavy casualties. Quiet night.[9]

Sherman 33 Armoured Brigade sticking to the tracks of the tank in front to avoid mines during CHARNWOOD.

Chapter Eleven

The Fall of Caen

During the evening of 8 July, the 3rd and the 3rd Canadian Division sent patrols from their recce regiments into Caen. They and the infantry patrols that followed probed the outskirts, all reporting the city streets as being blocked by rubble; and although they observed plenty of German movement, there was little resistance. For the defenders, it was a case of extricating themselves from destruction in and around Caen under the dark shadow of Hitler's prescriptive *Führerbefehl* that there was to be no withdrawal.

As the fighting gradually died down and the Allied divisions accepted that they would not be in possession of Caen that evening, 21st Panzer Division had started to stabilize a defence on the northern lip of the bowl in which Caen lies. During the afternoon General Obstfedter, commander of LXXXI Corps, had ordered General Feuchtinger to resume command of the sector that he had handed over to 16th *Luftwaffe Feld* Division days before, as its commander General Sivers, had lost control of his collapsing front. It was estimated that his infantry facing the 3rd Division had suffered 75 per cent casualties. Feuchtinger's orders were:

> After a heavy bombing attack the enemy has achieved a breakthrough and has advanced to the northern edge of the city of Caen. The situation is unclear. Orientate yourself on the situation at the division command post of the *16. Luftwaffe Feld* Division, which is in Caen. Relieve the commander of the *16. Luftwaffe Feld* Division and assume command there. All elements of the *16. Luftwaffe Feld* Division are subordinated to you for that purpose. If the situation permits, a counter-attack by the elements of the *21. Panzer Division* that have been brought in is to restore the situation.

In the I SS Panzer Corps area *Standartenführer* Meyer, having seen for himself the parlous situation that the remnants of 25 SS *Panzergrenadiers* were in, returned to his headquarters in the city:

> The enemy target practice at our Volkswagen started again. Erich Holsten drove and I clung onto the side. With a lot of luck, we reached the rubble of the city. After my return from Ardenne, I reported the critical situation to the [I SS Panzer] corps and urgently asked for permission to withdraw the remnants of the division to the east bank of the Orne. I left no doubt that Caen could not be held without the remnants of the division bleeding to death. The corps turned down the request. The Führer had ordered that the town had to be held at all costs! All protests and my reference to the senselessness of further sacrifices achieved nothing. We were to die in Caen![1]

Feldmarschall Rommel and SS-*Obergruppenführer* Dietrich, the commander of I SS Panzer Corps, photographed during July 1944.

At 2100 hours Rommel arrived at General Eberbach's Headquarters Panzer Group West and authorized a limited withdrawal from Caen and surrounding areas. Orders were promptly telephoned to LXXXI Corps, I SS and II SS Panzer Corps. Eberbach's *Kriegsbuch* recorded:

> The Caen bridgehead is to be cleared, inconspicuously, of the mass of heavy weapons during the night 8 to 9 July. Sufficiently strong forces, reinforced by Pioneers and numerous forward [artillery] observers, will remain behind and offer resistance along the line Calix–Point 64 (north of Caen)–northern edge of St Germain–airfield 300m south of the eastern town edge of

Oberst Fritz Kraemer (left), the 1a of Dietrich's command, photographed as an Army officer in July 1944. He was transferred into the SS on 1 August as an *Oberführer*. *Sturmbannführer* Hubert Meyer (right), the *Hitlerjugend*'s 1a or chief of staff.

> Carpiquet. Only in the face of a superior enemy attack, withdrawal to a line eastern bank of the Orne–northern edge of Vernoix–northern edge of Bretteville [the line of the forward outposts].[2]

At the same time, the counter attack on 3rd Division that was being prepared by 21st Panzer Division's *Kampfgruppe* Rauch (based on 192 Pz Gr Regt) was cancelled, and they were ordered to re-cross the Orne river and canal to the east. This they reported having achieved by 0900 hours the following morning.

These orders were in fact only formalizing what was already being planned as a necessity, as it was obvious that Hitler's order to hold Caen was no longer tenable. The *Hitlerjugend*'s 1a (chief of staff), *Sturmbannführer* Hubert Meyer, rang *Oberst* Kraemer, the 1a at headquarters I SS Panzer Corps, and explained the situation. Kraemer, now realizing the impossibility of holding on for another day without destruction, and considering the implication of ignoring a *Führebefehl*, quietly said that 'being thrown back while fighting a superior enemy could never be considered a withdrawal contrary to orders.' Kraemer was a first-rate Army staff officer who had been brought into the SS to add military practicality and expertise to the inspirational Corps commander, Sepp Dietrich, who was fiercely loyal to Hitler. This was an example of a man of stature taking responsibility.

Orders for the withdrawal were promptly prepared and disseminated to *Hitlerjugend*'s regiments. This was possibly Hubert Meyer's most important piece of staff work as the divisional 1a in the entire battle:[3]

> Regiment 25 will withdraw its battalions to the edge of Caen after nightfall. Before this, the battle-ready heavy weapons will have moved positions and be ready to fire …
>
> Together with the units still in action in the bridgehead, the artillery and mortars will move positions to the southern bank of the Orne. They will cover the disengagement of Regiment 25 and I/1 LAH [*Leibstandarte*] with fire strikes, and then delay any pursuit with harassing fire.

The movement of the artillery and surviving support weapons was quickly underway and, as noted by the divisional commander, 'After the onset of darkness, the battalions were withdrawn to the edge of Caen.' During the night the limited withdrawal of heavy weapons, as indicated above, became more general, with LXXXI Corps also ordering all its forces to withdraw at 0200 hours. The time taken to plan and execute the movement, with only a few hours of darkness left, meant that most of the infantry were still beyond the cover of the city at dawn.

With Allied patrols probing forward, especially in 25 *Panzergrenadier* Regiment's area, where some of the defenders were surrounded or bypassed, the Germans' routes into the city had to be cleared by groups of panzers. The numbers making their way back were small; III/25 SS *Panzergrenadiers*, for example, having just 100 soldiers and non-commissioned officers left.

Between 0300 and 0400 hours, divisional headquarters also moved south of the Orne into the Faubourg de Vaucelles, from where it could control the division's withdrawal. Main divisional headquarters was then established a further 5 miles to the rear at Garcelles. *Sturmbannführer* Hubert Meyer wrote: 'During the last hours of the night and the early hours of the morning of 9 July, the worn-out and totally exhausted survivors of Regiment 25 marched through the ruins of Caen and across the only usable Orne bridge to the south bank of the river.'

Standartenführer Meyer provides a vivid impression of the withdrawal of I/25 SS *Panzergrenadiers* from their trench system that night:

> They had arrived in Normandy with fresh, blooming faces. Now, camouflaged, muddy steel helmets hid emaciated faces whose eyes had, all too often, looked into another world. The men presented a picture of deep human misery. But it was immaterial; they couldn't be allowed to rest any longer. They had to defend the Orne. Waldmüller received his new orders and dragged his men from their leaden sleep, with every grenadier having to be woken individually. They staggered drowsily out of their bunkers and hung their ammunition around their necks; the heavy machine-gun belts dragged the half-asleep soldiers forward. Swearing, they hitched themselves to two of the heavy infantry guns and headed down towards the burning city. Two panzers on the northern approaches covered the withdrawal.

RAF intruder aircraft from Second Tactical Airforce were in action overnight south of Caen and formed the opinion that most German vehicle movement was away from the city. However, this information took until well after dawn to reach I Corps, and the movements could anyway have been interpreted as routine re-supply traffic. Also, on hearing the sound of movement and vehicles, patrols sent forward by the 59th Division withdrew, without gaining information indicating a German withdrawal.

I Corps' Plans

An accurate picture of the extent of the advances made by the three divisions only arrived in Corps headquarters late in the evening. It was, however, already readily apparent that 59th Division had made the least ground and at the time still seemed to have strongly defended villages and trench systems in front of them. On the other hand, with the 3rd and 3rd Canadian division already probing into Caen, the basis of Lieutenant General Crocker's plans for 9 July was obvious. The 59th would concentrate on attacking the enemy defences immediately in front of it, while the two flanking divisions would strike into the city, with the Canadians having the additional task of closing up to the Odon immediately west of Caen. Second Army's report summarized the situation:

> 59 Division was to clear the villages, which were still strongly defended, down to the 70 Northing grid line. South of this grid a new boundary between 3 Canadian Division and 3 British Division was drawn from North to South, cutting the city approximately into halves. Within these boundaries the two divisions were to clear as far as the river but were not to press a crossing of the river if strongly opposed; in addition, 3 British Division was charged with blocking the Northern exits to the city in order to cut off any enemy attempting to escape the advance of 59 Division.[4]

The 3rd Division with 9 Brigade leading was to advance into the city from the north with the tanks of 33 Brigade, while 2 Lincolns on the left at Hérouville were ordered to make limited advances parallel to the canal. The advance on Caen from FUPs around Ring Contour 60 would be preceded by a renewed bombardment at 1000 hours. The Canadians, with squadrons of Corps and divisional recce, were to renew their advance from the west, followed by battlegroups based on the North Nova Scotia Highlanders (NNS) and the companies of the Stormont, Glengarry and Dundas Highlanders (SGD).

Advance into Caen

The pattern of advance and resistance varied widely across the front, dependent on many factors, such as when and where the German units' withdrawal had started from, the time the Allied advance began in a particular area, ground cover, the quality of troops and the extent to which the withdrawal of anxious German troops could be controlled. *Sturmbannführer* Hubert Meyer noted that, certainly in the early stages, many of the Germans encountered by the Allies on the

Craters and ruined houses on the northern outskirts of Caen.

morning of 9 July were 'very likely ... individual pockets of resistance which had, regrettably, not received the order to withdraw.' The *Hitlerjugend* tended to fight on when pinned down, while the men of the *Feld* Division were inclined to surrender when cornered.

Deployed on the northern outskirts of Caen to cover the withdrawal of 25 SS *Panzergrenadiers* and to delay the Allied advance was the *Divisionsbegleitkompanie* (Divisional Escort Company). As described by *Unterscharführer* Freund, they found themselves under I Corps' opening barrage:

> The sector of 1. Zug [Platoon] contained a quarry where the Zug command post was located. The 2. Gruppe [Section] of 1. Zug, with its leader Werner Richter, had moved into a position on the left wing. Everyone was waiting for the expected English attack on Caen. In this situation, Werner Richter had a premonition that something would soon happen to him. He called me over and told me of his apprehension. He asked me to send his personal effects to his family. This I promised to do and asked Werner Richter for the same favour in case anything happened to me, trying to dispel Werner's sad thoughts. We separated then, but not without a joke about who would get it first.
>
> While still on the way from Werner Richter's foxhole to the Zug command post, I was caught by an artillery fire attack. Leaping through the

explosions, I made it to the command post. While I was still telling *Untersturmführer* Erwin Stier about Werner Richter's bleak forebodings, and shells were hammering our positions without pause, the MG gunner 1 of the Richter *Gruppe* rushed into the command post. He reported that his *Gruppe* leader had been killed. Without paying any regard to the exploding shells, I ran to my dead friend together with the MG gunner. I found him in his foxhole almost exactly as I had left him, sitting on the edge. However, his upper body had toppled over. Shell shrapnel had penetrated his neck and ripped open his right shoulder. We carried him to the quarry in a tarpaulin. We all knew that, after this fire attack, the English attack would have to start right away. And then they were there! They advanced on our positions on a wide front. We would not be able to withstand this superiority for long.

The importance of a force to cover a significant withdrawal has not changed. There was an ever-present threat that the withdrawal, when heavily pressed by the enemy, could become a disastrous rout, especially when attempting to negotiate choke points such as bridges. In this case, with I Corps not resuming operations until 1000 hours, the Germans with a head start were not under significant pressure, conducting what the 3rd Canadian Division considered to be 'an expertly executed withdrawal'.

British medics following the advancing infantry through the rubble of Caen.

3rd Division

The previous evening, 9 Brigade had passed through 185 Brigade to occupy positions on the high ground immediately north of Caen, but with patrols having reported the devastation in the city, Brigadier Orr decided to pause operations until daylight. He planned to advance into the city with the 2nd Battalion, Royal Ulster Rifles (2 RUR) on the right, 1st Battalion, King's Own Scottish Borderers (1 KOSB) to the left, and the tanks of the 1st Northamptonshire Yeomanry (1 NY) in support. However, given the reports of 'mountains of rubble', it was appreciated that there would be only a limited role for armour inside the city. As a preliminary operation both battalions dispatched patrols supported by tanks to the outskirts of Caen. The RUR's war diary recorded:

> Before the march into CAEN was begun, two patrols were sent out. The first, consisting of a platoon of 'A' Coy under Lieut R. WISE and a troop of tanks, moved down to CALIX on the Eastern outskirts. The second, a platoon of 'A' Company under Lieut B.R. BURGES with another troop of tanks, went to St JULIEN on the North West outskirts. Both patrols felt their way forward into CAEN and both suffered casualties from such snipers and infantry that still remained in the town. Both Platoon Commanders were wounded and within their commands were three killed and four wounded. Both patrols rejoined the Bn within the next 24 hours.

As dawn rose, the troops on Ring Contour 60 and the high ground overlooking Caen came under increasing artillery and mortar fire which inflicted mounting casualties. 2 RUR alone noted eighty such casualties on 9 July. The battalion's war diary records their entry into the city:

> 'B' Company led the way, clearing houses systematically and climbing over and through the ruins as best they could. Little resistance was encountered and the Bn reached the Boulevards in the centre of the town without incident.

On 9 Brigade's left flank, 1 KOSB advanced with C and D Companies leading. Their war diary for 9 July reads:

> The attack on CAEN. The plan. The Canadians were to attack from the West. The RURs in the centre from the North and 1 KOSB from the East. The Bn moved off at about 0930 hrs over Ring Contour 60, which was under shell fire, to FUP on the Eastern outskirts of CAEN. The ghostlike houses slowly came to life as civilians began to realise we were entering the town. They came running out with glasses and bottles of wine. As the Bn was forming up on the start line and trying to re-establish wireless contact with companies and Bde, four Boche were seen to withdraw towards the centre of the town. Soon afterwards our HQ was mortared leaving one killed and one wounded. The Bn then proceeded to clear the town. Little opposition was met. Progress was slowed down by snipers and an occasional MG.

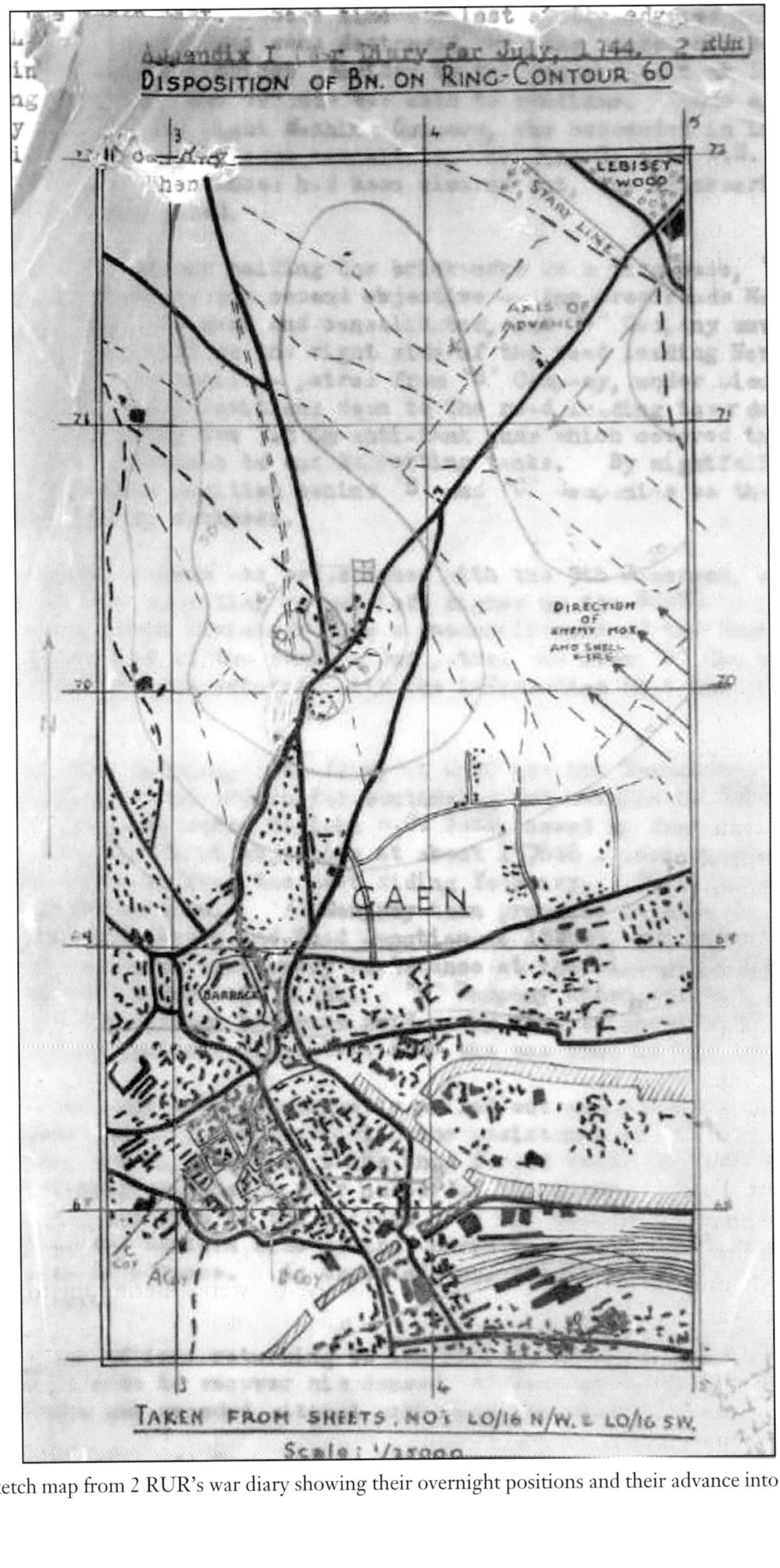

A sketch map from 2 RUR's war diary showing their overnight positions and their advance into Caen.

> Much assistance and information was offered by eager civilians. Debris and cratered streets also made progress extremely difficult. We eventually reached the RV in the Old Town and established contact with the RUR and pushed forward patrols to the river. Patrols met quite heavy fire from across the river and a number of casualties were sustained.[5]

Entering Caen, the battalions found destruction that far surpassed anything they had seen during the previous month. Great piles of rubble from collapsed building blocked the streets in the northern districts, and B Squadron of 1 NY along with armoured bulldozers quickly gave up the attempt to get into the city. The Royal Engineers with a mix of armoured and ordinary bulldozers were left 'to start carving canyons through the rubble'. This of course took time, as recorded by a CANLOAN machine-gun officer with 2nd Middlesex, Lieutenant Fendick, who waited, along with other supporting vehicles, in his carrier at the Y junction on Point 64:

> I sat in my carrier for most of the morning at the top of what had been the long straight road leading down to the city centre, watching a Royal Engineer armoured bulldozer work. He was clearing a path just wide enough to allow one lane of vehicles to pass, for several hundred yards through mountains of rubble higher than the bulldozer. Once he had a way open, I led my platoon on down.
>
> We travelled down the hill past the old Conqueror's castle, which was also pretty badly smashed. Further down into the centre of the city, I remember passing one church which still had its steeple upright, but its tower was split vertically from top to the ground by a wide crack. The roof was gone. Close to the bottom of the hill and the harbour the damage was less and the streets relatively clear.
>
> I had been ordered by Pat to take my platoon through to an eastern suburb, a district called Calix, where there was a suspected pocket of Boche on our side of the river.[6]

3rd Canadian Division

The 3rd Canadian Division's battle though the *Hitlerjugend*'s forward defences the previous day had been a hard and bruising fight, with considerable losses, but they had been able to make greater progress than the 59th Division on their left. From the city's western flank, the previous evening, the Canadians had launched an attempt to drive into the centre of Caen and secure the Orne bridges. The armoured cars and carriers of the Inns of Court Yeomanry and 7 Cdn Recce Regiment had probed east through positions held by 32 Guards Brigade. The Yeomanry's war diary describes their action on the evening of 8 July:

> D Sqn on right and A Sqn on left (N. & S.) of CARPIQUET recc'd as far as the Bretteville-sur-Odon rd, but darkness and the presence of dug-in Panthers cut the recce short: no concentration was seen, however. During

> this recce A Sqn was heavily fired on by Panthers, etc. which allowed the first two troops to proceed before opening up: Major Scott lost touch with these two troops and on their return it was found that their A-set aerials had been cut to 2 inches by enemy fire. One Daimler A/Car was lost, Sgt Thorp being killed. It appears that a Coy of Coldstream Guards through which A Sqn passed failed to warn them that the road was under fire from Panthers. A Sqn withdrew under cover of smoke, D Sqn found buildings on N. & S. of aerodrome strongly held. At the same time heavy tps of A & B Squadrons were ordered to the main road and rail bridges in CAEN: this, however, they were unable to carry out, owing to enemy opposition and except for the troop of B Sqn which blocked the road at ST GERMAIN, all Sqns were withdrawn and concentrated before 2359 hrs.

With the enemy still very much in place, there was every expectation of a stiff fight for the rest of Carpiquet and the villages around the western side of Caen during 9 July.

Major General Keller's plan for his division on CHARNWOOD's second day was to clear up the remainder of his divisional area and complete the advance into Caen. The latter operation was again to be led by the corps and divisional recce squadrons, followed by a mobile column provided by 9 Cdn Brigade, based on the Stormont, Glengarry & Dundas Highlanders; they would be followed by the North Nova Scotia Highlanders and the Highland Light Infantry of Canada, in that order. Further south, the attack to complete the capture of the Carpiquet hangars and barracks, Operation TROUSERS, delayed from the previous day, was to be carried out by 8 Cdn Brigade.

Amidst the battle procedure the North Nova Scotia Highlanders received battle casualty replacements. 'It was rather a shock when the 4 (four) officers and 61 (sixty-one) other ranks reinforcements [were] received that morning who had not even time to meet their platoon and company commanders . . . They were simply detailed to companies and platoons by numbers.' This was a less than perfect introduction to their new battalion and to the battle.

The SDG's Adjutant recorded the planning process and intent in the battalion's war diary:

> C.O. returns and orders and 'O' Gp for 0500 hrs. 'A' and 'B' coys will pack up and move from GRUNCHY via VIEUX CAIRON to area WOODS 970728. 'D' and 'C' coys will prepare to advance immediately and follow up the enemy who is withdrawing. 'D' coy leading with one sec carriers and one sec 3″ mortars. Comd post with 'C' Coy, remainder of Supt coy less one sec carriers in rear. Remainder of details to be tied up later. The role is advance to contact, and not to engage in heavy fighting. Coy comds are to get reorganized on this basis and return at 0730 hrs. The C.O. will move 'D' coy by wireless in a series of bounds. These bounds are lettered 'A' 'B' 'C' etc. to 'K' and are localities of enemy resistance on the way from FRANQUE-VILLE to CAEN.

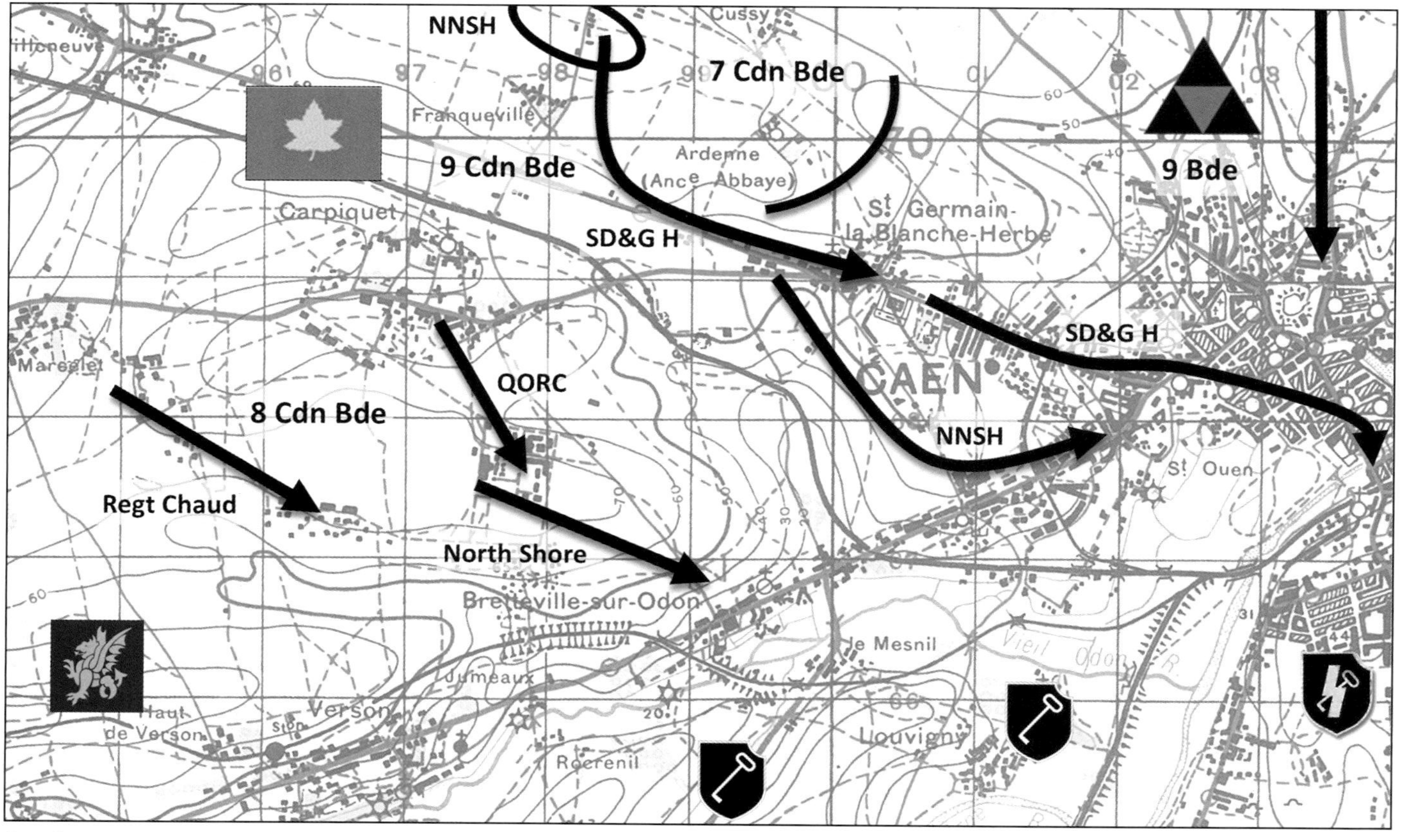

Canadian operation west of Caen on 9 July 1944.

A wounded *Hitlerjugend* soldier taken prisoner by men of the 3rd Canadian Division.

The battalion was, as ever, under pressure to get moving. The Adjutant noted at 0658 hours, 'Brig enquires how we are getting on. He is being pushed from higher formations: we work as urgently as possible, but we are very tired'; and an hour later, 'The Brig calls; he is most anxious that we push on in a hurry.' Despite mounting delays, Brigadier Cunningham ordered the advance to begin at 0900 hours.

Following closely behind the armoured cars of the recce squadrons, the SDG's mobile column was on the move with the Shermans of B Squadron of the Sherbrook Fusiliers, which passed through a firm base between Authie and Franqueville provided by the NNS Highlanders. Having cleared through Franqueville, they were soon astride the Caen–Bayeux road, advancing on their next objective, Saint-Germain-la-Blanche-Herbe.

On the western approaches to the city soldiers of the *Hitlerjugend* Panzer Division, who had put up so much resistance to the Canadians the previous day, were not going to be bundled out of their positions and chased south of the Orne. Instead, they were conducting a controlled withdrawal with a proper rearguard that was now well ahead of the Canadians. To the west of the city, this consisted of the remnants of III/26 *Panzergrenadiers* supported by the division's remaining two batteries of 88mm guns and Pioneers, whose task it was to delay the Allied advance. In this respect they were successful, the Canadians noting that the Germans had laid 'a carpet of mines to slow down our entry into the stricken city'. On the western approaches to Caen, although there was plenty of battle damage to the roads and houses following a month of bombardment, the obstructions were not nearly as severe as on the routes from the north. In addition to mines and some rubble there were groups of *Panzergrenadiers* of the delaying

Canadian troops entering Caen from the west.

force, who opened fire but withdrew as the SDG prepared to attack. Between 0900 hours and 1125 the companies cleared a succession of six enemy delaying positions.

At this point, while the SDG, 'impeded by MG and Snipers', continued through Saint-Germain into Caen, the NNS Highlanders passed to the south of them to clear the suburb of Venoix. After a hasty Orders Group, the Battalion moved forward once again under heavy mortar fire, down the railway track to Venoix. 'It was found that this road was mined and no vehicles were able to go through. However, the marching troops moved on, the vehicles returning to Carpiquet and going through St. Germain and south into Venoix.' By 1330 hours the leading companies of the SDG were entering the centre of Caen, followed by A and B Company.

Operation TROUSERS and the Advance on Bretteville-sur-Odon

A month into the campaign, the process of getting Brigadier Blackadder's 8 Cdn Brigade into battle further south in the Carpiquet area was swift. Divisional orders were given to brigade commanders by General Keller at 0030 hours, with brigade orders groups recorded as being called for between 0230 and 0300 hours. Battle procedure at battalion level followed, with planning, orders and preparations down the chain of command to section level. Despite it by now being a familiar process, the North Nova Scotia Highlanders described this as 'hasty'. The first moves were underway just after dawn at 0618 hours Double British Summer Time.

The plan for 8 Cdn Brigade was for two companies of the Queen's Own Rifles of Canada to attack the airfield control tower and the Carpiquet barracks from the village. Meanwhile, Le Regiment de la Chaudière was to advance from Marcalet to capture the southern hangars, with tank support provided by B Squadron, the Fort Garry Horse. The brigade's third battalion, the North Shore Regiment, was initially in reserve but, following the Queen's Own Rifles of Canada, was to be prepared to cross the Orne and secure the southern suburb of Cormelles if ordered.

According to the Fort Garry Horse, in expectation of the determined resistance by the defenders that the Inns of Court and 7 Cdn Recce Regiment had reported the previous evening, the attacks were preceded by 'an artillery barrage which rivalled that of the original barrage'. At 1000 hours the Chaudières advanced and noted that 'The advance is very fast and at noon the objective is captured.' The Queen's Own Rifles' C and D Company fared equally well and recorded:

> Few actual enemy are encountered although some casualties are sustained by arty and mortar fire. However forward coys report 'ABLE' by 1030 hrs and are soon in posn and consolidated. F Ech Vehs [Fighting Echelon vehicles] move up to bn and outside of the occasional shell, things are quite peaceful.

> Tac headquarters is established in a former air raid shelter which is very solid – too bad we didn't have it in our former spot.

With the Germans having withdrawn overnight, the Chaudières were also soon consolidating around the remnants of the hangars.

> We reorganized and noted that the losses had been very light despite the large number of Germans dead on the ground. Once installed, the German guns and mortars sent us a first rate burst but fortunately this caused no damage. We organize ourselves in a defensive position and the regimental pioneers clear the ground of mines and 'booby traps' which have been left there.

Facing little opposition, 8 Cdn Brigade took the opportunity to exploit their advantage. The Canadian report noted:

> This affair came off with such light opposition that Brigadier Blackadder, assuming that the Germans had withdrawn across the river, urged N. Shore R. to push on over the hillside into Bretteville-sur-Odon. His appreciation proved to be correct; the enemy had gone although the approaches to the place were still defended by intense mortar fire directed from the hills on the opposite bank.

Canadians enter Caen via the N13 Bayeux road.

The North Shore Regiment's war diary provides a detailed account of the next phase of the advance east towards Caen that would take the battalion into the village of Bretteville on the outskirts of the city:

> At 1025 L/Col Buell was called to Bde O Gp regarding move of Bn to Bretteville-sur-Odon. This move was a follow up of the move by Q.O.R. and R de Chaud. At 1025 hrs 'C' Coy moved to take over position formerly occupied by a Coy of the R de Chaud and were in position at 1053 hrs. Coy Comdrs were called to Bn 'O' Gps at 1200 hrs and were briefed regarding the occupation, clearing and holding of Bretteville-sur-Odon. This town was situated in a valley and could only be approached over open country but as it was vitally necessary to the Bde plan that this be seized; it was decided to move the Bn well dispersed with 'A' & 'C' Coys leading and 'B' & 'D' Coys follow up. The Carrier Pl made a recce around to the left of Bretteville-sur-Odon as both a recce and a diversionary move and at 1515 hrs all Coys reported that they were on the start line and at 1527 hrs the advance began. At first as the Bn moved under cover of the high ground in front of the Airport the only shelling was the normal harassing fire that the enemy had been putting down right along, but as the first Coys came into his view over the crest of the hill, he started to range with mortars, 81mm and 105mm, and by the time the two reserve Coys had started down the slope the shelling had reached a terrific pitch and it could be seen that 'B' & 'D' Coys were suffering casualties. Still they went on – dropping to avoid shrapnel when a shell burst behind them, but always getting up to continue the advance to their objective. At 1630 hrs the leading elements were on their objective.

As was the case with the brigade's other battalions, 'Resistance was very light in the town itself and the enemy had evidently moved out in a great hurry.' However, now across the high ground and on a forward slope in sight of the *Leibstandarte* south of the Odon, 'during the whole time arty and mortar fire was extremely heavy and very accurate.'

While the Canadian infantry was clearing the villages in detail, the recce regiments, avoiding contact with the enemy, were slipping through into the city. The Inns of Court Yeomanry recorded:

> Situation at midday was: A & D Sqns in CAEN with patrols on almost all the brs. all of which were strongly held by the enemy: B Sqn S. of CAEN–BRETTEVILLE Rd ... Progress through CAEN was found to be difficult, owing to craters and mountains of rubble and opposition from snipers and mortars: a rapturous welcome was given by the population, some of whom assisted our patrols by guiding them round obstructions etc.[7]

59th Division

With the formations to its flanks preparing to advance into the city, the 59th Division during 9 July was to complete its first- and second-phase tasks, fully securing

A rubble-filled street in the centre of Caen.

villages 'taken' the previous day and capturing those that the enemy apparently still held. To prevent clashes with the other divisions, their southerly limit of exploitation was set at the 70 Northing.

Major General Lyne's plan (see map on page 246) for was for 176 Brigade, supported by Shermans of the East Riding Yeomanry's C Squadron, to continue working its way south via the troublesome Trench System and Mâlon to Couvre Chef. In the centre, 197 Brigade was too properly secure the Bitot area, Mâlon and then La Folie. Tasks for 177 Brigade included the clearance of snipers who continued to bother 1/6 S Staffs in Cambes and the elimination of the remaining German positions in their area, including that at Galmanche. They were aided by the ERY's C Squadron, while the depleted B Squadron provided a reserve following its mauling the previous day.

The operations of 176 Brigade began with a resumption of the attack on the Trench System by 6 N Staffs and A Squadron ERY at 0930 hours. In the open country there was plenty of machine-gun and small-arms fire from those defenders who had been left behind, men the order to withdraw had not reached, or wounded soldiers unable to be evacuated. The Trench System was bombarded and worked through methodically by the Staffords' infantry this time, with tanks in close support. Lieutenant Brown explained that it was 'a fantastic deep trench system, similar to those used in the 1914–18 war, with deep slits, dug-outs and dug-in Tiger tanks [*sic*].'

> Now we had to clear these dug-outs, and in groups we wandered through the trenches, making sure they were empty. The recognised method of doing this was to heave a couple of grenades into every dug-out, and if nothing came out it was considered to be clear ... Then I came face to face with a steel-helmeted German, head and shoulders out of a slit trench, rifle pointing straight at me. In sheer panic I fired several times with my pistol; but as there was no reply, I advanced cautiously. I needn't have worried; he had been dead some hours. The poor fellow's intestines were hanging from a gaping hole in his stomach.

With the Trench System reported as clear at 1200 hours, the hamlet of Couvre Chef was the brigade's next objective. The adjacent villages of Épron and Auberge had eventually been entered during the night of 8/9 July by 7 R Norfolks, with A Company of 7 S Staffs under command. This company was sent forward to occupy Couvre Chef, but finding itself out on a limb, with communications having broken down and enemy machine-gun posts still active, it had been withdrawn.[8] Consequently, on the morning of 9 July, 7 R Norfolk were ordered to fully secure Épron and Aubers and capture Couvre Chef, this time with the help of 144 RAC. In a preliminary operation, the tanks were ordered to conduct an offensive reconnaissance of Couvre Chef. A Squadron left their overnight position near Ring Contour 60 and headed west across the boundary into 59th Division's area. As was the case with other surrounding villages, at 0700 hours the tanks reported that Couvre Chef had been abandoned by the Germans. However, following their experience the previous day, 7 R Norfolk did not believe them and ordered A Squadron's Shermans to withdraw. The squadron duly pulled back into fire positions on the railway line, where they were intermittently shelled and mortared. The Norfolks completed the clearance of Épron but when advancing from Épron to Auberge, in an example of poor coordination, they were shot up by A Squadron 1st Northamptonshire Yeomanry (1 NY) in friendly fire from the 3rd Division's area – fortunately, without casualties. The Norfolks then went ahead with the planned artillery bombardment of Couvre Chef before they 'attacked', with, according to Captain Cunliffe, 144 RAC 'watching with some derision'. Nonetheless, during the day A Squadron of the East Riding Yeomanry lost two tanks knocked out and two disabled. Once the village was confirmed as being in their hands, the Norfolks dispatched patrols a mile south to the division's limit of exploitation, this time with 1 NY correctly engaging Germans, who retreated before the Norfolks' advance.

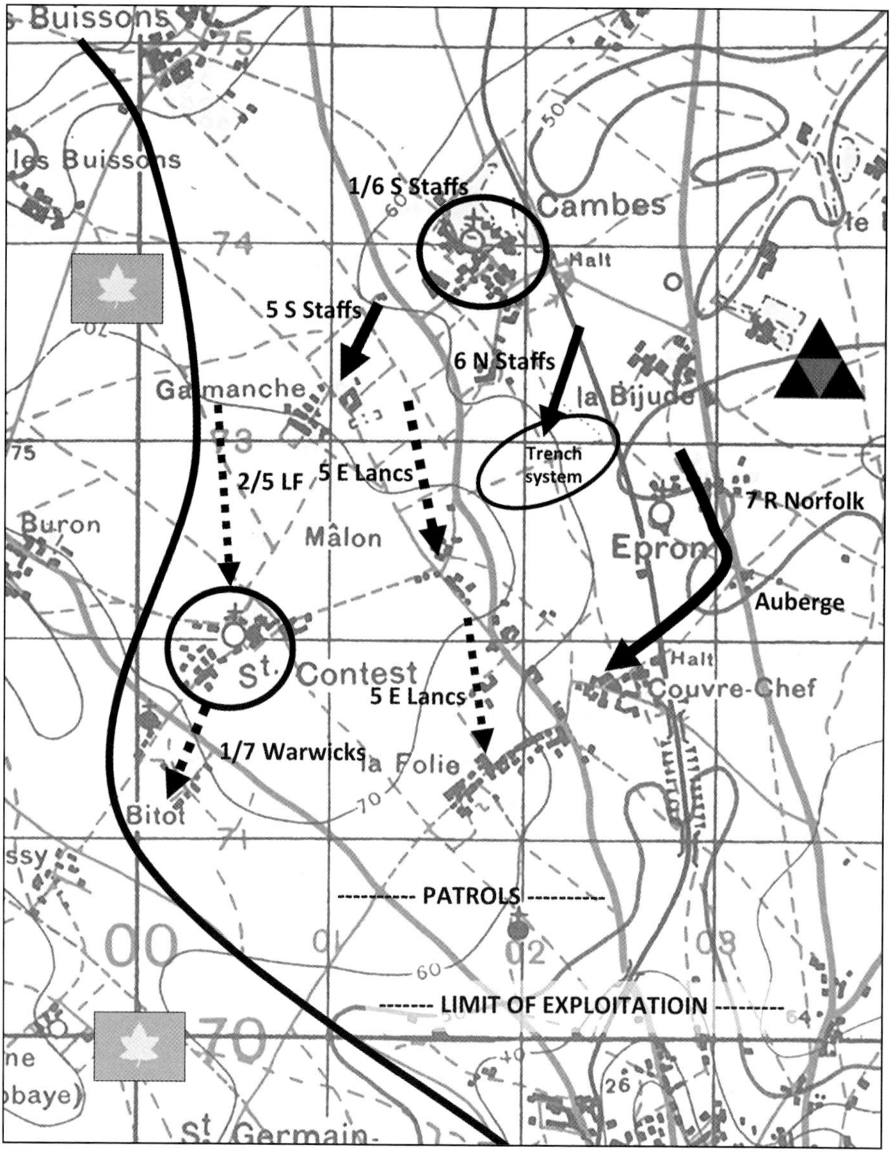

Operations of 59th Division to clear villages in their area during 9 July 1944.

In 177 Brigade's area, overnight, the 5 S Staffs had shared parts of Galmanche, not just the château, with groups of *Hitlerjugend* soldiers who had become separated and left behind. In one incident that made the national papers, they even found themselves in the same house:

> Two men of D Company of the 5th Battalion, unknown to each other, had spent the night inside the chateau with the Germans without the enemy knowing of their presence, although both knew the Germans were there [in the village]. As dawn broke one man crawled away, but was quickly followed by a German with a bayonet clenched in his hands. The other man, Private Parker, looking through a slit, saw what was happening and set off in pursuit. Just as the German was about to rush forward to make his kill, Private Parker killed him with his bayonet, thus saving his comrade's life. Private Parker, who was killed at a later date, was awarded the Military Medal.[9]

The diarist of 177 Brigade noted that serious action in Galmanche began somewhat later once the Trench System had been attacked:

> At approx 1100 hrs one coy 5 S Staff sp by tks and AVRE made a successful attack on the chateau at Galmanche and destroyed the enemy there. 5 or 6 odd snipers gave themselves up during the morning. At mid-day 2/6 S Staffords moved to LE MESNIL.[10]

The artillery pounded the ruins of the château, and when the bombardment lifted the tanks of C Squadron ERY took over with 75mm HE and fire from their Browning machine guns. This covered the AVREs forward to within the 80-yard range of the 230mm demolition rounds. With the last of the defenders stunned by this demonstration of firepower, the S Staffs company cleared the château, taking a dozen Germans prisoner and counting forty dead.

In the central southern part of the divisional area, once the objectives further north had been captured by 176 and 177 brigades, 197 Brigade was to secure the straggling hamlets of Bitot, Mâlon and La Folie. Orders were issued at 0800, and at 1230 hours patrols from 1/7 Warwicks advancing from St Contest reported, 'Objective [Bitot] clear of enemy'. At 1400 hours D Company led an unopposed advance to secure the village, while 2/5 Lancashire Fusiliers took over the defence of St Contest.

According to their account, during the fighting the previous day, the 5th East Lancashire Regiment (5 E Lancs) had been the reserve battalion of 197 Brigade and had spent the previous day 'moving up to successive positions in preparation for attacks that never happened'; this, the regimental historian noted, was 'a tiresome feature of any large battle'. On 9 July, with the Trench System taken by 6 N Staffs, the battalion was committed to an advance on Mâlon, from which the 2/5 Lancashire Fusiliers had been beaten back the previous day. By midday the battalion noted that 'After some 24 hours . . . the whole movement developed into a "mopping-up" role,' during which Mâlon was secured and patrols sent forward to La Folie.[11]

Tanks of 144 Regiment RAC in St Contest during 9 July 1944.

The ERY's historian added a comment on that day's 'mopping-up' – 'A phrase glibly used as if it represented something very minor. But for those who have to do it, it is hard and difficult combat with unseen groups of determined enemy who exact all too great a toll for their numbers, in a most demoralising manner.'[12]

One incident during the morning illustrates that the animosity between the Allies and the *Hitlerjugend* was not shared by the soldiers of the 59th Division, despite the brutal fighting of the previous day. Three members of the *Hitlerjugend*'s Escort Company were burying a comrade who had been killed during the morning's preliminary artillery bombardment, in a quarry on the northern outskirts of Caen. They were surrounded by a group of soldiers of the 59th Division but continued digging; having put up a very basic cross and said prayers, they were allowed, much to their surprise, to walk away.[13]

The 59th's divisional war diary appended a note at the end of the entry for 9 July which is worth quoting at length:

> For most of the Div it was the first experience of direct contact with the enemy. Fresh from UK with no gradual introduction to battle or battle conditions, the Div was given the task of assaulting and capturing a thoroughly org German def posn. This formed the bulk of the defs of CAEN. These defs had been assaulted previously and had succeeded in holding up the British. All ranks of the Div displayed confidence and ability and the attacks were carried out with great gallantry. Tps stood up to the strain remarkably

> well. Cas were by no means lt, totalling approx 70 offrs and 1,000 ORs killed, wounded and missing. All the Divisional objectives were taken; the capture of CAEN was made possible and the German losses in personnel and equipment were substantial. Known German personnel losses were 186 PW and the Div buried approx 230 German dead. It is estimated that German wounded would be at least 1,000 based on normal averages. The resistance of the Hitler Youth Div was fanatical, the GAF Div standard was not so high, but they made the task of breaching and capturing this portion of the German West Wall an outstanding feat, which reflects great credit on the fighting qualities of the div, particularly so in its very first action and experience of war.

Having congratulated his troops on their success, Major General Lyne added:

> I want every officer and man to think out for himself the lessons learned from this operation, so that we may get the maximum value from it and ensure that mistakes made due to inexperience are not repeated when we next go into action.

With time to reflect on their experience in their first battle, an almost universal comment across the division was that they had 'not been realistic'. The divisional historian wrote: 'And that, for the 59th Division, was the end of the Battle of Caen ... and [we] withdrew to the area of Ryes, north of our original concentration area, to rest, reorganise and think over what we had learnt.'

In the City

While the 59th Division cleared the last of the villages north of Caen, the infantry of the two flanking divisions had made their way through light enemy resistance and the worst of the devastation into the lower part of the city. It is worth reiterating that the rubble that confronted 3rd Division as they entered Caen was not entirely due to the bombing of the city on the evening of 7 July. Concerns over French civilian casualties and damage to their towns and cities remained, but the known difficulty of overcoming German resistance had allayed some of the qualms. Consequently, key points in the city such as bridges over the Orne, railway and road junctions had been repeatedly and not always accurately attacked from land, sea and air since the opening of the campaign, resulting in significant damage before the bomber strikes.

In Caen, as was the case across the towns and cities of France liberated by the Allies, the Resistance and those who donned the armband to join them were of assistance in helping to drive the Germans from the city. The RUR's diarist recorded that 'At this point we were met by numerous Frenchmen of the Underground Movement who established an immediate liaison and led our troops down towards the ORNE.' Amidst the ruins and rubble, enemy positions were pointed out to British and Canadian soldiers, who were also shown advantageous fire positions and led around blockages. As the Germans fell back and Allied troops penetrated further into the city, thousands of civilians sheltering in the Bon Sauveur hospital and the Lycée Malherbe greeted the troops with enthusiasm, singing the Marseillaise and waving flags. Many Allied soldiers commented on their unlikely reception amidst such destruction. This account by 2 RUR describes their 'progress':

> When the main body of the Battalion arrived down in the town, the advance soon assumed the air of triumphant progress rather than a calculated operation of war: the people of Caen were determined to make it so. We discovered afterwards that they had suffered all the brutalities that had become commonplace in Europe. In addition, they had seen their town laid waste in a series of RAF attacks by their own friends, the British. If we were ever doubtful of a welcome reception, the first few hours in Caen put our minds at rest. Flags of France were draped out of windows, and the people poured out of their houses with greetings and glasses of wine.

Soldiers of I Corps in Caen with some of the civilians they liberated.

> On the boulevards, we were met by the Captain of the Resistance Movement with several of his comrades, who gave us 'Liberté' as the password agreed upon by themselves and their Headquarters in London. One of their number guided C Company along the boulevards and others proved themselves invaluable in disclosing hideouts of German snipers and machine gunners. It may be said here that through the complete mastery of the language displayed by Major J.C.S.G. de Longueuil we were able to take full advantage of their assistance.

The Canadians, with more French speakers amongst them, were received if anything even more warmly; their historical section added that 'Although many had suffered from our bombing and shelling, the acceptance of these measures as an accompaniment of war and the price of liberation gave most remarkable expression to the faith, forbearance, the courage, and perhaps, the fatalism of those who had endured it.' *The Times* correspondent added:

> In the streets were eager, excited groups of local people who pressed round anyone speaking their language. Their relief was indescribable, though it

An anti-tank gun belonging to 1 KOSB in the centre of Caen near the Church of St Pierre.

> would be false to pretend that one was not met now and again with the question: 'Why have you done this to us?' But the dominating sentiment was gladness that at last the British had come, that the Germans had been flung out.[14]

Further south in the city, the *Hitlerjugend* were still withdrawing across the Orne bridges, which were under fire, but it was reported to Headquarters I SS Panzer Corps that the division's main body was south of the Orne at 1300 hours. Here, as recounted by *Sturmbannführer* Hubert Meyer, there was no rest for the *Panzergreanadiers* once across the river, as they needed 'to build up new defensive positions. Their heavy weapons which had not been destroyed were already in position along with artillery and rocket launchers, all of which were ready for action, even though there was some shortage of ammunition.' For most of the SS, the withdrawal through the city was out of contact, and for the RUR, as their historian noted, 'The rest of the operation can be swiftly summarised. We pushed gradually to the line of the river Orne and then systematically mopped up such disorganised resistance as remained.'

With 21st Panzer Division's *Kampfgruppe* Rauch having completed its withdrawal to the east of the Orne during the morning, incorrect reports were received by General Feuchtinger that the area of Ring Contour 60 was unoccupied by the British. Consequently, *Oberst* Rauch was ordered to re-cross into the city via the Bellemais railway bridge with two companies of 46 *Jäger* Regiment, supported by the heavy weapons of 5/192 *Panzergrenadiers*. Crossing the railway bridge at 1500 hours and advancing towards the city centre, they came under heavy fire and were forced back across the bridge. Amidst the Allied euphoria it seems that this limited counter-attack was rebuffed so easily it has gone without record in accounts of the day. The war diary of the *Hitlerjugend*'s escort company records that their last patrols and survivors of III/26 SS *Panzergrenadiers* from the Carpiquet area of Caen eventually crossed the river in the south-eastern quarter at 1600 hours and that the divisional pioneers blew the last remaining usable bridge over the Orne. Two hours later, 9 Brigade had reached the Orne, but with the *Hitlerjugend* visibly in position on the opposite bank, I Corps confirmed the cancellation of CHARNWOOD's final phase. 9 Brigade's war diary summarized the latter stage of the advance to the river and canal in Caen:

> 2 RUR reached the line of the river by 1430 hrs and 1 KOSB on the LEFT reached the canal EAST of BASSIN ST. PIERRE after encountering opposition from MG posts by midday. Both bns closed up to the line of the canal and river East and WEST of BASSIN ST PIERRE, 2 RUR having to dislodge enemy MG-posts in built up areas near the river, a task in the performance of which they received enthusiastic assistance from the local population, and 1 KOSB coming under MG and mortar fire from the other side of the canal and river banks. By 1700 hrs 2 RUR had affected a junc on their RIGHT with elements of 3 Cdn Div. During the afternoon 1 KOSB were

> brought further into the towns WEST of BASSIN ST PIERRE. Enemy MG fire and sniping prevented close br recce.

BBC reporter Frank Gillard and his fellow journalists had spent the morning of 9 July waiting at the junction on Point 64 to be allowed to go down into Caen:

> It was close on two o'clock when the commander received a message which made him turn to us and say, 'All right; if you want to go in, you can go.' Feeling very much like a military target, we shot over the open brow of the hill in our jeep, until we reached a crossroads beyond which there was so much German fire that it was obvious that the only way was to continue on foot, 'playing musical chairs from slit trench to slit trench', as one officer on the spot put it. In any case, a vehicle would have been out of the question, for 100 yards or so ahead, just round a bend, we came across the beginnings of the destruction. Rubble and masonry were being shovelled into a great bomb-crater which completely blocked the whole road. Beyond that, the scene was one of absolute and complete devastation. Every building a total wreck, trees and poles and petrol-pumps lying askew across the road, wires trailing everywhere. We picked our way ahead, thankful for the fierce counter-battery fire of our guns which were pouring concentrations into Colombelles factory at that moment and keeping the enemy up there quiet.
>
> I made some progress by climbing through into the back gardens and breaking through from one to the other down the hillside. But even then the going was so hard that I had to give it up. I went back to the top of the road and took the right fork. This was the track roughly cleared by bulldozers. But even now it was like a switchback railway. We got down among the ruined houses and met our first two civilians – two men. They told us that

BBC reporter Frank Gillard at work in Normandy.

General Crocker finally in Caen.

> there were thousands of refugees taking shelter in the huge buildings of the asylum and in a school.
>
> Away ahead of us we could hear the sharp rattle of machine-gun fire as our forward troops pushed on through the city. There was stiff resistance at points, but the Germans weren't making a house-to-house fight of it. In some more open ground on our left – goodness knows how they ever got into it – a handful of our [Canadian] tanks were taking on enemy targets, perhaps across the river.[15]

In their final battle for Caen, the Allied soldiers of I Corps suffered losses of 3,817 troops during CHARNWOOD, and some eighty tanks. The Germans lost more than 2,000 men and thirty-two panzers.

Conclusions

On 10 July operations to round off the capture of Caen continued. On the west bank of the Orne canal 2 Lincolns attacked German bridgeheads between Hérouville and Caen, and on the east side of the river 153 Brigade of the 51st Highland Division conducted Operation STACK to capture the Colombelles steel works. The latter was a disappointing failure for the below-par Highlanders, and it contributed to Major General Bullen-Smith being relieved of his command. On the same day, to the west, 43rd Wessex Division conducted a much larger affair in Operation JUPITER, with a brigade of 15th Scottish Division and a brigade of 3rd Canadian Division under command. It, too, was less than fully successful, with Hill 112 remaining in enemy hands and the Wessex's advance on the Orne crossing thrown back at Maltot; but ground immediately west of Caen was secured.

Hill 112 was to remain in German hands for another six weeks before being abandoned, but the eastern and southern suburbs of Caen were secured in Operation ATLANTIC by the Canadians operating on the flanks of GOODWOOD on 18 July 1944. In subsequent First Canadian Army attacks south, the roads through the rubble of Caen and over the bridges of the Orne were important arterial routes. During this time the city was still within the range of artillery, this time German, whose turn it was to shell the bridges. During Operation TOTALIZE Caen's southern suburbs were mis-bombed. It was indeed a tortured city.

After a month in action north of Caen, the 3rd Division was withdrawn from the city, having been relieved in place by the recently arrived 2nd Canadian Division of Lieutenant General Guy Simmons' newly activated II Canadian Corps. Captain Scarfe wrote:

> The fall of Caen meant much more to the Division than was really warranted by the tactical gain. And when, on July 11th, the Infantry were brought back out of the line in the transport of the Divisional R.A.S.C. Companies, there was a general feeling of relaxation. Even the Gunners felt it, though the guns had to remain in action. The amenities of the Div Club at Luc-sur-Mer were in great demand; so were such footballs, darts, or any other sports gear as could be obtained from Army Welfare Services. The supreme pleasure was to have a bath and a long, undisturbed sleep. So far there had only been biscuits to eat with the tinned food in the compo packs. On the 13th of July the Biscuit-Eaters were given their first half-slice of bread. It was only half a slice, but it was eaten with greater relish than can be imagined even by those

> who, two years later, feel the rationing of bread most keenly. Then, on the 14th, after only three days of rest and reorganisation, the Division suddenly learnt that a move into action across the Orne was imminent.[1]

In its next battle the 3rd Division was to advance on the left flank of Operation GOODWOOD. Meanwhile, 3rd Canadian Division also joined the II Canadian Corps, with its old ground north west of Caen being taken over by XII Corps and its positions in the city by the 2nd Canadian Division. Finally, the 59th Division moved back to the coast.

> By the evening of 12th July, the whole division was in its rest area, rather bitterly conscious of the truth of 'what goes up must come down', as the great concentration of AA guns around the beaches harried the occasional intruder. The HQ War Diary records, '2100 hrs –first bread issue – 3oz in lieu of 1½ oz biscuits'; a landmark indeed in the progress of the build-up. Mobile laundry and bath units worked round the clock and the Divisional Concert Party – including a luscious brunette female impersonator – played till it dropped. More seriously, we reaped the fruits of the Divisional Commander's insistence on a thorough 'left out of battle policy', and the battered infantry quickly regained its battle trim as it absorbed the officers, NCOs and specialists who had been left protesting in 'B' Echelon while their comrades went into battle. These were not raw reinforcements, but men

Canadian engineers bulldoze routes through the rubble of Caen.

> who had long been normal members of their battalion and were ready to slip straight into any place allotted to them.[2]

However, even though 'The division needed a rest, but it did not need – and did not get – a long one', the 59th marched south-west to join XXX Corps on 13 July, when they were inserted in the line between the 53rd and the 49th divisions for Operation POMEGRANATE, the attack on Noyers.

Views of the Future Course the Battle

With Caen in the hands of I Corps, the two sides looked to the future of the battle for Normandy. The German view of the situation that kept nineteen divisions fixed in the Pas de Calais, thanks to the remarkable longevity of Operation FORTITUDE, was this:

> Once the Caen area has been occupied completely, and suitable bridgeheads established across the Orne, the enemy will launch his drive for Paris. Now, as before, one must reckon on a major landing by the First American Army Group in the zone of Fifteenth Army for an operation in combination with Army Group Montgomery and for the elimination of the *Vergeltungswaffen* [V, or revenge weapons]. [Army Group B report, 3–9 July 1944]

Montgomery stuck to his basic concept:

> My broad policy remains unchanged. It is to draw the main enemy forces into the battle on our eastern flank, and to fight them there, so that our affairs on the western flank may proceed the easier. But the enemy has been able to bring reinforcements to oppose the advance of the First [US] Army. It is important to speed up our advance on the western flank; the operations of the Second Army must therefore be so staged that they will have a direct influence on the operations of the First Army, as well as holding enemy forces on the eastern flank. [Montgomery's Directive M510, 10 July 1944]

General Dempsey's headquarters, however, acknowledged that the next stage of the fighting in Normandy would not be easy:

> Tactically in the west [i.e. Normandy], in spite of very severe losses, great difficulties in finding divisions to stem the tide and long lines of communication, the German is as tough a fighter as ever and determined to give up nothing without a fight. He may be helped, and not too brilliantly, by Poles, Russians, Alsatians and even a Persian, many of whom are deserting to our lines, but as long as there are live Germans with ammunition, weapons and petrol, the fight will go on whatever the cost.
>
> [Second Army Intelligence Summary No. 36]

None of these predictions was wrong. The battle for Normandy ground on for another seven weeks.

* * *

Despite fighting under many disadvantages, the German soldier remained a doughty opponent in battle.

A Question of Airfields

The issue of ground for airfields on the left flank around Caen was one of the central factors in the criticism of General Montgomery's conduct of the campaign in Normandy during July and into August 1944.

When Montgomery's recast plans for the assault landing and the campaign were presented to senior Allied commanders, as early as March 1944, Air Marshal Leigh-Mallory objected and urged strongly that 'Second Army should push east at an earlier stage than is envisaged in the present forecast of operations.' As commander of the Allied Expeditionary Air Force, he wanted to see more ground south of Caen taken for airfields at an early stage. The country elsewhere in much of Montgomery's proposed lodgement, he argued, was not suitable for quickly or easily establishing Advanced Landing Grounds (ALG) for the squadrons of the Second Tactical Air Force (2 TAF) or the Ninth US Air Force to operate from.

Air Marshal Sir Trafford Leigh-Mallory.

In his presentation of plans on 7 April, Montgomery tried to address Leigh-Malory's concerns:

> Second Army is to assault west of the River Orne and to develop operations to the south and south-east in order to secure airfield sites and to protect the eastern flank of First U.S. Army while the latter is capturing Cherbourg. In its subsequent operations the Second Army will pivot on its left and offer a strong front against enemy movement towards the lodgment area from the east.

This did not satisfy the airmen's requirements for sufficient airfields in Normandy; they wanted firm objectives further south-east to plan against. These Montgomery was reluctant to provide, and the dispute rumbled on into May, with Leigh-Mallory refusing to sign up to the campaign plan. Finally, Montgomery and his chief planner drew up illustrative maps that placed the pivot well the south of Caen in the Falaise/Argentan area. Brigadier Belchem, while believing Montgomery was

> sincere in his statements ... thought that short of a miracle – such as a complete German collapse – there was little hope of the British Second Army reaching Argentan, or even Falaise, in the early stage of the Battle of Normandy.[3]

Montgomery repeatedly stressed that the enemy's likely reaction on the left flank would heavily influence the progress of the battle. In addition, he questioned whether resources for such an extensive drive south were possible in the time frame demanded by the air forces. It was only once Montgomery had confirmed that he would endeavour to deliver the ground demanded by Leigh-Mallory that the 21st Army Group's detailed master plan was finally agreed. However, with evidence of the German reinforcement of Lower Normandy growing daily, the prospect of a speedy advance from the coast was receding; no matter what commander's plans are, 'the enemy always has a say'.

Although Montgomery always expected to fight hard around the left flank, he cannot have expected the Germans to fight so determinedly to hold Caen, despite being in range of the guns of the Allied fleet. Chester Wilmot wrote:

> At the start of the invasion, Montgomery had believed that Second Army, in order to fulfil its role of 'protecting and threatening', would have to secure the area south-east of Caen at the outset. In the first week, however, when Rommel had to commit his panzer divisions defensively, the capture of the Caen area became more difficult, but also less necessary, for the German armour was already pinned and contained there ... The conversion of this possibility into a reality in the first week of the invasion brought about prematurely the strategic situation which Montgomery's plan required, and made it difficult, if not impossible, for him to meet Leigh-Mallory's request that Second Army should secure the Caen airfield zone without delay.[4]

By early July, a combination of factors caused criticism to be heaped on Montgomery for the failure to capture Caen and ground to the south and south-east. Firstly, the airmen, headed by Air Marshal Tedder, General Eisenhower's deputy

Men of the airfield construction groups laying Square Mesh Trackway (SMT) at an Advanced Landing Ground (ALG).

commander, wanted space in which to deploy the whole of 2 TAF and fulfil their ambition of shaping the campaign with the might of air power. Secondly, Lieutenant General Morgan, the COSSAC planner, whose basic strategy to break out on the left flank had been rejected by Montgomery, led a chorus of criticism that Montgomery was defensive and was failing to break out. Finally, Eisenhower, who espoused the US doctrine of the day of attacking everywhere, despite being well briefed on Mongomery's campaign plan, complained about a lack of progress on Second Army's front.

However, with the Luftwaffe being severely reduced before the campaign opened, Montgomery believed that operating from airfields in southern England and from fifteen ALGs which would be open in Normandy by the end of June would meet the Second Army's need for air cover and close support. Wilmot commented:

> This view was rejected and resented by Leigh-Mallory and by the Commander of the Second British Tactical Air Force, Air Marshal Sir Arthur

Coningham. They tended to present their claims for more airfields almost as demands of right which Montgomery should be obliged to fulfil. This attitude sprang from a genuine eagerness 'to play their full part in the battle'.

Resentment built as Montgomery left his staff to deal with air commanders – this appeared to cast the airmen as advisers, not equals. Wilmot recalled a press conference at which Coningham blurted out, 'It's always "Monty's Army", "Monty's victory", "Monty strikes again". You never say "Coningham's Air Force".'

Criticism continued to build, with space for airfields becoming a significant issue not only in military and political circles but in the press as well. Since Montgomery was unable, of course, to publicly explain his strategy, this continued right up to the fulfilment of his 'master plan' and the breakout at the end of July, with the Seine and Loire being reached as projected by D+90.

Air Marshal 'Māori' Coningham with Generals Montgomery and Dempsey.

Over the years, many have commented on and argued over the month-long battles for Caen. The controversy started with the discredited Ingersoll and aberrant Wilmot and continued to be pursued vigorously by the regiments that fought there. The battle lines were drawn long before the contents of ULTRA files became available in the late 1970s, and before information on the enemy's reinforcement of Normandy from Germany and the east became readily accessible. Opinion has now shifted towards accepting that the rates of advance inland by the other two Second Army D Day divisions were not that dissimilar, and neither faced a panzer division or the type of pre-D Day layered defences that had been prepared to cover Caen. Several contemporary or near-contemporary thoughts are, however, worth considering.

Based on his experience of fighting the Red Army, *Standartenführer* Meyer was critical of the way the Allies used their armour, of which they had a considerable superiority in numbers, on 8 July. Rather than overwhelm the German defenders with bold dashes for the Caen bridges that would have unhinged the defences, he believed that the British and Canadian tanks were instead hanging back, supporting their infantry, and thus making themselves vulnerable. He wrote:

> With the exception of the … artillery, the attack lacked momentum and initiative on the battlefield and was conducted … along tactical principles employed in World War I. You could only afford to conduct such warfare against an army that had already been bled white.

It should, however, be noted that Meyer had himself tried an Eastern Front-style armoured charge against the Canadians on those same fields on D+1 and had failed badly.

A French family returning to the ruins of Buron on 18 July 1944.

21 ARMY GROUP
Personal Message from the C-in-C
To be read out to all troops

1. A great deal has happened since my last message to you on 10 June – one month ago; the battle in Normandy has been fierce and hard since then, and much has been achieved.

2. Our gains have been definite and concrete; and we have held everything we have gained, despite the desperate efforts of the enemy to push us back into the sea. On the west flank – CHERBOURG One the east flank – CAEN And much territory in between.

And all the time a tremendous struggle with a skilful enemy, whose good fighting qualities and tenacity in battle cannot but attract our admiration. The pace has been hot, and it was clear that someone would have to give ground sooner or later; it was equally clear that the Allied soldiers would see the thing through to the end and would never give up; and so the Germans have been forced to give ground -- which is very right and proper.

3. And to-day, the Allied Armies fighting in Normandy have good grounds for solid satisfaction. We have taken over 54,000 prisoners. We have given the enemy forces a tremendous pounding, and we know from prisoners what great losses they have suffered. And we have enlarged and extended our lodgement area, and in all that area we are very firm and secure, and we are developing our offensive operations in accordance with our plans.

4. And so, to every Allied soldier in Normandy I say: "Well done. Well done indeed. You have performed a great task in a manner which is fully in keeping with the great traditions of the fighting stocks from which we all come. And your families and friends in the homeland may well be very proud of their menfolk serving overseas."

5. It is the earnest desire of every Allied soldier in Normandy to finish this business off as quickly as possible, and to pull his full weight and do his duty until it is so finished off. That we all know. And I cannot do better than to conclude this message by quoting the favourite prayer of Sir Francis Drake: "O Lord God, when Thou givest to Thy servants to endeavour in any great matter, grant us also to know that it is not the beginning, but the continuing of the same until it be thoroughly finished, which yieldeth the true glory."

6. Let us fight on to victory in the spirit of that prayer.

7. Good luck to each one of you.

B. L. Montgomery
General
C-in-C 21 Army Group.

11 July 1944
FRANCE

General Montgomery s message to 21st Army Group on 11 July 1944.

The words of Lieutenant General Guy Simmons, although he was writing a rebuttal of criticism of Operation SPRING, which took place after the fall of Caen, neatly sum up the purpose of fighting around the 'city hinge' from D Day until early August 1944:

> Of all the operations of war the 'holding attack' is that least understood by the layman, for the casualties seem out of all proportion to apparent gains. It is also, for the same reasons, the most trying for a commander and his troops. Yet to achieve great decisive results against a skilful enemy, the hostile reserves must be drawn in and pinned and worn down before the real coup-de-grace can be delivered. In all military history, to force an able [enemy] commander to expend his reserves there has been discovered no alternative to the 'holding attack'. To affect its purpose, such an attack must be directed against an objective about which the enemy is highly sensitive and for the protection of which he is certain to react.[3]

In the context of the Normandy Campaign, General Montgomery had identified that 'objective' as Caen and the surrounding country on Second Army's left flank. If, following the German reinforcement during the spring, he was unlikely to capture Caen quickly or cleanly, he would make the enemy fight hard to keep it. As one veteran put it, Caen was 'The Anvil of Victory'.

The Warwicks' universal carrier, nicknamed 'Dog Star' (see page 195).

Notes

Introduction

1. TNA CAB 44/246.
2. Edwards, Commander Kenneth, *Operation Neptune* (Collins, London, 1946).

Chapter 1: D Day and the 'First Phase'

1. Saunders, Tim, *The Advance on Caen: From SWORD Beach towards the City 6–9 June* (Pen & Sword, Barnsley, 2025).
2. TNA WO 205/532.
3. Bletchley had delivered into the hands of Allied commanders a decrypt of von Rundstedt's plan for the defence of Normandy.
4. TNA WO 171/1325.
5. Kortenhaus, Werner, *The Combat History of the 21. Panzer Division* (Helion, Solihull, 2014).
6. Edwards, Commander Kenneth, *Operation Neptune* (Collins, London, 1946).
7. Saunders, Tim, *Battle for the Bocage – Normandy 1944* (Pen & Sword, Barnsley, 2021).
8. Sanders, Geoffrey, *Soldier, Sailor* (The Bombardment Units Association, Gloucester, 1947).
9. Saunders and Hone, *12th Hitlerjugend Panzer Division in Normandy* (Pen & Sword, Barnsley, 2021).
10. The No. 68 Set was developed for combined operations use by amphibious and airborne forces. It was a low-frequency version, giving longer range, of the No. 18 set that was typically used at infantry company level.

Chapter 2: The Long June into July

1. TNA CAB 44/246.
2. Anon., *History of the 2nd Bn: The Royal Ulster Rifles in North-West Europe, 1944-45* (Regimental publication, 1946).
3. The CANLOAN scheme was to loan 673 junior Canadian officers, principally to the British infantry, to fight in the North-West European Campaign.
4. Fendick, Reg, *A CANLOAN Officer* (Revised edition, Vickers MG Collection & Research Association, 2022).
5. Edwards, Commander Kenneth, *Operation Neptune* (Collins, London, 1946).
6. *Administrative History of 21 Army Group 6 June 1944–8 May 1945* (HQ BAOR, Germany, 1945).
7. Sanders, Geoffrey, *Soldier, Sailor* (The Bombardment Units Association, Gloucester, 1947).
8. It sounds as if the anti-tank mines were to be fired electronically and used in the manner of a Claymore.
9. On 14 June Fritz Witt was killed by a naval fire strike, following which Kurt 'Panzer' Meyer took command of the 12th *Hitlerjugend* SS Panzer Division.
10. Meyer, Hubert, *The History of the 12. SS-Panzerdivision Hitlerjugend* (J.J. Fedorowicz, Winnipeg, 1994).
11. As in the Great War, the Germans experienced persistent vermin problems, but the Second British Army, thanks to well organized RAOC mobile bath and laundry units, were largely on top of the issue.
12. The officer map reading was the division's Assistant Director of Medical Services (ADMS).
13. There were other exacerbating factors, including the dilution of the division's Scottishness, and 'Why us again?'

14. Kortenhaus, Werner, *The Combat History of 21. Panzer Division* (Helion & Co, Warwick, 2014).
15. Zeltling, Niklas, *Normandy 1944, German Military Organisation* (J.J. Fedorowicz, Winnipeg, 2000).
16. The Germans had copied Michelin maps of France. The colours used were identical to the original maps, but highlighting of tourist routes and intermediate distances were deleted.
17. Belchem, Major General David, *All in the Day's March* (Collins, London, 1978).
18. Edwards, Kenneth, *Operation Neptune* (Collins, London, 1946).
19. IWM, Montgomery Papers, vol. 1.
20. Logistic Branch HQ BAOR, *Administrative History of 21 Army Group, 6 June 1944–8 May 1945* (BAOR, November 1945).
21. Montgomery's directive M 505 of 18 June 1944.
22. Ibid.
23. IWM, Montgomery Papers, vol. 1.
24. Scott, Wing Commander Desmond, *Typhoon Pilot*, Leo Cooper (Secker & Warburg, London, 1982).

Chapter 3: Château de la Londe

1. The farmhouse is today known as Le Petit Londel.
2. TNA WO171/1332.
3. https://ww2talk.com/
4. Carell, Paul, *Invasion – They're Coming!* (Bantam Books, New York, 1967).
5. https://ww2talk.com/
6. German divisional headquarters had very effective radio intercept platoons, which noted an increase in radio chatter when attacks were imminent and were able to triangulate the source of the signals to generate target data for mortars or artillery.
7. There is evidence that the 75mm gun that was also captured was probably a PaK 97/38, which was a lash-up of a First World War French barrel that fired hollow charge ammunition mounted on a PaK 38 gun carriage.
8. It was a German principle that no matter what their trade was, soldiers were first and foremost fighting men, and all were expected to take part in battle alongside the infantry.
9. Saunders and Hone, *141 Regiment RAC (The Buffs) – Flamethrowers in Normandy* (Pen & Sword, Barnsley, 2024).
10. Bailey, Harry, *The Playboys* (privately published).
11. IWM Sound Archive. Lacey interview 1964.
12. This is sometimes mistakenly referred to as a purely diversionary attack. Its aim was also to take tactically important ground.
13. The Crocodiles did not feature in the renewed attack but were to remain on call. This was probably because in their first operation with the brigade, a single troop had, as their 2iC Captain Bailey said, contributed 'precisely nothing at all'. The regiment and those they supported were having to learn on the job how to use flame to best effect and save infantry lives.
14. Lummis, Colonel Eric, *1st Suffolk in Normandy* (https://www.arrse.co.uk/community/).
15. Scarfe, Norman, *Assault Division* (Collins, London, 1947).
16. The powerful II SS Panzer Corps was being tracked by ULTRA from Ukraine back to the west. Finally, on its approach to Normandy, the intelligence was released to General Dempsey, and offensive operations were halted.
17. https://ww2talk.com/
18. Myrvang, Folke, *MG34 – MG42, German Universal Machineguns* (Collector Garde Publications, USA).
19. D 166/1 of 1943

Chapter 4: Operation WINDSOR

1. Some have added as a motivation for WINDSOR the desire to capture one of only two hard airfields in Normandy.

2. Eisenhower, *Report by the Supreme Commander to the Combined Chiefs of Staff* (CMH reprint, Washington, 1994).
3. Quoted in CMHQ report no. 147.
4. Quoted in CMHQ report no. 162.
5. This battalion had four batteries, each of four guns. Three of them had 150mm *Schwere Feldhaubitze* 18 guns and one had 100mm *Kanonen*. However, virtually all the guns of I SS Panzer Corps were within range, but German artillery procedures lacked the speed and flexibility of the British and Canadian regiments of the Royal Artillery.
6. Számvéber, Norbert, *Waffen SS Armour in Normandy* (Helion, Solihull, 2011).
7. Meyer, Hubert, *The History of 12 SS-Panzer Division* (Fedorowicz, Canada, 1994).
8. Interview with the author, 2005.
9. Quoted in CMHQ report no. 162.
10. The 22nd Dragoons was a war-raised regiment formed from cadres of the 4th/7th Dragoon Guards and the Inniskilling Dragoons in 1940. They were converted to Flails in 1943.
11. Bailey, Harry, *Playboys* (Apple iBooks, 2014).
12. Milner, Marc, *D-Day to Carpiquet – The North Shore Regiment and the Liberation of Europe* (New Brunswick Military History Project, Fredericton, 2007).
13. The linear creeping bombardment was little used after WINDSOR.
14. Laurier Military History Archive (translated from the French).
15. Captain Bailey makes the point that 'Because of its trailer a croc will get ditched or bogged long before any other tank ...'
16. The National Archives: WO 171/877.
17. Laurier Military History Archive.
18. Whitsted, Roy, *Canadians: A Battalion at War* (Burlington Books, Ontario)
19. Számvéber, Norbert, *Waffen SS Armour in Normandy* (Helion, Solihull, 2011).
20. Library and Archive of Canada RG24-C-3.
21. Lehmann and Tielmann, *The Leibstandarte Vol IV/1* (Fedorowicz, Canada, 1993).

Chapter 5: Operation CHARNWOOD: The Attack on Caen

1. JAB, *The Short of 33rd Field Regiment* (Höxter, Germany, June 1945).
2. TNA WO 205.
3. Neave, Airey, *The War Diary of Julius Neave* (privately published, 1994).
4. TNA 106/1065.
5. Montgomery, *Normandy to the Baltic* (BAOR Stationary Services, Germany, 1946).
6. The Air Historical Branch RAF – the Army 'knowingly gave the RAF an exaggerated account of the defences in the target area' and 'the major achievement [was] the raising of morale of our own troops.'
7. The deployment of First Canadian Army and its army troops was delayed due largely to a lack of space in the beachhead. Similarly, the last three armoured divisions (Guards, 4th Canadian and Polish) were put back in favour of infantry divisions. The II Canadian Corps and the 2nd Canadian Division were, however, in the process of deployment.
8. BBC, *People's War*, July 2005.
9. The B-17 aircraft of 422nd 'Special Leaflet Squadron' of the USAAF dropped leaflets on the city and across the surrounding area thirty minutes before the bombing.
10. 21 AG Intsum 11 July 1944. TNA WO 171/132.
11. Meyer, Kurt, *Grenadiers* (J.J. Fedorowicz, Winnipeg, 2001).
12. A call for a MIKE target was for all twenty-four guns of a regiment to fire on a specific grid reference; UNCLE was for the seventy-two guns of an infantry division; VICTOR target was for all corps guns within range; and YORK for all army guns.
13. Townend and Baldwin, *Gunners in Normandy* (The History Press, Cheltenham, 2020).
14. TNA WO 171/1325.

Chapter 6: Attack of the 3rd Division

1. Brigadier Smith handed over command of 185 Brigade on 7 July and sent the following message to his troops: 'On relinquishing command 185 Inf Bde I wish to thank all ranks for their loyal co-operation, and above all, for their gallantry and endurance on D Day and D+1. I also wish to thank them for their stoic endurance of the very real hardships of training. I wish all ranks the very best of good luck for the future and know that I can safely rely on 185 Inf Bde to continue the good work and contribute in no small measure to the successful conclusion of the war.' Later in the NWE campaign, Brigadier Eric Bols was promoted to major general and to command of 6th Airborne Division in time for the Rhine crossing.
2. TNA WO 171/1387.
3. Lincoln, John, *Thank God and the Infantry* (Amberley Publishing, Stroud. 2009).
4. TNA 171/703.
5. Weight, Gary J., *Mettle and Pasture – The History of the Second Battalion, The Lincolnshire Regiment during World War II* (Helion, Solihull, 2015).
6. St George's Church inside the castle has been repaired and is open to the public.
7. Not quite destroyed: 31 *Jäger* Regiment reported that they had suffered 65 per cent infantry casualties.
8. TNA WO 171/1325.
9. Anon, *The 1st and 2nd Northamptonshire Yeomanry 1939–1946* (Meyer, Brunswick, 1946).
10. TNA WO 171/1384.
11. TNA WO 171/703.
12. Bailey, Harry, *Playboys* (Apple iBooks, 2014).
13. Major Spearpoint, having recovered from his wounds, later commanded a squadron of Churchills in 107 Regiment RAC.
14. Saunders and Hone, *12th Hitlerjugend SS Panzer Division in Normandy* (Pen & Sword, Barnsley, 2021 and 2023).

Chapter 7: The Attack by the 59th (Staffordshire) Division

1. Finlinson, quoted in Staff College papers, TNA 106/1065.
2. Knight, Peter, *The 59th Division – Its War Story* (Trinity Press, Worcester).
3. Anon, *Your Men in Battle – The South Staffordshire Regiment 1939–1945* (second edition).
4. TNA WO 171/705
5. TNA WO 171/705
6. Ellison, V.C., *Europe Revisited: The East Riding Yeomanry in the Liberation of Europe and the Defeat of Germany* (Brown & Sons, 1946).
7. Brigadier Lingham was awarded the DSO later in the Normandy campaign.
8. Meyer, Hubert, *12th Hitlerjugend Panzer Division* (Fedorowicz, Canada, 1984).
9. The M48A2 fuse for the American 75mm HE round had a superfast setting of 0.05 seconds and an alternative delay setting of 0.15 seconds. Shells with delay were often ricocheted into difficult targets.
10. Anon, *Introduction to Recollections of the Operations Undertaken by A Squadron of the 13th/18th Royal Hussars during the 1944–45 Campaign in Europe* (http://www.lightdragoons.org.uk/).
11. TNA WO 373/49/413.
12. Knight, Peter, *The 59th Division – Its War Story* (Trinity Press, Worcester, 1957).

Chapter 8: Enter the 3rd Canadian Division

1. Sanders, Geoffrey, *Soldier Sailor* (The Bombardment Units Association, Gloucester, 1947).
2. LMH Archive.
3. There are documentary indications, confirmed by this account, that the half-tracks previously only found in III/26 *Panzergrenadiers*, were now being issued to both of the division's III battalions. This was happening across the *Panzerwaffe*.

4. *Hauptsturmführer* von Ribbentrop was the son of the German foreign minister.
5. *Kompanie-kameradenschaft. Die 3. Kompanie* (Edition Zeitgeschichte).
6. *Hauptmann* Steger was one of those Wehrmacht officers attached to the division and was the holder of a Knight's Cross. Recently his gas mask container came to light in farm building south-east of Caen. Interestingly, it is named on the inside with both his army and SS ranks. Later, he was taken prisoner, but his wife was mistakenly told that he had been killed.
7. *Kompanie-kameradenschaft.*
8. Meyer, Hubert, *The History of the 12. SS-Panzerdivision Hitlerjugend* (J.J. Fedorowicz Publishing Inc, Canada, 1994).
9. CMHQ report No.58.
10. Kurt Meyer and his namesake, the division's 1a, disagree on which of 25 SS *Panzergrenadiers'* heavy companies held Grunchy. Hubert Meyer has it held by 14 (Recce) Company, with 16 (Pioneer) Company in Authie.
11. CMHQ report No.162.
12. LMH Archive
13. CMHQ report No.162.

Chapter 9: The Afternoon Attack of the 59th Division

1. Royal Regiment of Fusiliers Museum (Royal Warwickshire) (Facebook, 8 July 2020).
2. https://film.iwmcollections.org.uk/record/36323.
3. Saunders and Hone, *12th Hitlerjugend SS Panzer Division* (Pen & Sword, Barnsley, 2021).
4. TNA WO 171/1388.
5. TNA WO 171/1329
6. Bailey, Harry, *Playboys* (ibooks, 2014).
7. The 50mm PaK 36 had been given a new lease of life by the introduction of an extraordinary hollow charge anti-tank round which could theoretically penetrate any Allied armour at up to 800m (realistically, 300m).

Chapter 10: Abbaye d'Ardenne and Cussy

1. Meyer, Kurt, *Grenadiers* (J.J. Fedorowicz, Canada, 2001).
2. Brown, Gordon, *The Capture of the Abbaye D'Ardenne by the Regina Rifles, 8 July 1944* (Canadian Military History, 1995).
3. LMS Archive.
4. LMS Archive.
5. LMS Archive.
6. Meyer, Kurt, *Grenadiers* (J.J. Fedorowicz, Canada, 2001).
7. University of Victoria Libraries.
8. Meredith, Captain J.L.J., *The Story of the Seventh Battalion, The Somerset Light Infantry* (privately published, 1945).
9. TNA WO 171-258. Translation in the war diary.

Chapter 11: The Fall of Caen

1. Meyer, Kurt, *Grenadiers* (J.J. Fedorowicz, Canada, 2001).
2. Quoted in CHHQ report 162.
3. See Saunders and Hone, *12th Hitlerjugend SS Panzer Division in Normandy* (Pen & Sword, Barnsley, 2021) for the full set of *Sturmbannführer* Meyer's orders.
4. *An Account of the Operations of Second Army in Europe 1944–1945*, Vol. 1 (HQ Second Army, August, 1945).
5. https://www.royalscotskosbwardiaries.co.uk/war-diaries-kosb.
6. Fendick, RF, *A CANLOAN Officer* (Vickers MG Collection & Research Association edition, 2022).
7. TNA WO 171/845.

8. War diaries and battalion accounts are at best vague about the 'capture' of these villages during 8 July. The I Corps map issued with its CHARNWOOD report shows the northern half of Épron held but the others villages still in enemy hands.
9. Duckworth, L.B., *Your men in battle; the story of the South Staffordshire Regiment 1939–45* (Express and Star, Wolverhampton, 1945).
10. TNA WO 171/700.
11. Various, *History of the East Lancashire Regiment in the War 1939–1945* (Lancashire Infantry Museum reprint, Preston, 2016).
12. Elliston, V.C., *Europe Revisited; The East Riding Yeomanry in the Liberation of Europe* (Privately published).
13. Meyer, Hubert, *The History of the 12. SS-Panzerdivision Hitlerjugend* (J.J. Fedorowicz, Canada, 1994).
14. *The Times* (London, 2 July 1944).
15. Hawkins, Desmond (ed), *War Report D-Day to VE-Day* (Ariel Books/BBC, 1985).

Conclusions

1. Scarfe, Norman, *Assault Division* (Collins, London, 1947).
2. Knight, Peter, *The 59th Division; Its War Story* (Frederick Muller Ltd, Worcester).
3. Belchem, Major General David, *Victory in Normandy* (Chatto & Windus, London, 1981).
4. Wilmot, Chester, The Struggle for Europe (Collins, London, 1952).
5. CMHQ report. Simonds to Chief of Staff Canadian of the Military HQ, 21 Jan 46. Operation SPRING was a continuation of ATLANTIC and GOODWOOD that was launched on the same day as COBRA. It was designed to fix German formations in the east and to put II Canadian Corps on the high ground at Verrières and Bourguébus and advance south on the Caen–Falaise road to Point 122. The cost was 1,550 casualties for a toehold on the high ground.

Index